Shippie Townsend

Gospel News

Divided into Eleven Sections

Shippie Townsend

Gospel News
Divided into Eleven Sections

ISBN/EAN: 9783337253141

Printed in Europe, USA, Canada, Australia, Japan

Cover: Foto ©Lupo / pixelio.de

More available books at **www.hansebooks.com**

GOSPEL NEWS,

DIVIDED INTO ELEVEN SECTIONS.

PEACE AND JOY:

Being a Brief Attempt to confider the Evidences of the Truth of the Gospel, in which we have the witnefs of Peace with God, through Jesus Christ, drawn from the Old and New-Teftaments, together with our Obligations to keep the Foundation of our Peace, thus evidenced always in Remembrance; with feveral other Pieces connected with and built upon this foundation, part of which was not before publifhed:

By SHIPPIE TOWNSEND.

Isaiah lvii. 19. I create the Fruit of the Lips; Peace, Peace to far off and to near, faith the Lord.

John xvi. 33. Thefe things have I fpoken unto you, that in me ye might have peace.

Acts x. 36. Preaching peace by Jesus Christ.

Collosians i. 20. He hath made peace by the blood of his crofs.

PRINTED AT BOSTON;
By ALEXANDER YOUNG and THOMAS MINNS,
FOR THE WRITER, AND SOLD AT THE SEVERAL
BOOK-STORES IN TOWN.
MDCCXCIV.

DEDICATION.

As an expression of unfeigned Thanksgiving, for the exceeding Riches of Divine Grace, exhibited in the Gospel, the following Collection is dedicated by the Writer, to the Honour and Glory of the Author and Finisher of our Faith; and as an expression of Love to the purchased possession, they are published for their perusal. That the blessing of God may attend the work, to those who read or hear, is the prayer of the Writer.

AMEN.

The Occasion of the following Treatise.

ON the publication of Peace in *Boston*, a number of friends were collected together an evening after, and a speech delivered on the occasion; the substance of which is the foundation of the present discourse: When the importance of understanding the evidence of the truth of the gospel, which publishes peace with God, through Jesus Christ, in order to satisfy distressed, perplexed minds, and for the consolation of believers, gave occasion briefly to go over these evidences, as they appear in the law of *Moses*, the *Prophets* and the *Psalms*, in the birth, life, death, and resurrection of Jesus Christ: In the testimony of the *Apostles*: In the miracles wrought by the power of the Holy Ghost, in confirmation of their testimony: The difference between those miracles and the deceivable miracles of antichrist: The evidence arising from the rise, reign, and consumption of antichrist, and that arising from the state of the *Jews*, according to what Jesus Christ said concerning them, agreeable to the *Prophets* and *Apostles*. These things being often read in the course of reading the bible, as histories of the events that took place, and not as evidences of the truth testified of Jesus Christ, for which they were designed; and so our minds remain at a loss about the evidences of the truth of the gospel, which is, I apprehend, the source of much of our darkness and perplexity.

Herein I have endeavoured to keep close to the scriptures, and to speak of those things in scripture language, in words that the Holy Ghost teacheth, comparing scripture with scripture: Such as wish patiently to search the scriptures to see if these things are

are so, may be assisted in turning to many of them that may tend to lead their minds to the evidences therein contained. When I had gone through the consideration of the evidences above-mentioned, the importance of the truth thus evidenced being kept in memory, struck my mind, which occasioned the consideration of many passages to that end. I have endeavoured to keep as close to the obvious meaning of the scripture, and as free from the traditions of men as I was able: Having gone through in as brief and plain a manner as I am capable of, I now devote it to the honour and glory of our LORD REDEEMER, and to the benefit and comfort of that part of his purchased inheritance into whose hands it may come.

PEACE

PEACE AND JOY.

SECTION I.—CHAPTER I.

The Bleſſings of Peace *between* England *and* America.

IN every piece of news our minds are anxious about the evidence of its truth, in proportion to the importance of it to us: And in order to our rejoicing, with full ſatisfaction in good news; theſe two things are neceſſary.

Firſt. That we are fully ſatisfied of the evidence of its truth.

Secondly. That we underſtand the greatneſs of the good therein contained.

The good tidings of peace we now contemplate with joy, come to us with the fulleſt evidence of their truth that can be deſired, ſo as to leave no room for the leaſt doubt or heſitation: It is only requiſite for the fulneſs of our joy, that we underſtand the greatneſs of this mercy; in order to which it would be needful to conſider 1ſt, what we are hereby delivered from; and 2dly, what we are hereby put in poſſeſſion of.

[The reſidue of the firſt chapter being more peculiar to the time when it was firſt publiſhed, it is here paſſed over, and we proceed to chapter 2d.]

CHAP.

CHAP. II.

The News of PEACE *with* GOD.

WHILE I am speaking of the ground of rejoicing in the glad tidings of peace, national peace, or peace from war, is there not an anxious spot in the mind that is not yet reached an objection to fulness of joy after this manner? These things are bounded by time which is swiftly passing, but there is a long eternity before me, *and my concern is whether my peace is made with* GOD.

If there be any news about that matter which would make it certain, then, I could rejoice. Is there any? Yes, and it is published by an angel, *Luke* ii. 9 to 14: It is good tidings of great joy, *which shall be to all people*; for unto you is born in the city of *David*, a SAVIOUR which is CHRIST the LORD; on which a multitude of the heavenly host appearing praising and saying, glory to GOD in the highest, and on earth peace; good will towards men; unto you: To who? To the shepherds, exclusive of all others? No, it shall be *to all people*. On earth peace, good will towards men: Not a corner of the earth, nor any of the inhabitants finally excluded from it. If I am on earth, no matter what part of it, there is peace there. If I be of the race of men, there is good will to them. This is a short account of this good news: But what is contained in it, *unto you*; to all people? *is born in the city of David*, the place whence the scripture saith that CHRIST should come, *John* vii. 42, *Micah* v. 2. A SAVIOUR which is CHRIST *the* LORD; a SAVIOUR appointed and anointed to this office; who is also the LORD, having all power in Heaven and earth; able to accomplish the salvation of all people. He was born a SAVIOUR, *Galations* iv. 4. *When the fulness of time was come,* GOD *sent forth his* SON, *made of a woman,*

woman, made under the law, to redeem them that were under the law, that we might receive the adoption of sons.

He lived a SAVIOUR, and made it manifest by forgiving sin, by healing diseases, by testifying he came not to destroy mens' lives, but to save them, that the world through him might be saved.

He saves by his holy life, in which the law is perfectly obeyed, even to that precept, *Matt.* v. 48. *Be ye perfect as your Father in Heaven is perfect*: This JESUS spake under the law while that dispensation lasted, and it must be to lead to himself, where alone it could have its fulfilment; and every son and daughter of *Adam* must despair of attaining any other way than as they are compleat in him in whom the divine will was done on earth as it is in Heaven.

Again, he saves by his death, by answering the penalty of the law for the sins of the people, 1. *Cor.* xv. 3. CHRIST *died for our sins according to the scriptures;* and the apostle says, *We thus judge, if one died for all then all died*; all being comprehended in the one, the head of every man for whom he tasted death: And thus we are said *to be reconciled to* GOD *by the death of his Son.*

Again, he saves by his resurrection, as that evidences the truth of his character and the perfection of his work and sacrifice, and of the perfect satisfaction thereby made to law and justice; so that he could not be holden of death, as he is declared, determined, manifested, the SON of GOD with power according to the spirit of holiness, by the resurrection from the dead, he being our head. The scripture saith, *he rose again for our justification.* So the apostle speaks of the answer of a good conscience towards GOD *by the resurrection of* JESUS CHRIST: *It is* GOD *that justifieth, who is he that condemneth? It is* CHRIST *that died, yea rather that has risen again from the dead.*

Further,

Further, he saves by his exaltation and intercession, *who is at the right hand of* God, *who also maketh intercession for us:* He is able to save to the utmost them that come to God by him, seeing he ever lives to make intercession for them, and to them that look for him he will appear the second time without sin unto salvation. He told his disciples, *I go to prepare a place for you; I will come again and receive you to myself, that where I am ye may be also.*

This is a brief account of our peace, being made with God, *for he is our peace, and he hath made peace by the blood of his cross.* Now the truth of this news depends on the true character of Jesus Christ. If he be the Christ, the Son of God, the news is all true, the salvation is accomplished.

CHAP. III.

The Evidence *of the Truth of this News, from the Scriptures of the* Old Testament.

THE inquiry then is, where is the evidence of the truth of this good news? The answer is in the whole volume of the book which is written of him, which would carry us back to the first promise of the seed of the woman that should bruise the serpent's head. To the promise to *Abraham, Gen.* xxii. 18. *And in thy seed shall all the families of the earth be blessed.* It would lead us to his way, which the Psalmist says was made known to *Moses*, his way of shewing mercy: This was made known to him in *Exodus* xxxiv. 6. *Moses* had prayed in the preceding chapter, verse 13. *Shew me now thy way that I may know thee, that I may find grace in thy sight.* Verse 18th, *And he said, I beseech thee shew me thy glory.* The answer is, verse 19. *I will make all my goodness pass be-*
fore

fore thee. In chap. xxxiv. 5. *The* LORD *defcended in a cloud, and ftood with him there, and proclaimed the name of the* LORD. Verfe 6. *And the* LORD *paffed by before him, and proclaimed the* LORD, *the* LORD GOD *merciful and gracious, long fuffering and abundant in goodnefs and truth, keeping mercy for thoufands, forgiving iniquity and tranfgreffion and fin, and that will by no means clear.* How is this name of the LORD to be made manifeft? How is iniquity, tranfgreffion and fin to be forgiven confiftent with juftice, but with refpect to the furety in which juftice is fatisfied, who was by no means cleared until all the divine attributes harmonized in him, he having paid the utmoft farthing? *He fpared not his own fon, but gave him up for us all.* We cannot poffibly conceive of peace and forgivenefs of iniquity, tranfgreffion and fin, and the guilty tranfgreffors not cleared. The words the guilty are fupplied as we fee by the different character.

It is added, *Vifiting the iniquities of the fathers upon the children unto the third and fourth.*

Under the former difpenfation there was a remembrance of fin every year; the priefthood and facrifice could not take it away? The children of *Ifrael* are afked what they mean by ufing this proverb. *The fathers have eaten four grapes, and the childrens' teeth are fet on edge?* Ezekiel xviii. 2. So *Jeremiah* xxxi. 29. *In thofe days they fhall fay no more the fathers have eaten four grapes and the childrens' teeth are fet on edge; but every one fhall die for his own iniquity.* Muft not this have its fulfilment in him who when he was lifted up from the earth, drew all men unto him, and tafted death for every man, and dying for all, all died. Is not this thought ftrengthened by comparing verfe 34? *For I will forgive their iniquity, and I will remember their fin no more;* which refers to the one facrifice of JESUS CHRIST, in which there is remission and no more sacrifice for sin, as in *Hebrews* x. 17, 18. And thus only have we a consistent view of every man dying for his own iniquity, and the forgiveness of iniquity, and the remembrance of sin no more.

So then the visiting the iniquities of the fathers on the children was to continue until the coming of CHRIST and his perfect sacrifice, in which there was remission, and no more offering for sin, no remembrance of it by repeated sacrifice as under the law, it being taken away by the one sacrifice. Why this is called the third and fourth is matter of inquiry; but this is plain, that JESUS CHRIST came under the law, and closed that dispensation, and brought in the gospel dispensation.

Which gospel, or way of shewing mercy in consistence with justice was made known to *Moses*, as it was also in the passover institution, *Exodus* xii. In which the unblemished LAMB was a type of JESUS the LAMB without blemish and without spot, the LAMB of GOD that taketh away the sin of the world; wherein is pointed out what GOD had respect unto in passing over the children of *Israel*, in verses 13, 23. *And when I see the blood* I will pass over you, and *when he seeth the blood* he will pass over the door, and not suffer the destroyer to come in unto your houses to smite; leading us to the price of our redemption, the precious blood of CHRIST as a LAMB without blemish and without spot, in which we have the fulfilment of this word of GOD.

This was also shewn to *Moses* in the brazen serpent that typified the lifting up the SON of MAN, *that whosoever believeth on him might not perish, but have eternal life.* And in the various things under that dispensation, that had a shadow of good things to come, which centring in JESUS, and having their fulfilment in him, are so many undeniable evidences of the truth of the gospel, the good news of salvation by JESUS CHRIST. The

The like may be said of the prophets, who all gave witness to him; see *Isaiah* liii. 3 to 6. *He is despised and rejected of men; a man of sorrow and acquainted with grief: He hath borne our griefs and carried our sorrows: He was wounded for our transgressions: He was bruised for our iniquities; the chastisement of our peace was upon him, and with his stripes we are healed. All we, like lost sheep, have gone astray, and turned every one to his own way; the* Lord *laid upon him the iniquity of us all.* Verse 8. *for the transgression of my people was he smitten.*

Was he wounded for our transgression, bruised for our iniquities, and the chastisement of our peace upon him, and we healed by his stripes, surely then according to *Jeremiah* xxiii. 6. This is the name whereby he shall be called *the* Lord *our righteousness*. *Ezekiel* also prophetically proclaims the glad tidings, chapter xxxiv. 29. *And I will raise up for them a plant of renown, and they shall no more be consumed with hunger in the land:* Which is the same spoken of by *Isaiah* in his 49th chapter, from 8 to 10. *They shall not hunger nor thirst, neither shall the heat or sun smite them; for he that hath mercy on them shall lead them; even by the springs of water shall he guide them:* Which is explained, *John* vi. 35. *And* Jesus *said unto them, I am the bread of life, he that cometh to me shall never hunger, and he that believeth on me shall never thirst.*

When *Daniel* was speaking and praying, and confessing his sin and making supplication, he is informed by the angel *Gabriel*, that *seventy weeks were determined to finish transgression and make an end of sin.* This could not be done under the *Mosaick* dispensation, where the priests stood daily offering oftentimes those sacrifices which only brought sin to remembrance, and could not take it away: But this was to finish and make an end of it, *and to make reconciliation for iniquity*

iniquity, *and to bring in everlasting righteousness.* All typical legal righteousness was in its own nature transitory, only pointing to this, and must fade as a leaf when its antitype is made manifest, and everlasting righteousness brought in.

And to seal up the vision and the prophecy, and to anoint the MOST HOLY.

The sealing up the vision and the prophecy leads to the completion of it, as when any writing is to be sealed, care is taken that it is completely finished. This vision and prophecy, or what was revealed to and delivered by the prophets, had its completion in the anointing of the MOST HOLY.

To whom all the prophets gave witness, and who is brought in by the prophet *Hosea*, chapter xiii. 9, saying, *O Israel, thou hast destroyed thyself, but in me is thy help.* V. 14. *I will heal their back slidings ; I will ransom thee from the power of the grave ; I will redeem thee from death.* And ch. xiv. 4. *I will love them freely ; for my anger is turned away from him.* This is good news, glad tidings of great joy ; of which *Joel* also speaks, ch. iii. 24. *For I will cleanse their blood that I have not cleansed ; for the* LORD *dwelleth in* Zion.

And although *Amos* was called to prophecy of the various judgments, the desolations and destructions that were to come on *Syria*, the *Philistines, Tyrus, Edom*, the children of *Ammon* and *Moab*, with *Judah* and the kingdom of *Israel*, or the ten tribes, of whose utter destruction, as a kingdom he prophecyeth : Yet he tells us, ch. ix. v. 11. *In that day,* or as the apostle expresses it, *after this will I return and raise up the tabernacle of* David *that is fallen, and close up the breaches thereof, that they may possess the remnant of* Edom, *and of* ALL *the heathen that are called by my name, saith the* LORD.

All the heathen are called by my name. Yes, and blessed be his name, with Amen, ecchoing from the utmost

utmost ends of the earth: In CHRIST JESUS is this prophecy fulfilled; this tabernacle of *David* raised up; that as *James* expresses it, the residue of men might seek the LORD, AND ALL THE GENTILES upon whom my name is called, saith the LORD, that doeth all these things.

It would draw me to too great length to mention the other prophets, which write in their prophecies of JESUS, to whom they all gave witness, as so many undeniable evidences of the truth of the news of salvation by JESUS CHRIST. The exhortation in *Isa.* xli. 27, may be here introduced: *Behold, behold them, and I will give unto* Jerusalem, ONE *that bringeth good tidings;* even good tidings of great joy, which shall be to *all people.* If we pass from the Law of *Moses* and the prophets to the *Psalms,* they are concerning him; and we see not the meaning of them until we see them center in him, and testify of him. The perfect character of the BLESSED MAN in the 1st, 14th and 21st *Psalms,* is no where to be found but in CHRIST JESUS: The many prayers that are made in the various *Psalms* where uprightness and love to the divine precepts, testimonies, commandments, &c. are pleaded as the ground of being heard, belong to none but JESUS, who ever did the things that pleased the FATHER; and are the prayers, supplication, strong crying, with tears to him that was able to save him from death, that he offered in the days of his flesh, and was heard for his piety; that these were his prayers, we have a specimen in his uttering the 1st v. of the xxiid *Psalm* on the cross; the other part of the *Psalm* was as undoubtedly a prophetical description of the prayers of the MESSIAH, as that though it was not vocally expressed. The assurance of being heard, and the happy fruits of his sufferings, expressed from the 21st v. to the end of the *Psalm*, bring to view that expression, FATHER, *I thank thee, that thou hast heard me, and I know that thou hearest me always.* If

If we cast our eye on the 18th *Psalm*, where the Prophet brings in the MESSIAH under the sorrows, the snares of death and the sorrows of hell, in distress calling upon the LORD, and crying to his GOD: *It is added, he heard my voice out of his temple, and my cry came before him into his ears.* The following most majestick description would lead to the answer of the prayers of JESUS on the cross, in the earthquake: *Then the earth shook and trembled, the foundations of the hills moved and was shaken because he was wroth.* The darkness that was under his feet would lead to the darkness that was over all the earth: *He made darkness his pavillion, round about dark waters and thick clouds of the sky.*

Verse 16 and on. He sent from above, he took me, he drew me out of many waters, he delivered me from my strong enemy, and from them that hated me. *Though they appeared to the view of the world* too strong for me, he brought me forth into a large place, he delivered me, because he delighted in me, *because in me he was well pleased.* This deliverance leads our minds to his resurrection from the dead. *The* LORD *rewarded me according to my righteousness, according to the cleanness of my hands hath he recompensed me; for I have kept the way of the* LORD, *and have not wickedly departed from my* GOD; *for all his judgments were before me, and I did not put away his statutes from me: I was also upright before him, and kept myself from mine iniquity; therefore hath the* LORD *recompensed me according to my righteousness, according to the cleanness of my hands in his eye-sight.* Now when we view *David* in the *Psalms* speaking of himself, we are led to blunder in the dark after creature righteousness, and wish to be as good as *David,* that we may pray, as he did; and hope we are sincerely desirous of it, &c. So to compass ourselves about with sparks of our own kindling, which will be for-

ever

ever disappointing, but when we see him testifying of JESUS, we find a righteousness that is perfect, that is safe to trust and be found in: for with him who perfectly fulfilled the law and endured the curse in mercy to us *with* him who is *the merciful thou wilt shew thyself merciful; with this upright man thou wilt shew thyself upright; with* this *pure,* this HOLY ONE *thou wilt shew thyself pure,* while thou wilt contend with the perverse that slight this perfect righteousness, and go about to establish their own: *For thou wilt save the afflicted people* through the divine righteousness, that are altogether destitute of righteousness in themselves, *but wilt bring down high looks.* Surely he scorneth the scorner, he resisteth the proud; the loftiness of man shall be bowed down, and the hautiness of man shall be made low, and the LORD alone shall be exalted. In that day, according as it is written, let him that glorieth glory in the LORD. But to consider the good news of salvation by JESUS CHRIST from the *Psalms,* would open too large a field for the present design; if what has been brought to view may be an help to open this field, to walk in at our leisure, a good end may be answered.

CHAP. IV.

The Evidences *of this Truth from the* New-Testament.

IF we turn over to the New-Testament, the evidences multiply upon us from the birth, life, death and resurrection of JESUS, from the testimony of the apostles, from the prophecy of the rise and reign, consumption and destruction of antichrist, from the state of the *Jews,* agreeable to the prophecy of CHRIST and the apostles' testimony concerning them.

PART

PART I.

Of the Birth, Life, Death and Resurrection of JESUS CHRIST.

TO begin with his birth. When an inquiry is made for the place for the LORD, an habitation for the MIGHTY ONE of *Jacob*, it is said, *Psalm* cxxxii. 6. *Lo, we heard of it, at Ephrata*, when this habitation is found for the LORD. It is added, v. 7. *We will go into his tabernacle, we will worship at his foot-stool.* The prophet *Micah* foretells the place of his birth, chap. v. 2. *And thou Bethlehem Ephrata, thou art little among the thousands of Judah;* * *out of thee shall he come forth unto me, that shall be the* RULER *in Israel, whose goings forth have been from the beginning, even from the days of eternity.* The evangelist *Mat.* ch. ii. 1, gives an account that JESUS was born in *Bethlehem*, of *Judah*, *in the days of Herod the king*; who upon hearing of his being born king of the *Jews*, he gathered the chief priests and scribes of the people together, and demanded of them where CHRIST should be born? as being satisfied that that event was foretold: They said unto him, in *Bethlehem*, of *Judah*, and quoted the prophecy of *Micah* just mentioned.

Poor deceived, mistaken *Herod*, supposing JESUS CHRIST to be a temporal prince, feared himself in danger, (alas, in danger from the SAVIOUR, from him who came not to destroy mens' lives but to save them) and sought the young child's life, which occasioned the being sent to *Egypt* for the fulfilment of the prophecy; *out of Egypt I have called my son.* Upon his return from *Egypt*, *Joseph* was afraid of king *Archelus*, who reigned in the room of his father *Herod*, so

---

* It is said the *Jews*, the daughter of troops, divided their country, so that for every thousand there was a Chief Captain; and because *Bethlehem* was not able to make up a thousand, the prophet calleth it little, but GOD would raise up *Israel's* RULER therein.

so did not return to *Judea*, but turned aside into the parts of *Gallilee*, and came and dwelt in the city called *Nazareth*; that it might be fulfilled that was spoken of by the prophets, he shall be called a *Nazareen*: As the prophets in the plural number are here spoken of, and I have not been able to turn to any of them, in which this is particularly expressed, it has exercised my mind in way of inquiry, and that which appears most likely, is, that it was what was testified by the prophets concerning JESUS, in other expressions that denote the same thing.

Now when I consider that the holiness of the *Nazarites* under the law was only typical, and could not make the *Nazarites* perfect, as pertaining to the conscience, but they must offer their sin-offering when the days of their separation were fulfilled, *Num.* vi. 13. 14. Though all the days of their separation they were called holy unto the LORD, I look for this holiness thus typified; in him of whom it is said, he shall be called a *Nazareen*. In him alone can I view that inimitably grand, majestick description of her *Nazarites*, we have in *Lam.* iv. 7: *Her Nazarites were purer than snow; they were whiter than milk; they were more ruddy in body than rubies; their polishing of sapphire.* This was what their holiness, all the days of their separation, pointed to, which dwelt in perfection in JESUS the HOLY ONE. When we consider *Sampson*, who was a type of him, a *Nazarite* from the womb, as the angel told *Manoah's* wife, *Judges* xiii. 5. She added, when she told her husband in v. 7. 'till the day of his death; but this might not be, no perfection was to be found in the typical *Nazarites*, that was reserved to the antitype.

Now considering these things, if what is said of the *Nazarites* referred only to themselves, those scriptures would be of private interpretation; but we are told no scripture is so, therefore they must point to

C   JESUS

Jesus who is the public interpretation of them: So what is spoken of them is fulfilled in his being called a *Nazareen*; and as the *Nazarites'* holiness, pointed to his perfect holiness so the multitude of texts where he is spoken of as the Holy One, all point to him. In this character, the purer than snow, the whiter than milk, the more ruddy than rubies, whose polishing is of sapphire, the *Nazarite* indeed, in whom is no blemish; this is the most satisfying view I can at present take of that passage, that it might be fulfilled that was spoken of by the prophets, he shall be called a *Nazareen*.

If we take notice of the life of Jesus, we shall find the prophesies fulfilled herein as so many evidences of the truth under consideration. The psalmist, in the ciiid psalm, blesseth *the* Lord *who forgiveth all thy iniquities, who healeth all thy diseases.* That Jesus is the Lord is evidenced in his pronouncing to the sick of the palsy, son be of good cheer, thy sins be forgiven thee. To prove himself the Lord that forgave iniquity, he healed the man with his word, as we see *Matt.* ix. begining, *Mark* ii. 3.

When the disciples of *John* were sent to inquire, if he were the true Messiah, *Luke* vii. 21, *in the same hour he cured many of infirmities, and plagues, and of evil spirits; and to many that were blind he gave sight*, and gave them this as an answer to *John; the blind see, the lame walk, the lepers are cleansed, the deaf hear, the dead are raised, to the poor the gospel is preached*, as if he had said, tell *John* the things you hear and see, and let him compare them with the prophesies of the Old-Testament concerning the Messiah, and collect the answer to his inquiry.

The blind see; *Psalm* cxlvi. 8. *The* Lord *openeth the eyes of the blind*, *Isaiah* xxix. 18. *And the eyes of the blind shall see out of obscurity and out of darkness. Isa.* xlii, 6. 7. *And I will keep thee and give*

give thee for a covenant of the people, to open the blind eyes, Isa. xxxv. 5. *Then the eyes of the blind shall be opened.* Isa. xlii. 16. *And I will bring the blind by a way which they knew not; I will make darkness light before them, and crooked things streight; These things will I do unto them, and not forsake them.*—Thus the many that were blind, to whom he gave sight while *John's* messengers tarried, appeared as so many evidences of his being the true MESSIAH, prophesied of by the prophets: So do the two blind men whose eyes were opened, recorded in *Matt.* ix, from the 27th v. and the blind man that was restored and saw every man clearly, *Mark* viii. from 23d to 25th v. With blind *Bartimeus* the beggar, who received his sight and followed JESUS in the way, *Mark* x. from 46 to 52; and the other beggar man, who was blind from his birth, of purpose *that the works of* GOD *might be made manifest in him,* that he should be an evidence of the truth of the character of JESUS CHRIST, as a means made use of to bring others to believe in him; for this is the work of GOD, that ye believe on him whom he hath sent. If we consider these as not only restored to their bodily sight, but having the light of the knowledge of the glory of GOD, in the face of JESUS CHRIST, worshipping him, calling him LORD, following him in the way, the evidence will increase upon us; and we shall see the following character exemplified spiritually as well as literally, THE LAME WALK. Those ignorant and incapacitated to go one step of the way, having received sight, follow JESUS in the way, as well as those literally lame, who when we see them coming to JESUS in the temple, and being brought to him in other places, and healed by him, are we not constrained to join with the multitude in *Matt.* xv. 31, *who wondered when they saw the dumb speak, the maimed to be whole, the lame to walk, and the blind to see? And they glorified the* GOD *of Israel.* And do we not see, *Isaiah*, xxxv. 6. *Then shall the lame leap as an hart*, fulfilled in Jesus causing the lame to walk ? See the man lame from his mother's womb, *leaping and walking and praising* God, *Acts* iii. 8.

The lepers are cleansed.—Under the law there were directions to the priest to discover the leprosy and put the leper out of the camp, and shut him up, &c. but no means directed to, for the healing of it, that was the work of God.

Even when king *Uzziah* was smitten with leprosy, he continued so to the day of his death, and dwelt in a several house ; the wealth of his kingdom could not procure him healing or inlargement.

When the King of *Syria* sent to the king of *Israel* to recover *Naaman* of his leprosy, no wonder that the king of *Israel* was so struck as to rend his cloaths and say, am I a God, to kill and make alive ! That this man doth send to me to recover a man of his leprosy.

But behold ! when Jesus came down from the mountain, among the multitude that followed him, *there came a leper and worshipped him, saying*, Lord *if thou wilt, thou canst make me clean ; and* Jesus *put forth his hand and touched him, and said, I* will, *be thou clean, and immediately his leprosy was cleansed.* This was done under the law dispensation ; so Jesus saith to him, *see thou tell no man, but go thy way, shew thyself to the priest, and offer the gift that Moses commanded for a testimony unto them.* Though the priest could do nothing towards cleansing the leper, yet he was directed when to pronounce him clean ; and when he was obliged to pronounce one clean that Jesus had healed by his word, it was an evidence unto them of this truth, that Jesus was the Christ, the true Messiah. Even *Naaman* the *Syrian*, when healed of his leprosy, acknowledges the God of *Israel* to be the one only living and true God, 2 *Kings*, v. 15. *Behold, now I know that there is no* God *in all the*

the earth but in Israel: So then when JESUS said to the leper with immediate success, I will, be thou clean, it was a testimony unto them, that the GOD that could kill and make alive, and recover a man of his leprosy, was manifest in the flesh, in JESUS of *Nazareth*, that JESUS was the true MESSIAH, he that should come; and *John* would know when the lepers were cleansed; he need not look for another; especially when he understood him to heal with a word without hesitation: Even when ten of them joined their voices in JESUS, master have mercy on us, he only says, go shew yourselves to the priest; and as they went they were cleansed.

The deaf hear. The prophet *Isaiah* says, chap. xxix. 18. *In that day shall the deaf hear the words of the book;* and xxxv. 5. *The ears of the deaf shall be unstopped.* In *Mark* vii. from 32 to 37, JESUS manifests himself the true MESSIAH, by healing the deaf and dumb, to the astonishment of beholders, who acknowledge he hath done all things well: *He maketh the deaf to hear and the dumb to speak.*

The dead are raised up. JESUS raising the widow's son from the dead, *Luke* vii. 12, caused the much people that were present at the young man's funeral to glorify GOD, and gave occasion to *John* to send his disciples to him: He likewise manifested himself in calling *Lazarus* out of his grave, on which many of the *Jews*, believed on him.

And to the poor the Gospel is preached. This passage contains ample matter to fill the mind with admiration, at the exceeding riches of divine grace contained therein. Oftentimes poverty of spirit is looked upon as a qualification, or good disposition, wrought in, or attained by, religious people, as that which distinguishes them as objects of the divine favour, to the exclusion of the destitute and worthless among the children of men; and there is nothing more natural to us than to admire ourselves for some such supposed attainment, to the despising of others. When JESUS brought this passage to the view of his hearers, in the 4th of *Luke*, where it is written, the spirit of the LORD is upon me, because he hath annointed me *to preach the gospel to the poor*, &c. and said unto them, this day is this scripture fulfilled in your ears: They all bear him witness, and wondered at the gracious words which proceeded out of his mouth; undoubtedly imagining it had a particular direction to them, as thus qualified, as well as that they had a claim upon him as their countryman, he shewed them from the scriptures of the old testament, that the widows of *Israel* were passed by, and *Elias* sent to *Serepta* of *Sidon*, to a despised *Gentile*, a woman that was a widow; and though many lepers were in *Israel* in the days of the prophet, yet none of them were cleansed, saving *Naaman* the *Syrian*; which soon evidenced their destitution of poverty of spirit, by their being filled with wrath, highly offended at the aspect of the gospel toward the destitute.

To the poor the gospel is preached. What do we understand by gospel? It is good news, glad tidings.

The poverty, distress and perplexity of mankind is about acceptance with GOD, and it is natural to us all to look for it in a way of establishing our own righteousness, which is ever accompanied with distress and perplexity, as inadequate to satisfy justice, or give peace of conscience; and the distressing inquiry, what lack I yet?, dwells upon the mind that is conscious of inability of doing any thing that can satisfy justice, or atone for past transgressions: But the gospel brings glad tidings of peace by JESUS CHRIST, the MEDIATOR of GOD and man, the end of the law for righteousness; in whom alone we are made accepted: His righteousness being perfect and the sole ground of acceptance, no one can ever look for *acceptance*

ceptance by virtue of any other righteousness, without sinking disappointment, be his character ever so fair in the eyes of men, or in his own apprehensions.

Neither can any one ever so vile look for acceptance solely from this quarter and be disappointed, *Isaiah* xxviii. 16. 1 *Pet.* ii. 6. *He that believeth shall not make haste: He that believeth on him shall not be confounded*: Shame and confusion belongs to those who make lies their refuge, and hide themselves under falshood: For the hail shall sweep away the refuge of lies, and the waters shall overflow the hiding-place; which must bring on haste and confusion of mind when the refuge and hiding-place fails, which those who believe the gospel report shall not be subject to; for, *Rom.* ix. 33. *Whosoever believeth on him shall not be ashamed.*

The gospel brings the sure and everlasting foundation to view, in the perfect character and finished work of JESUS CHRIST. 'Tis good news, glad tidings to the destitute children of men: Let *John* judge if it can come from any but the true MESSIAH, he that should come, &c.

To the inquiry, why *John*, who before this bare witness of him, should now send to ask this question, whether for the confirmation of his own faith, or the satisfaction of his disciples, it may be said, it appears likely he might have himself and them both in view; for both they and he might be stumbled to see that he was left confined in prison, while JESUS, to whom he bare testimony as the true MESSIAH, did not relieve him; JESUS lets him know he was about the work the MESSIAH was to do, and the blessedness he was to look for was not a temporal deliverance from his confinement, but in not being offended in him.

As *John*'s testimony hath been mentioned, it may be needful to attend to it as an evidence of the truth before us; for as the prophet prophesied of *John* as

the

the forerunner of the true MESSIAH, *(as the voice of him that crieth in the wilderness, prepare ye the way of the* LORD, *make straight in the desert a high-way for our* GOD : *Every valley shall be exalted, and every mountain and hill shall be made low, and the crooked shall be made straight, and the rough places plain; and the glory of the* LORD *shall be revealed, and all flesh shall see together, for the mouth of the* LORD *hath spoken,* Isaiah xl. 3, 4, 5. *Behold I will send you Elias the prophet before the coming of the great and dreadful day of the Lord,* Malachi iv. 5. This event must take place: So the disciples when they had a view of his glory on the mount of transfiguration, and heard the voice, this is my beloved Son, in whom I am well pleased, asked this question, why say the scribes that *Elias* must first come? JESUS answered and told them, *Elias* verily cometh first. *Elias* is come already, and they have done to him whatsoever they listed: (They had beheaded *John* in prison) likewise shall also the son of man suffer of them. Then the disciples understood that he spake to them of *John* the Baptist, of whom *Matthew* says, *this is he that was spoken of by the prophet* Esais, *saying, prepare ye the way of the* LORD, *make his paths straight*. Perhaps we have the reason of his being called *Elias*, in *Luke* i. 17. And he, i. e. *John*, shall go before him; i. e. JESUS in the spirit and power of *Elias*, and shall turn the hearts of the fathers to the children, &c.

The spirit and power of *Elias* was manifested in bringing the idolatrous *Israelites* to acknowledge JEHOVAH is GOD, 1 *Kings*, 18, 21 to 29. *John* the baptist comes in the same spirit to turn the disobedient to the wisdom of the just, and make ready a people prepared for the LORD. *John* calls them off from every error, to view the glory of the LORD, that was to be revealed in the MESSIAH that should come after him, and be preferred before him, until he comes

to

to know him. Says he, *I knew him not, but that he should be made manifest to Israel:* At his baptism, when he saw the HOLY GHOST descend and remain on him, and heard the voice from heaven confirming the prophetick word, This is my beloved Son, in whom I am well pleased. He says, *he that sent me to baptize with water, the same said unto me, upon whom thou shalt see the spirit descending and remaining on him, the same is he that baptizeth with the* HOLY GHOST; *and I saw and bear record that this is the* SON *of* GOD.

What *Isaiah* prophesied of him had an exact fulfilment in him and his ministry, calling every exalted character, that looked for preference in the MESSIAH's kingdom on that account, to repentance; it was not an earthly kingdom, but the kingdom of Heaven that was at hand. None were there admitted on account of personal excellencies, or excluded for want of them; but every one admitted by the good pleasure of the KING, in virtue of his own righteousness; which, while it brought low mountains and hills, it exalted every valley, every one depressed and despairing for want of personal righteousness, to recommend them to the divine favour, upon the knowledge of his perfect character and finished work, or upon the glory of the LORD being revealed. See the ground of their acceptance in him;—*All flesh shall see together; for the mouth of the* LORD *hath spoken.* Thus were the vilest characters encouraged by *John's* preaching; the publicans and harlots believed him, whose characters were depressed low as valleys. The apostle speaking to the *Ephesian Gentiles,* who in time past, or before they believed the gospel, sustained the same worthless characters, says, *Eph.* ii. 4. *But* GOD *who is rich in mercy, for his great love wherewith he loved us, even when we were dead in sins, hath quickened us together with* CHRIST, *and hath raised us up together, and made us sit together in heavenly places*

D

in CHRIST JESUS. Surely here, the valleys are exalted, sinners of the *Gentiles* quickened together with CHRIST, and raised and made to sit together in heavenly places in CHRIST JESUS. JESUS the high-priest of our profession, when he had offered one sacrifice for sin, sat down as having finished his work. We sinners of the *Gentiles,* as low as valleys, are quickened together with CHRIST, and raised and made to sit together in him; sit as those come to a place of rest and safety. Surely here is the place in which the brother of low degree may sit and rejoice with exceeding great joy, in that he is exalted, and the rich in that he is made low; that he hath discovered the fading nature of his riches, by the knowledge of JESUS CHRIST. If we pursue *John*'s testimony of him, after JESUS was manifested to him, as in *John* i. 29, 36. *Behold the* LAMB *of* GOD *that taketh away the sin of the world: Behold the* LAMB *of* GOD, &c. It will join in yielding evidence that JESUS is the CHRIST; for so sure as the prophet's testimony of the voice crying in the wilderness, was fulfilled in *John* the baptist, so sure he bare witness to the truth which he thus expresses; *I saw and bare record that this is the* SON *of* GOD.

This is the character JESUS claimed; this is the truth he bare witness to, through his whole life; this is what his works bare witness of. This is the character he claimed, *John* viii. 24, 28, 58. *Before Abraham was I am;* which was the character of the GOD of *Israel,* as given to *Moses, Exodus.* iii. 13, 14. *Moses* inquires, what answer he shall give, when the children of *Israel* shall ask the name of the GOD of their fathers? *And* GOD *said unto Moses, I* AM *that I* AM: *And he said, thus shalt thou say to the children of Israel, I* AM *hath sent me unto you.* JESUS conversing with their descendants who had this record, says to them, if ye believe not that I AM, ye shall die in your sins. When ye have lift up the SON of MAN, ye
shall

shall know that I AM. When the band came to apprehend Jesus, he said unto them, Whom seek ye? They said, JESUS of *Nazareth*: JESUS saith unto them, I AM. As soon as he had said unto them, I AM, they went backward and fell to the ground. He asked again, whom seek ye? They said, JESUS of *Nazareth*: JESUS answered, I have told you that I AM.—When JESUS said, *before Abraham was, I* AM, they took up stones to cast at him, *John*, viii. 59. The reason of their several attempts to stone him, they gave, *John* x. 33, *for blasphemy*: *And because thou being a man maketh thyself.* GOD, he still claimed this character, and referred them to his works. *If I do not the works of my father, believe me not; but if I do, though you believe not me, believe the works; that ye may know and believe that the father hath sent me: I have greater witness than that of John, for the work which the father hath given me to finish, the same works that I do bare witness of me, that the father hath sent me: Believe me that I am in the father and the father in me, or else believe me for the very works sake.*

Thus JESUS claimed the character and did the works which the MESSIAH was to do, and referred the *Jews* to the works, as bearing witness of him: They constantly opposing and accusing him as having a devil, being mad, speaking blasphemy, until he is pursued to death as a blasphemer; in which death we have the fulfilment of the prophesies, and the accomplishment of the types of the old Testament. And although JESUS was put to death as a blasphemer, and is despised and rejected of men; despised and we esteemed him not: but esteemed him stricken, smitten of GOD and afflicted; yet he was wounded for our transgressions, he was bruised for our iniquities; the chastisement of our peace was upon him, and by his stripes we are healed: The LORD hath laid on him the iniquities of us all: For the transgression of my people

people was he smitten. The various other prophesies concerning the death of CHRIST (which had their fulfilment therein) in the old-testament, would lead to too great length to take a view of here. All the types and sacrifices have their fulfilment here, as the LAMB GOD would provide himself, of which *Abraham* told *Isaac*, who was typified by the lamb caught in the thicket by his horns, that was offered instead of *Isaac, Genesis* xxii. 13, as the antitype of the passover lamb, the blood of which being sprinkled on the door, &c. the destroying angel should pass over and not come into their houses. These types no doubt *John* had in view when he points to the antitype with, behold the LAMB of GOD that taketh away the sin of the world : Behold, the LAMB of GOD. So had *John* the beloved, when he says, *Unto him that loved us and washed us from our sins in his own blood.* So had *Paul*, when he says, *Even* CHRIST *our passover is sacrificed for us:* and when he speaks of the *church of* GOD *which he had purchased with his own blood,* of being *justified by his blood,* of having *redemption through his blood,* and of his *sanctifying the people with his own blood,* And *Peter*, when he says, for as much as ye were not redeemed with corruptible things as silver and gold, from your vain conversation, received by tradition from your fathers, *but with the precious blood of* CHRIST, *as of a* LAMB *without blemish and without spot.* Here the whole redeemed company will join without a dissenter, *Thou art worthy, for thou wast slain and hast redeemed us to* GOD *by thy blood.*

The fulfilment of the prophesies of the old-testament in the circumstances of the death of JESUS might here be taken brief notice of, such as the reproach he underwent, spoken of *Psalm* xlii. 3, 10. *My tears have been my meat day and night, while they continually say unto me, where is thy* GOD ? *With a sword in my bones mine enemies reproach me, while they say continually,*

ally, where is thy GOD? *They that sit in the gate speak against me, and I am the song of the drunkard. Reproach hath broken my heart.* Is it possible to express the most keen reproach in stronger language? With a sword in my bones mine enemies reproach me; reproach hath broken my heart. These were fulfilled in the dying JESUS, *Where is thy* GOD? He trusted in GOD, let him deliver him now, if he will have him. They spit upon him: What more ignominious? They blind-folded and smote him: What more distressing? The prophesy says, they shout out the lip, they wag the head. The history says, they that passed by reviled him, wagging their heads. The prophesy of their giving him vinegar to drink, is then fulfilled, and the prophetick language of the xxiid *Psalm* uttered; *my* GOD, *my* GOD, *why hast thou forsaken me?* And we have a specimen of the accomplishment of the prophesy in the ciid *Psalm*, of his regarding the prayer of the destitute, hearing the groaning of the prisoner, and saving the sons of death, in his answer to the dying thief. Here we have him uttering the language of *Psalm* xxxi. 5. *Father, into thy hands I commend my spirit.* The prophet *Daniel* says, *he shall finish transgression and make an end of sin, make reconciliation for iniquity, and bring in everlasting righteousness.* JESUS upon the cross says, *it is finished.* *Isaiah* says, *he made intercession for the transgressors.* Dying JESUS prays, *Father forgive them for they know not what they do.* Those circumstances that at first view seemed merely accidental, were ordered for the fulfilment of the scriptures: The zeal of the *Jews* for the the observation of the sabbath, made them urge that the legs of those that were crucified might be broken, and that they might be taken away. Consequent upon which the soldiers came and brake the legs of the first, and of the other that were crucified with him; but when they saw that *he* was already dead they

they break not *his* legs, but one of them with a spear pierced *his* side, and forthwith came there out blood and water, *which things were done that the scriptures should be fulfilled,* The type in the passover lamb, *Exodus,* xii. 46, *Numbers* ix. 12. *Neither shall ye break a bone thereof,* has its fulfilment here. And the prophesy in *Psalm* xxxiv. 20. *He keepeth all his bones, not one of them is broken,* is accomplished in him.— (Doth the apostle say, we are members of his body, of his flesh, and of his bones! and shall not one of them be broken! here is strong consolation.) So likewise the piercing the spear is spoken of by another prophet: *They shall look on him whom they have pierced,* for *every eye* shall see him, *and they also that pierced him.*

Thus the subject is pursued until Jesus is dead: The soldiers found him so, and therefore they break not his legs. When *Joseph* asked the body of *Pilate,* he would not give it until he knew from the Centurion that he was certainly dead. *Joseph,* who before had been a secret disciple for fear of the *Jews,* went in boldly to *Pilate* to ask the body of Jesus, and laid him in his own new tomb, that was hewed out of a rock, wherein never man before was laid.

Well, his crucifiers have prevailed—are they satisfied? Alas! they are still afraid! they remember that Jesus put the issue of the controversy upon his *resurrection* from the dead, which he spake of so often as to be a known fact among them: And they say to *Pilate,* Sir, we remember that that deceiver said while he was alive, after three days I will *rise* again; command therefore that the sepulchre be made sure until the third day: *Pilate,* answered, *You have a watch, go your way, make it as sure as you can. So they went and made the sepulchre sure, sealing the stone and setting a watch.* The design of the watch was to prevent any deception about the resurrection of Jesus Christ,

Christ, by his disciples coming by night and stealing him away. Alas! what fear could arise from the disciples; who all forsook him and fled? *Matthew* xxvi. 56, *Mark* xiv. 50. And though *Peter* and *John* afterwards followed him, yet *Peter* followed afar off, and was afraid to own his Lord, even before a damsel, but denied three times that he knew him: And *John* who was the only male of the disciples that we have an account of that stood by the cross, he did not understand the scriptures concerning the resurrection of Jesus Christ, until it was accomplished, nor any of them, *John* xx. 8. 9. The sepulchre was hewn out of a rock, and no way to it but by the door. The very great stone that was rolled to the door was sealed, and the watch set to keep it, who if they fell asleep, forfeited their lives; but divine power interposed, there was a great earthquake; *the Angel of the Lord descended and rolled back the stone from the door and sat upon it; his countenance was like lightning, and his raiment white as snow, and for fear of him the keepers did shake and became as dead men.* The earthquake mentioned in *Matthew* xxvii. 51, 54, and xxviii. 2, appears to be one and the same, though at first view the mention that is made of it in *Matthew* xxvii. 51, seems to be immediately connected with his giving up the ghost; yet the 53d verse shews it belonged to his resurrection. The vail of the temple was rent in twain from the top to the bottom; the vail that always hung to divide the holy place from the most holy, where none might enter but the high-priest once a year, upon the day of atonement, with the blood of the sacrifice, which he offered for himself and the errors of the people: This was rent to shew that the antitype was now come, and the way to the holiest of all was opened by Jesus Christ.

The centurion and those that were with him watching Jesus, when they saw the earthquake, and those
things

things that were done, feared, saying, *truly this was the* SON *of* GOD. The centurian and they that were with him watching JESUS, mentioned in the 54th verse, I conceive to be the watch at the sepulchre, although the appointment of them by *Pilate* and their being set is mentioned after in verses 65, 66; this watch being set to prevent, finally strengthen the evidence of our LORD's resurrection, being themselves constrained to acknowledge, truly this man was the SON of GOD. Some of them returning to the city shewed the chief priest all the things that were done, and when they were assembled with the elders, they gave large money to the soldiers, to hire them to say, his disciples came by night and stole him away while we slept; and although this will expose you to death, yet we will interpose if it come to the governor's ears; we will persuade him and secure you: So they took the money and did as they were taught; and this saying is commonly reported among the *Jews* until this day, *Matt.* xxviii. from the 11th to the 16th verse. By this report it is evident that JESUS was not in the sepulchre on the third day, by the confession of the *Jews*. The angel that thus overcome and dispirited the soldiers comforted the women with the tidings of the resurrection: *Fear not ye; for I know that ye seek* JESUS: *He is not here; for he is risen as he said: Come, see the place where the* LORD *lay.*

Mary Magdalene was the first at the sepulchre: *John* xx. 1. *Early while it was yet dark, and seeth, the stone rolled away from the sepulchre.* This was all that *John* gives account of her seeing at that time of her going to the sepulchre; upon which she runneth and cometh to *Peter* and *John*, saying, they have taken away the LORD out of the sepulchre, and we know not where they have laid him: They ran both of them, and went into the sepulchre, and saw the linen clothes lie, and the napkin that was about his

his head wrapt together in a place by itself. It is said of *John, he saw and believed, for as yet they knew not the scriptures that he must rise from the dead.* He saw and believed what? that JESUS was not in the sepulchre: Also it appears most highly probable that what the scriptures of the Old-Testament had said, pointing to the resurrection of JESUS CHRIST, with what he had said concerning it, which as yet, or until that time they did not understand, now struck the mind of *John,* as what was accomplished in his resurrection; while *Peter* returned wondering in himself at what had happened, and went away again unto their own home; (but *Mary* was back again the second time to the sepulchre after them:) And when *they* went home she stood without at the door of the sepulchre weeping, and stooping down into the sepulchre, *and seeth two angels in white, sitting one at the head, and the other at the feet where the body of* JESUS *had lain;* who inquired, why she wept? Because, said she, they have taken away my LORD; and she turned herself back and saw JESUS standing, and knew not that it was JESUS: He was pleased, by calling her by name, to make himself known to her, and bid her go to his brethren, and speak to them of his ascension. She went and told the disciples that she had seen the LORD, and that he had spoken these things unto her.

She is now ready to accompany the women to the sepulchre with the spices they had prepared, as *Matthew* relates, who came at the rising of the sun. They said, who shall roll us away the stone from the door of the sepulchre, for it was very great. But why should they make the inquiry, if *Mary* had been there before and seen the stone rolled away? Probably they might not credit her testimony; might suppose her to be easily mistaken, being there so very early, while it was yet dark. But when *they* looked *they* saw that the

F. stone

stone was rolled away, and entering in *they saw a young man sitting on the right side in a long white garment.* Saith *Mark, and behold two men stood by them in shining garments.* Saith *Luke,* which spake to the women, saying, *be not affrighted, ye seek* JESUS *of Nazareth, which was crucified: He is not here; but is risen. Mark* mentions a young man sitting, and *Luke* two men standing, which testimonies do not contradict each other; for it often happens when two are together the one that strikes the attention most, as being chief speaker, is made mention of; especially when the evidence of the fact they testify is the matter to be attended to, and it is not uncommon for a person who is first seen sitting, to be presently and at the same interview standing or moving from place to place. Those who were in long white garments, or shining garments, I suppose, were angels appearing in the likeness of men; and, no doubt, the same angel that *Matthew* speaks of, who came and rolled back the stone, and sat upon it, whose countenance was like lightning, and his raiment white as snow, was one of them, and the chief speaker. Their joint testimony is, that JESUS CHRIST is risen from the dead, as he said unto the disciples: And each evangelist reports, that they sent the women with the news to the disciples, informing them that he goeth before them into *Gallilee,* where they should see him, as he said unto them before he was crucified, *Matt.* xxvi. 32, and *Mark* xvi. 7.

Now as they went to tell his disciples, JESUS *met them and said, All hail,* and sends them on the same errand they had before from the angels. *Mary* had before told the disciples she had seen the LORD, and that he had spoken such things unto her. Now JESUS meets and shews himself to *Mary Magdalene,* the other *Mary, Salome* and other women, with them, and sends them with their joint evidence to tell his disciples.

disciples. The view that I have taken of JESUS CHRIST shewing himself to *Mary Magdalene* alone, as recorded by *John* previous to and distinct from his appearing to the women, is proved and strengthened by *Mark* xvi. 9. *Now when* JESUS *was risen, early the first day of the week he appeared first to Mary Magdalene, out of whom he had cast seven devils;* and it seems to me to be most plainly to be gathered from the history, as related by the four evangelists.

The disciples did not believe *Mary Magdalene*, *Mark* xvi. 11. They did not believe the joint testimony of her and the other women, *Luke* xxiv. 11. So JESUS after appeared to two of them as they walked and went into the country; the account of which we have, *Mark* xvi. 12, and the particulars related, *Luke* xxiv. 13, &c. And they went and told it to the residue; neither believed they them: The cure of their unbelief, or the further evidences that was given of the truth to them, are multiplied evidences of the same truth to us. He after appeared to the eleven as they sat at meat, and upbraided them of their unbelief and hardness of heart, because they believed not them that had seen him after he was risen, *Mark* xvi. 14. But *Thomas* was not with them when JESUS came, *John* xx. 24. The other disciples therefore said unto him, we have seen the LORD: *But he said unto them, except I shall see in his hand the print of the nails, and put my finger into the print of the nails, and thrust my hand into his side, I will not believe.* Thus we see the disciples did not any of them give in, to this truth, without evidence to their full satisfaction. After eight days, (I suppose, on the return of the first day of the week) his disciples were within, and *Thomas* with them; when JESUS again manifested himself to them, and satisfied *Thomas* of the evidence of the truth he had before heard from the other disciples, by saying to him, *Reach hither thy finger and behold my hands:*

and

and reach hither thy hand and thrust it into my side, and be not faithless, but believing. Thomas, satisfied with the evidence, answered and said, *My Lord and my God.* Jesus *said unto him, Thomas, because thou hast seen me thou hast believed; blessed are they that have not seen and have believed:* Those that believe on the credit of divine testimony; that believe through the word of the prophets and apostles, jointly centring in this truth; although they see not Jesus with their bodily eyes; of whom *Peter* speaks, 1st epistle, i, 8. *In whom, though now ye see him not, yet believing, ye rejoice with joy unspeakable, and full of glory.*

We find him not only shewing himself to them, but eating and drinking with them after his resurrection. The evening of the day of his resurrection, when he walked unknown with two of the disciples, when they came to sit at meat with them, *he took bread and blessed, and brake and gave to them; and their eyes were opened and they knew him.* They rose up the same hour, and returned to *Jerusalem;* and found the eleven gathered together, and they that were with them, saying, *The* Lord *is risen indeed, and hath appeared unto Simon:* And they told what things were done in the way, and how he was known of them, in breaking of bread. And as they thus spake, Jesus himself stood in the midst, and said, peace unto you. When they were terrified and affrighted, supposing they had seen a spirit, he bid them behold his hands and his feet, that it was he himself; bid them handle him, and be satisfied he had flesh and bones; and shewed them his hands and his feet. And while they believed not for joy and wondered, he said unto them, have ye any meat? And they gave him a piece of a broiled fish and a honey-comb; and he took it and did eat before them, *Luke* xxiv. 43. We have another account of his dining with them, *John* xxi. from the 10th to the 13th. And *Peter* speaks of it, *Acts* x. 40, 41. Him
God

God raised up and shewed him openly; not to all the people, *but to us who did eat and drink with him after he rose from the dead.* This part of the evidence may be closed with the testimony of Paul, 1st, Cor. xv. 4th to the 8th. *That he rose again the third day, according to the scriptures: And that he was seen of Cephas, then of the twelve. After that he was seen of above five hundred brethren at once; of whom the greater part remain unto this present, but some are fallen asleep. After that he was seen of James; then of all the apostles. And last of all he was seen of me also, as of one born out of due time.*

PART II.

The gift of the HOLY GHOST :—*The spread of the Gospel: The miracles wrought in confirmation of the Truth :—The difference between them and the deceivable miracles of Antichrist.*

THE gift of the HOLY GHOST, according to the promise of JESUS CHRIST to his disciples, is another evidence of this truth, with which is connected the Apostles' testimony, or their bearing witness of the resurrection of the LORD JESUS. When JESUS CHRIST *told his disciples,* John xiv. 2, *I go to prepare a place for you.* Chap. xvi. 5, 7, *But now I go my way to him that sent me. Nevertheless, I tell you the truth; it is expedient for you that I go away: For if I go not away, the Comforter will not come unto you; but if I depart I will send him unto you. I will pray the Father, and he shall give you another Comforter, that he may abide with you forever; but the Comforter, the* HOLY GHOST, *whom the Father will send in my name, he shall teach you all things, and bring all things to your remembrance, whatsoever I have said unto you.* And *Luke* tells us in the history

of

of the *Acts* of the *Apostles*, chap. i. 4, 5. That JESUS *being assembled together with them, commanded them that they should not depart from Jerusalem, but wait for the promise of the Father, which ye have heard of me; for John truly baptized with water, but ye shall be baptized with the* HOLY GHOST, *not many days hence.* This having its accomplishment after the ascension of JESUS CHRIST, while the disciples tarried together at *Jerusalem*, waiting for it, according to the LORD's direction, as we have account, *Acts* ii. evidences the truth before us, that JESUS CHRIST is the Son of GOD, which will more fully appear, if we consider the office of the Spirit, or the design of his being sent, as expressed by JESUS CHRIST unto his disciples before his death, *John* xvi. 13. *When he, the Spirit of truth, is come, he shall guide you into all truth; for he shall not speak of himself; but whatsoever he shall hear, that shall he speak: And he will shew you things to come. He shall glorify me: for he shall take of mine, and shew it unto you, John* xv. 26. *But when the Comforter is come, whom I will send unto you from the Father, the spirit of truth, which proceedeth from the Father, he shall testify of me. And ye also shall bear witness, because ye have been with me from the beginning, Acts* i. 8. *But ye shall receive power after that the* HOLY GHOST *is come upon you: And ye shall be witnesses unto me, both in* Jerusalem, *and in all* Judea, *and in* Samaria, *and unto the uttermost parts of the earth.*

There appears *three things* to be taken notice of.

First. He shall shew you things to come. This had its fulfilment, I conceive, in what the Apostles spake concerning the rise, reign consumption and destruction of Antichrist; as in 2 *Thess.* 2; 2 *Pet.* 2; 1 *John* ii. 18, 19; 1 *Tim.* iv. 1; 2 *Tim.* 3; and in the book of the *Revelations:* And in what is spoken of *Israel* in the xith of *Romans*, particularly from the 26th verse. Secondly.

Secondly. He shall not speak of himself, he shall glorify me; for he shall receive of mine, and shew it unto you. All that the Father hath are mine; therefore said I that he shall take of mine, and shew it unto you.

He shall not speak of himself, of his work on the hearts of men, so as to make men the objects of admiration and attention, because they can tell of the work of the Spirit on their hearts, and so are led to give out that they are some *great ones*, some peculiar favourites of heaven.

He shall glorify me, he shall take of mine and shew it unto you. The office of the spirit is to shew the glory of CHRIST, as a guide points us forward to the way in which we should go, or to the object to which we should look; and is the voice behind us, saying, this is the way, walk ye in it. We are taught to call JESUS LORD, by the HOLY GHOST, and to view his glory as our all-sufficient relief, in our destitute circumstances, to be looked to: Not to call ourselves and one another experienced Christians, that have the Spirit, and so to admire ourselves and one another as the favorites of Heaven, in preference to others. If we should take notice of the many ways in which the work of the spirit is manifested in the New Testament, they would be all found to center in the display of the glory of CHRIST, which will be more easily brought to view in considering the *third particular;* wherein the witness of the Spirit and the Apostles' testimony are connected together.

Thirdly. He shall testify of me, and ye also shall bear witness, because ye have been with me from the beginning; ye shall receive power after that the HOLY GHOST is come upon you; and ye shall be witnesses unto me in *Jerusalem,* and in all *Judea,* and *Samaria,* and to the uttermost ends of the earth.

When

When the Apostles were filled with the HOLY GHOST, on the day of Pentecost, they received power to be witnesses of the resurrection of the LORD JESUS, to men of other tongues, as the Spirit gave them utterance, though there were together at that time dwellers in *Jerusalem Jews, devote men out of every nation under heaven.* There are about fifteen different parts of the earth mentioned, from whence they came, where they were born; (probably collected together to the feast of Pentecost.) *They heard every man in his own tongue, wherein they were born.* What they heard was proving from the Scriptures that JESUS was the CHRIST, as evidenced by his resurrection from the dead: as may be seen by *Peter*'s discourse to them, v. 36. *Therefore let all the house of Israel know assuredly that* GOD *hath made that same* JESUS *whom ye have crucified both* LORD *and* CHRIST; the effect of which was the addition of about three thousand souls, to the number of those that called JESUS LORD, by the HOLY GHOST. The apostles did not arrogate any thing to themselves; for when the *lame man* was healed in the next chapter, by the gift of healing from the same Spirit, and the people ran together into *Solomon*'s porch, greatly wondering, *Peter* answered to the people, Ye men of *Israel*, why marvel ye at this? Or why look ye so earnestly upon us, as tho' by our own power or holiness we had made this man to walk? *The* GOD *of Abraham, and of Isaac, and of Jacob, the* GOD *of our Fathers hath glorified his Son* JESUS, *whom ye delivered up, and denied in the presence of Pilate, when he was determined to let him go; but ye denied the* HOLY ONE *and the just, and desired a murderer to be granted unto you, and killed the Prince of Life, whom* GOD *hath raised from the dead, whereof we are witnesses, and his name, through faith in his name, hath made this man strong, whom ye see and know; yea,*

yea, the faith that is by him hath given him this perfect soundness in the presence of you all. And tho' on their speaking to the people, the priests and the captain of the temple and the Sadducees came upon them, being grieved that they taught the people, and preached through Jesus, the resurrection from the dead, and laid hands on them, and put them in hold until the next day; yet many of them that heard the word believed; and the number of the men were about five thousand.

The next day, being brought before the rulers, they received power to be witnesses to this truth, before these rulers in *Jerusalem;* being filled with the Holy Ghost, *Peter* said unto them, Ye rulers of the people and elders of *Israel,* if we this day be examined of the good deed done to the impotent man, by what means he is made whole, *be it known to you all, and to all the people of Israel, that by the name of* Jesus Christ, *of Nazareth, whom ye crucified, whom* God *raised from the dead, even by him doth this man stand before you whole:* This is the stone set at nought by you builders, which is become the head of the corner. Neither is there salvation in any other; for there is none other name under Heaven given among men, whereby we must be saved. Thus with great power gave the apostles witness of the resurrection; and though they straitly threatened and commanded them not to speak at all, nor teach in the name of Jesus, they received power to answer; Whether it be right in the sight of God to hearken to you more than unto God, judge ye? We ought to obey God rather than man; we cannot but speak the things which we have heard and seen.

Thus hath the apostles, bearing witness unto Jesus at *Jerusalem,* and *Judea* been hinted at. The History of the *Acts* of the *Apostles* abounds with other like instances: But I pass to mention their being witnesses in *Samaria*, and to the uttermost ends of the earth. Upon the persecution against the church at *Jerusalem*, they that were scattered went every where preaching the word. Then *Philip* went down to *Samaria* and preached CHRIST there. And when the apostles heard that *Samaria* had received the word of GOD, they sent to them *Peter* and *John*: And they, when they had testified and preached the word of the LORD, returned to *Jerusalem* and preached the gospel in many villages of the *Samaritans*. *Philip* was sent to the desert, where he met the *Ethiopean* Eunuch, and preached CHRIST to him, from the liiid of *Isaiah*. *Philip* was after found at *Azotus*, and passing through he preached in all the cities until he came to *Cesarea*.

In the above-mentioned history *Luke* gives an account of the apostles' being witnesses in *Antioch, Ataliah, Berea, Cesarea, Cyprus, Cyrean, Cicillia, Damascus, Derbe, Ephesus, Galatia, Joppa, Iconium, Illyricom, Lydda, Lystra, Macedonia, Missa, Paphos, Phenicia, Perga, Pisidia, Pamphilia, Salamis, Selucia, Syria, Troas* and *Thessalonica*: Which are here mentioned to illustrate the fulfilment of the promise of JESUS CHRIST to his disciples: Ye shall receive power after that the HOLY GHOST is come upon you; and ye shall be witnesses unto me in *Samaria*, and to the uttermost parts of the earth.

Here it may be added, that the Apostles in their testimony, and first Disciples, appeared sincere; they really believed the truth they testified, because they worshipped JESUS CHRIST as GOD. In endeavouring, for my own satisfaction, to look into the New Testament, to see who were believers, that, laying aside tradition, I might find what was the faith of the Gospel: From thence I could not but draw this conclusion, that those who saw the glory of CHRIST in so satisfactory a manner as to call him LORD, and address

dress him as the object of their worship, were believers: These appeared to understand the mystery of godliness, that God was manifest in the flesh. When I came to *Matt.* viii. 2. And behold a leper worshipping him, saying, LORD! if thou wilt thou canst make me clean, I was satisfied I found a New Testament Believer: And reading on to ver. 6, 7, 8, I saw a Centurion beseeching him, saying, LORD, my servant lyeth at home sick of the palsy, grievously tormented. JESUS *saith, I will come and heal him. The Centurion answered, and said,* LORD, *I am not worthy that thou shouldst come under my roof, but speak the word only and my servant shall be healed;* I thought I had found another, and was confirmed that I was right, by reading down to the 10th verse; *When* JESUS *heard, he marveled and said, I have not found so great faith, no not in Israel.* In looking into the 9th chapter I saw a number of believers, whose faith was manifested by their works, in bringing a man sick of the palsy to JESUS. I call them Believers with good authority; for JESUS saw their faith. Proceeding to verse 18th, I find another Believer, a worshipper of JESUS, saying to him, My daughter is now dead; but come and lay thine hand upon her and she shall live. A diseased woman, in the crowd, is next brought in, in a parenthesis, who had such faith in him, as to say within herself, If I may but touch the hem of his garment I shall be whole. Next we come to the two blind men, v. 27, who followed him, crying and saying, Thou Son of *David*, have mercy on us. And as they addressed him as Son of *David*, JESUS was pleased to give them opportunity to profess their faith, and worship him as LORD: *Believest thou that I am able to do this? They said unto him, Yea,* Lord. Were I to indulge myself further in this agreeable company, I might seem tedious, having already looked over two chapters; but this may suffice for a specimen,

that

that the first Disciples, together with the Apostles, worshipped Jesus as Lord; beholding his glory, the glory of the only begotten of the Father, full of grace and truth, they address him as the object of their worship; Lord increase our faith; Lord to whom shall we go but unto Thee? Thou hast the words of eternal life, and we believe, and are sure that thou art the Christ, the Son of the living God. Their testimony being most surely believed of themselves, it carried them to count all things but loss for the excellency of the knowledge of Christ Jesus their Lord. But I am told, that the addressing of Jesus Christ as Lord, is not an evidence that they believed the divinity of his Person, or worshipped him, seeing there are Lords many, and the term Lord is often used for a superior.

But I cannot think the instances that I have, or that might be mentioned, can be thus set aside; and I am happy to find it is the description and character of the first disciples, *Acts* ix. 21. Them that call on this name: And the 1st epistle to the *Corinthians* is not only directed to the church of God at *Corinth*; to them that are sanctified in Christ Jesus, called saints; but to all that in every place call upon the name of Jesus Christ our Lord, both theirs and ours. It seems *Paul* thought it the character of the sanctified in Christ Jesus. And dying *Stephen* addresses Jesus as the object of his worship, in the same language with which Jesus addresses the father. They stoned *Stephen*, calling upon, and saying, Lord Jesus receive my spirit. The word *GOD* is supplied by the translators. So we have *Stephen* addressing Jesus Christ, as the object of his worship in his most serious and important dying hour, calling upon and saying, Lord Jesus receive my spirit. Here I thought to have closed what I intended, upon the evidence of the sincerity of the apostles and first disciples,

ciples, in their belief of their testimony; being so satisfied therewith, as without hesitation, to direct their worship to him, as the true GOD and eternal life: But as the thought has been objected to as above, (and bringing the callers on that name to view is agreeable) I would a little further pursue the subject. In *Matt.* xv. 22, 25, we have a woman of *Canaan* crying unto him, saying, *Have mercy on me, O* LORD, *thou* SON *of David!* Then came she and worshipped him, saying, LORD, *help me.* She was a caller on that name, a New-Testament believer, as JESUS CHRIST himself testifies; O woman, great is thy faith! She appears to be divinely taught to understand the question the pharisees could not answer, what think ye of CHRIST, whose son is he? They say unto him the son of *David.* How then doth *David* in spirit call him LORD, saying, the LORD said to my LORD, sit thou at my right hand, until I make thine enemies thy foot stool. If *David* then call him LORD, how is he his son? She looks to him in this united character, which can be seen in GOD manifest in the flesh.

In the 17th chap. we find another believer, tho' a weak one, calling on that name, v. 14. a man kneeling down to him and saying, LORD *have mercy on my son, for he is lunatick,* and sore vexed. I call him a weak one, because *Mark* says, He addressed JESUS with, If thou canst do any thing, have mercy on us and help us. JESUS saith unto him, *If thou canst believe, all things are possible to him that believeth: And straitway the father of the child cried and said, with tears,* LORD *I believe, help thou my unbelief.* I might take notice of the multitudes that came and were brought to CHRIST for healing, whose faith in and worshipping JESUS is not particularly mentioned, though it is clearly implied; for who would come themselves, or bring their diseased friends to be healed, ed, if they did not believe him able to heal them? And such as were healed by him, previous to their knowledge of him, and without their application to him, were thereby brought to know and own him, as the man born blind; *John* ix. 38. He said, LORD *I believe, and he worshipped him.* I might take notice of the calling of the apostles; of *Peter*'s confession, that had CHRIST's approbation; of *Nathaniel*'s conviction and confession; of *Thomas*, who, upon conviction, with full satisfaction said, *My* LORD *and my* GOD: But shall close with the crucified thief; LORD *remember me when thou comest to thy kingdom.* Thus the apostles' bearing witness, with their sincerity herein, has been briefly hinted at. The HOLY GHOST testifying of CHRIST in connexion therewith, is to be seen in the miracles wrought by the apostles, in confirmation of their testimony, by which GOD bare witness with signs and wonders, and divers miracles, and gifts of the HOLY GHOST, according to his own will; when it was the divine will that miracles should be wrought, in confirmation of the witness of the resurrection of the LORD JESUS, which the apostles bare. Perhaps it would be too lengthy to recite the many miracles wrought by the apostles, in confirmation of their doctrine, the healing the lame man has been already mentioned. I shall only recite the passage in *Acts* v. 12. And by the hands of the apostles were many signs and wonders wrought among the people; insomuch as they brought the sick into the streets, and laid on beds and couches, that at the least, the shadow of *Peter*'s passing by might overshadow some of them. Then came also a multitude out of the cities round about unto *Jerusalem*, bringing sick folks, and them that were vexed with unclean spirits; and they were healed *every one*. With the miracles which *Philip* did, in confirmation of the preaching of CHRIST in *Samaria*, which are thus recorded; Unclean spirits, crying

crying with a loud voice, came out of many that were possessed; and many taken with palsies, and that were lame, were healed. And that God wrought special miracles by the hands of *Paul*, so that from his body were brought handkerchiefs or aprons, and the diseases departed from them, and the evil spirits went out of them.

But here may arise an enquiry, in that we are told of the coming of antichrist, whose coming is after the working of satan, with all power, and signs, and lying wonders, and with all deceivableness of unrighteousness, 2 *Thes.* ii. 9. 10. And of the beast, the spirit of devils, and the false prophet, *Rev.* xiii. 13, 14—xvi. 14—xix. 20; that wrought miracles, whereby men were deceived. How may the difference be known, between the miracles wrought by Jesus Christ and his apostles, under the influence of the Holy Ghost, in confirmation of the doctrine of Christ, and the signs, wonders and miracles of antichrist, the beast, false prophet and spirit of devils.

To which it may be replied, That there are *two things* ever observable in the miracles wrought by Jesus Christ and his Apostles.

Ist. They were to testify of Christ.

IIdly. To relieve the afflicted.

Ist. To testify of Christ. Those wrought by Jesus Christ were to manifest his true character; to prove his claim to be the Son of God, one with the Father. If ye believe not me, believe the works, the works I do in my Father's name bear witness of me.

So also those wrought by the hands of the Apostles were to testify of him, agreeable to what Jesus Christ said unto them, *He shall testify of me*, and ye also shall bear witness because ye have been with me from the beginning. While they bear witness to the resurrection of the Lord Jesus, miracles wrought

by

by the power of the HOLY GHOST, testified of the truth which they bear witness to. It was not the piety, power or holiness of the Apostles; they declared themselves to be men of like passions with their hearers: But it was the dignity and glory of CHRIST that was hereby made manifest.

IIdly. They were to relieve the afflicted, both in their bodies and minds. For instance, let us view the man sick of the palsy, believing JESUS, when he said, Son thy sins be forgiven thee, and his afflicted mind is relieved. He is of good cheer indeed, and that his faith might be confirmed, as well as that others might know he had power on earth to forgive sins, he is bid to arise, take up his couch and go to his house. His body is relieved, and he is able to carry that on which he lay, out before them all.

The like may be said of all the miracles wrought by JESUS CHRIST; they were all miracles of mercy to the blind, deaf, dumb, maimed, possessed, &c. not the poorest, meanest, most destitute and miserable, ever cast out, that came to him, nor any case beyond his power, whereby he was still manifesting himself mighty to save. These are left on record both as the ground of our faith in him, and as an encouragement for the most dejected and abject children of men, to look to him from all the ends of the earth and be saved, whatever be their distresses.

Thus were the miracles wrought by the apostles, miracles of relief to the afflicted, both in their bodies and minds. Let us view the instance of the lame man that never had walked, though above forty years old, to whom *Peter* said, Silver and gold have I none, but such as I have give I thee *in the name of* JESUS CHRIST, *of Nazareth, rise up and walk.* See him leaping and walking; and we see him relieved of his bodily infirmity; view him praising GOD; and we see his mind relieved. See the sequel;

sequel; and we see it is by Jesus of *Nazareth*, who was crucified, whom God raised from the dead, and to confirm the witness the apostles bare of him: But the deceivable miracles,

Ist. Testify of men.

IIdly. Establish falshood.

IIIdly. Lead men into slavish fear, darkness and perplexity.

Ist. They testify of men, *Acts* viii. 9. *Simon* used sorcery and bewitched the people, giving out that *himself* was some great one, to whom they gave heed. So antichrist, spoken of by the apostles, 2 *Thess.* ii. whose coming is after the working of satan, with all power, and signs, and lying wonders, and with all deceivableness of unrighteousness, is he who opposeth and exalteth himself above all that is called God, or that is worshipped; so that he, as God, sitteth in the temple of God, shewing himself that he is God. This was undoubtedly manifest when the authority of the church was held more sacred than the written word, and a measure of it is to be seen wherever the decrees, counsels, confessions and catechisms of men are preferred before the written word, or where they appear to have more weight and influence: The ground of this is, they were wonderfully pious, learned and holy men, who were not likely to be deceived, and we have been ready to say, if we were as good as they we should not fear, which is idolatry, putting the creature in the place of the Creator; so worshipping and serving the creature more than the Creator, who is God, blessed forever.

IIdly. To establish falshood, to lead the mind from the fountain of living waters, to broken cisterns that can hold no water; for while they testify of the piety and holiness of men, and lead to the above-mentioned idolatry, they testify of that which is not, of error and falshood: Because the scripture testifies of man, That there is none righteous, no not one; they are all gone out of the way; all we like sheep have gone astray. When we look to men there is no cluster to eat, the good is perished out of the earth, and none upright among men; the best of them is a briar, the most upright, sharper than a thorn hedge: So it leads

IIIdly. To slavish fear, darkness and perplexity. The fear of man bringeth a snare; the spirit of antichrist testifying of man, bringing their persons into admiration, tends to subject men to them for their supposed piety and importance, and to look to them as their guides, and to look to themselves, in order to qualify them to look to JESUS, in manner and form as they shall direct them, which will soon bewilder and perplex them with the anxious inquiry, what lack I yet, to adorn myself suitably to go to JESUS, that I may obtain salvation by him?

The sum of the answer to the above inquiry is, Every spirit that confesseth that JESUS is come in the flesh, is of GOD; for if JESUS is come in the flesh, he hath in our nature and in our stead, fulfilled all righteousness, obeyed the precept and suffered the penalty of the law, which is manifest, in his resurrection from the dead, when he rose for our justification; the belief of this truth relieves the mind, and gives the answer of a good conscience towards GOD.

But every spirit that confesseth not that JESUS is come in the flesh, is not of GOD; the spirit that leads us to look to men and to ourselves, to put forth a helping hand to interest us in the divine favour, and insists that the work of CHRIST is not itself alone all-sufficient to recommend us thereto, is the spirit of antichrist, 1 *John*, iv. 3. It may be said, antichrist holds forth the evidences of the truth of the gospel, as the apostles foretold of the rise, reign, consumption and destruction of antichrist, who hath arisen and reigned even over the kings of the earth, whom the LORD has been

been consuming with the spirit of his mouth, and will destroy by the brightness of his coming.

The spirit of antichrist, whose coming is after the working of satan, with all power, signs, and lying wonders, as it testifies of men, and has raised them into places of profit, worldly honour and power over their fellow creatures, has led men into bondage and slavery to those thus raised, and into darkness and perplexity, subjecting them to religious tyranny and persecution, so as to change the appearance of primitive christianity, and prejudice the minds of unbelievers, both *Jews* and *Gentiles*, against the christian religion.

The spirit of CHRIST which testifies of him bows down the loftiness, and lays low the haughtiness of men, so that the LORD alone is exalted: And where the spirit of the LORD is, there is liberty, light, joy and gladness; and men are taught thereby to love their enemies, to do good to them that hate them, and pray for them that despitefully use and persecute them, to love one another as he hath loved them, and by love to serve one another: The consideration of which evidences and manifests the New-Testament religion to be divine, and the author of it to be the Alpha and Omega, the begining and the ending, the first and the last; and so far as it prevails it cannot fail to recommend the religion that teaches and inforces it to the consciences of all men. By this shall all men know *ye are my disciples, if ye love one another.*

PART III.

The Jews an Evidence of the Truth before us.

I MIGHT farther add, that the *Jews* may be brought in as another evidence to the truth before us, as they are preserved in the providence of GOD, in their dispersions among the nations cleaving to *Moses,* who wrote of Jesus Christ, as living witnesses of the truth of the record of the Old-Testament scriptures, from which scriptures the apostles of the Lord and Saviour proved the truth of what they testified concerning Jesus, as being fulfilled in him. So likewise in the fulfilment of what Jesus Christ said concerning them, that should be consequent on their rejecting him and persecuting his disciples.

Ist. Their rejecting him; see the parable of the vineyard, *Matt.* xxi. 38, 41. *Mark* xii. 7, 8, 9. *Luke* xx. 14, 15, 16. He says in *Matt.* xxiii. 37, 38, and *Luke* xiii. 34, 35. *O! Jerusalem, Jerusalem! Thou that killest the prophets and stonest them that are sent unto you! How often would I have gathered you as a hen gathereth her chickens under her wings, but ye would not! Behold your house is left unto you desolate!* So also in *Matt.* xxiv. 12—*Mark* xxi. 5, 6, when his disciples called him to view the stones and the building of the temple, he said, *Verily I say unto you, there shall not be left one stone upon another that shall not be thrown down*; which had its literal accomplishment in the destruction of *Jerusalem* and the temple, and the very place where they stood ploughed as a field, according to the prophet *Micah*, which was consequent on their rejecting him: And,

IIdly. Persecuting his disciples; *Matt.* xxi. from 34. *Wherefore behold I send you prophets and wise men and scribes, and of them ye shall kill and crucify, and of them ye shall scourge in your synagogues, and persecute from city to city.* Jesus told them this should come upon them, previous to the destruction of *Jerusalem;* for when he was speaking of that event, he tells them, *Luke* xxi. 12, 16. *But before all these they shall lay their hands on you and persecute, delivering you up to the synagogues, and into prisons, being brought before kings and rluers for my name sake. And ye shall be betrayed both by parents and brethren, and kinsfolks and friends; and of you shall they cause* to be put to death. And as he foretold of the destruction of *Jerusalem* and the temple, and warned his disciples of what they should meet with, or what should befall them : So he gave them a token, which they understood, when to make their escape from those dreadful calamities, *Matt*. xxiv. 15 and onward—*Mark* xiii. from v. 14—*Luke* xxi. 20, &c.

I suppose there is a fund of evidence to the truth before us, in what befel the children of *Israel*, in all that came upon them, the blessing and the curse; and their being rooted out of their land, in anger and wrath, and great indignation, and cast into another land, as at this day, mentioned *Deut*. xxix. 28—xxx. 1; which will more fully appear when v. 6 shall have its accomplishment : *And the* Lord *thy* God *shall circumcise thy heart and the heart of thy seed, to love the* Lord *thy* God *with all thine heart and with all thy soul, that thou mayst live ;* which is similar to the prophecy *Isa*. lix. 20; which is thus quoted by the Apostle, *Rom*. xi. 26 : As it is written, *There shall come out of Zion the Deliverer, and turn away ungodliness from Jacob. For this my covenant unto them, when I shall take away their sins.* This is to take place, according to the Apostle, when the fulness of the *Gentiles* shall come in, and so all *Israel* shall be saved ; for notwithstanding they are, as concerning the Gospel, enemies for the sake of the *Gentiles*, yet, as touching the election, they are beloved for their Father's sake, for the gifts and calling of God are without repentance. I apprehend, Jesus Christ speaks of the same thing when he says, Ye shall not see me until ye say, *Blessed is he that cometh in the name of the* Lord. Thus the prophet spake of Jesus, *Psalm* cxviii. 26. Thus the multitudes, *Matt*. xxi. 9. that went before and that followed after Jesus, riding to *Jerusalem*, cried Hosanna! *Blessed is he that cometh in the name of the* Lord! And thus shall

the

the *Jews* do when their hearts are circumcised to love the LORD their GOD with all their hearts.

Thus have I hinted at many particulars, wherein the evidences of the truth of the good news of the gospel are contained, as knowing that where the character of JESUS CHRIST is understood, and the evidences of the truth testified of him are satisfactory to the mind, nothing can hinder rejoicing in him; for so sure as he is GOD manifest in the flesh, as his claim to Deity is just, as he rose again from the dead, so sure was his obedience in our nature perfect, and his one sacrifice did forever take away sin. The FATHER is well pleased for his righteousness sake, and we are made accepted in the beloved; for, says the Apostle, all things are of GOD, *who hath reconciled us to himself by* JESUS CHRIST; and least that should be looked upon as the privilege of the Apostles and first christians only, he adds, GOD *was in* CHRIST, *reconciling the world unto himself, not imputing their trespasses unto them; for he hath made him sin for us who knew no sin, that we might be made the righteousness of* GOD *in him.* Hence arises the answer of a good conscience towards GOD, by the resurrection of JESUS CHRIST, which the Apostle calls the baptism that now saves us; so that the person whose mind was just now perplexed with a sense of guilt, full of anxiety and distress, turning every way with disappointment to broken cisterns that can hold no water, upon understanding the import of the resurrection of JESUS CHRIST, finds that which quiets his mind and answers all objections, agreeable to the Apostle, *Rom.* viii. It is GOD that justifieth, who is he that condemneth? It is CHRIST that died; yea, rather that is risen again from the dead. We read of being begotten again to a lively hope by the resurrection of JESUS CHRIST from the dead, 1 *Pet.* i. 4.

CHAP.

CHAP. V.

The good contained in the TRUTH *thus evidenced, and our* Obligation *to keep it always in* Remembrance.

THIS leads to the consideration of the good contained in the glad tidings of the Gospel, which respects both the life that now is and that which is to come, being furnished with the answer of a good conscience towards GOD, by the resurrection of JESUS CHRIST, under a sense of our own guilt, inability and folly, and the various causes of shame, fear and terror that arise from a view of ourselves, to have assurance from the scriptures *that* CHRIST *was delivered for our offences, and rose again for our justification,* Rom. iv. 25. That CHRIST died for our sins according to the scriptures, and that he was buried and rose again the third day, according to the scriptures, 1 Cor. xv. 3, 4, shews our peace is made with GOD by him who is our peace, and hath made peace by the blood of his cross. The work is finished in his death, and witnessed in his resurrection; the hope we are begotten to is a lively hope, a hope that maketh not ashamed; of which the Apostle speaks, *Rom.* v. 5. For when he speaks of JESUS being delivered for our offences, and being raised again for our justification, ch. iv. 25, he adds, ch. v. 1. *Therefore being justified:* upon believing this truth, *we have peace with* GOD, *through our* LORD JESUS CHRIST, by whom we have access by faith into this grace wherein we now stand, and rejoice in the hope of the glory of GOD. This made them glory in tribulation, which wrought patience, experience and hope; and this hope maketh not ashamed, because the love of GOD is shed abroad in our hearts by the HOLY GHOST, which is given to us. How was the

love

love of God shed abroad in their hearts, but in their being satisfied and assured of the truth of the manifestation of it in the death and resurrection of Jesus Christ, as the Apostle adds in the next verse; For when we were without strength Christ died for the ungodly, who was delivered for our offences, and rose again for our justification: Therefore the hope that comes thereby is a lively hope, springing from the truth, from the perfect work of Christ; not the hope of the hypocrite; for what is that, *though he hath gained*; though he hath gained a good opinion of himself, as being distinguished from some of his fellow-creatures in point of acceptance with God, on account of something wrought in or done by him; will it do to mention before God when trouble comes? Will he hear his cry on that account? Will he hear him in his own name? Or though he hath gained the good opinion of others, what is it when God takes away his soul? Hopes from this quarter is as a spider's web, as the giving up the ghost: While the hope that comes by the resurrection of Christ maketh not ashamed, is a lively hope. This is the Gospel which the Apostle preached, by which, says he, ye are saved, if ye keep in memory what I preached unto you, unless ye have believed in vain. How believed in vain? If Christ be not raised your faith is vain, and you are yet in your sins: But, says he, Now is Christ risen and become the first fruits of them that slept. Hence it follows, their faith is not vain, they believed a truth; therefore did not believe in vain, therefore they are not in their sins, they are saved by the gospel, the hope is a lively hope.

Begotten to a lively hope; to an inheritance undefiled and that fadeth not away, reserved in the Heavens.

To an inheritance; to as many as received him, or believed the truth concerning him, or received his testimony,

testimony, to them gave he power to become the sons of God; and if children, then heirs; heirs of God, joint heirs with Christ; who inherits all things, and could say, All that the Father hath is mine; all mine are thine, and thine are mine; who has prayed for his disciples that they may be with him to behold his glory, and hath said unto them; Because I live, ye shall live also. This his inheritance is incorruptible, and will never fade away, because it is his in perfect righteousness, and altogether undefiled, and it is beyond the reach of moth, rust or thieves, being reserved in the Heavens.

These hints lead to a contemplation of that good which is contained in the gospel, which hath height and depth, length and breadth, that passeth knowledge, as it respects the present life, and leads to an understanding of the wise man's question and answer, in *Ecclef.* vi. 12—vii. 1. Who knoweth what good for man in life, or what is man's chief good all the days of his vain life, which he spendeth as a shadow? The answer is, a name better than precious ointment, the name above every name, the knowledge of which shews the day of a man's death better than the day of his birth; this is man's chief good in life. He that findeth me, findeth life, and shall obtain favour of the Lord; Whoso harkeneth unto me shall dwell safely, and be quiet from fear of evil, as knowing that all things shall work together for good, to them that love God; to them that are called according to his purpose. And with respect to the life to come, if the apostle saith, eye hath not seen, nor ear heard, neither have entered into the heart of man the things that God hath prepared for them that love him, well may I leave it in the admiring language of the Psalmist, O how great is thy goodness which thou hast laid up for them that fear thee! Thou hast wrought for them that trust in thee, before the sons of men.

May I never forget this truth, that is thus evidenced, and contains in it man's chief good in this life and the life to come. When the apostle would have *Timothy* be strong in the grace that is in CHRIST JESUS, and endure hardness as a good soldier of JESUS CHRIST, he tells him to *remember that* JESUS CHRIST, *of the seed of David, was raised from the dead*, as that which was all-sufficient to animate him hereunto; and when he gives the *Corinthians* a brief account of the gospel, that he and his fellow-apostles preached, how that CHRIST died for our sins, and was buried and rose again the third day, according to the scriptures, and that he was seen of his chosen witnesses, many of which were then alive, though some had fallen asleep, he says, of this gospel, *by which ye are saved, if we keep in memory what I preached unto you.* How is he to be understood? Doth the gospel save on condition of keeping in memory, so that if they forgot it they were lost?

I conceive the meaning of the apostle to be as if he had said, what I have preached is a precious truth, in which is all our salvation. Now then if those that believe this truth, keep it in memory, it will save them from innumerable evils they will otherways be exposed to: For in this truth there is a source of obligation and consolation which ought always to be kept in memory.

First. For obligation.

The remembrance that JESUS CHRIST died for our sins, and rose again for our justification, will always demonstrate to the mind, that we are not our own, but bought with a price, and obliged to glorify him in our spirits and bodies which are his: So that when temptation besets us, to induce us to act, according to our own lusts in opposition to his will concerning us; to act according to the prince of the power of the air, the spirit that now worketh in the children

children of disobedience. The remembrance of this truth, is like taking the shield of faith, which quenches the fiery darts of the devil. Under this head of obligation may be said, (1st,) We are hereby put in mind of the apostle's exhortation, be ye reconciled to God; which he inforceth from the certainty of this truth: For he hath made him to be sin for us, who knew no sin, that we might be made the righteousness of God in him. Seeing God was in Christ reconciling the world to himself, where is enmity? It must be in us; therefore be ye reconciled unto God; to his way of reconciling us to himself, to which we are by nature enemies, our pride of heart would not be thus beholden; but it is the way infinitely wise, in which mercy and truth meet together, righteousness and peace embrace each other, in which our salvation is secured, our haughtiness humbled and the Lord alone is exalted. Be ye reconciled to God, to all his dispensations towards us, which all come from him who is love, with a design of love to us: Be ye reconciled to be at his dispose through life, and resigned to him in death; to look on ourselves, our children, our estates, our time and talents, as all belonging to him, to be improved to his glory, while he intrusts us with them; to be resigned when he calls for them, with thankfulness that we have so long enjoyed them. Blessed Jesus, thou hast taught us to pray, Thy will be done! (2dly.) The remembrance of this truth obliges us to be reconciled one to another, and live in love and peace, one with another. For a person to have all his hopes solely founded on the free forgiveness of ten thousand talents, and have his brother by the throat for a few pence, how inconsistent and ungreatful must it appear! To see an injury, perhaps only a supposed one, not real, or an accidental one, not designed; or if it be real and designed, to see it hoarded up in the mind; to nurse

up

up alienation, anger, revenge, &c. how contrary is it to the spirit of the gospel! To the example of JESUS CHRIST, who prayed for his enemies, and hath directed his disciples, *But love ye your enemies*; as also to the direction of the apostle, *Dearly beloved, avenge not yourselves, but rather give place to wrath: for it is written, vengeance is mine, I will repay, saith the* LORD. *Therefore, if thine enemy hunger, feed him; if he thirst, give him drink; for in so doing thou shalt heap coals of fire on his head. Be not overcome of evil, but overcome evil with good.*

Secondly. This truth is always to be kept in remembrance as a source of consolation: He is the living spring of everlasting consolation. It is GOD that justifieth, who is he that condemneth? It is CHRIST that died, yea rather that is risen again from the dead, who is even at the right hand of GOD, who also maketh intercession for us. Who shall separate us from the love of GOD in CHRIST JESUS? JESUS CHRIST is justified in the spirit, declared to be the SON of GOD with power, according to the spirit of holiness, by the resurrection from the dead. Is the head risen? Is the head justified? Who shall separate the members from a participation therein? Shall the tribulation, or distress, or famine, or nakedness, or persecution or peril, or sword they may be exposed to? Nay, in all these things they are more than conquerors through him that loved them. Let this truth be forgotten in tribulation and distress, they lay hard on, look dark and gloomy; which we are saved from by keeping the truth in memory.

To illustrate my meaning by a similitude: If I have a family full of wants, and several creditors that ought to be paid, at the same time urging upon me; if I have a sum of money that is sufficient for all need, but have laid it away and forgot it, these wants and creditors sink my spirits and perplex my mind: If I remember

remember this sum, my mind is relieved, I am saved from this perplexity, I have enough to answer all exigencies and demands, and ward off the danger my creditors were ready to threaten me with.

The importance of keeping this in memory is further manifested in the care the apostle *Peter* shews for the disciples to this end, 2 ep. ch. i. v. 12, 13, 15, Wherefore I will not be negligent to put you always in remembrance of these things; yea, I think it meet as long as I am in this tabernacle, to stir you up, by putting you in remembrance. Moreover, I will endeavour that you may be able, after my decease, to have these things always in remembrance; *for they are certain truths.* We have not followed cunningly devised fables, when we made known unto you the power and coming of JESUS CHRIST, but were eye-witnesses of his Majesty. And as the apostles are thus careful to keep this in the memory of the disciples, look which way we will, every thing seems designed to bring JESUS to remembrance. If we sit at home at our own table, the bread, the meat, the wine brings to view the true bread, the meat that endures to eternal life; the wine of consolation. If we walk abroad, the apple-tree invites us to delight and sit down under *his* shadow and taste *his* fruits; the vine invites us to contemplate our union with, and nourishment from, and fruitfulness in the true vine. If the wind pierce us, and the tempest rise, he is a hiding place from the wind, and a covert from the tempest. If we reflect on poverty or riches, where shall we see them, but in him who was rich, and for our sakes became poor, that we through his poverty might be rich? If upon life or death we do not think to purpose, until it carry our minds to him that liveth and was dead, and is alive forever; who is our life, the life of our life, and our hope in death. We can scarce turn our minds any where, but something is calculated to bring him to remembrance. The

The Lord's supper, or the breaking of bread, is peculiarly so, for as the passover Lamb, was an eminent type of Christ sufferings in his individual capacity, and had its accomplishment in Christ our passover sacrificed for us; so the bread and wine manifests his body and blood in a collective view. The bread is not a single grain, nor the cup the juice of a single grape, but the many made one. So the body of Christ is not viewed as a single individual, but the many, made one: When he, the head was lifted up and drew all men unto him, and dying for all, all died; the apostles thus judge, if one died for all, then were all dead. As all distinctions of grains are swallowed up in one bread, and all distinctions of grapes, in one cup, so faith viewing all in him, sees both *Jew* and *Gentile* reconciled in one body by the cross, and the enmity slain thereby, so that there is neither *Greek* nor *Jew*, barbarian, Cythian, bond or free, but Christ, is all in all. When we view them individually, we see both *Jew* and *Greek*, &c. but when viewed in the head of every man, all distinction is lost, and we contemplate divine love to the whole human race, with gratitude and joy; and so our obligations to love him, who first loved us, and to love one another as he hath given commandment.

I would close with an address to the believers of the foregoing news, the news of salvation by Jesus Christ in two branches:—Inquiring, is it not the indispensible duty of every one of them.

Ist. To consider what was the effect of the belief of the gospel in the days of the apostles, whom Jesus Christ connected with himself, saying, he that heareth you, heareth me; and he that despiseth you, despiseth me; and he that despiseth me, despiseth him that sent me? Of whom Jesus Christ was seen for forty days after his resurrection, speaking to them of the things pertaining to the kingdom of God:
And

And after he had thus instructed them, he sent them forth to preach the Gospel to every creature, and to teach the believers of their testimony to observe all things whatsoever he had commanded them; adding, that he was with them to the end of the world. Now the practice of the apostles thus taught of him, among the believers of their testimony, was to gather them into distinct particular churches, that in connexion one with another, they might enjoy the fellowship of the gospel, and watch over one another, and together observe all things whatsoever was commanded them. Is not this evident from the instances of the places where the apostles preached, recorded in the *Acts*, where, after their preaching, churches were gathered, elders ordained over them, and epistles wrote to them, as standing together in that connexion.

We find *Paul* in the xvith of *Acts*, at *Philippi*;[*] whereupon we have an epistle wrote to the saints at *Philippi*, with the bishops and deacons.

In *Acts* xviith, at *Thessalonica*;[†] consequent upon it, we have two epistles to the church there.

In *Acts* xviiith at *Corinth*,[‡] where he continued a year and six months among them: Consequent upon it we have two epistles to the church at *Corinth*.

In *Acts* xixth, at *Ephesus*,[§] where he spake three months

---

[*] According to the notes in the margin of our Bibles, the Apostle *Paul* was at *Philippi* in 53, and wrote the epistle to that church in 64.

[†] At *Thessalonica* in 53, and sent both the epistles to the church there in 54.

[‡] At *Corinth* in 54, and wrote his first epistle to the *Corinthians* in 59; his second in 60.

[§] He was present at *Ephesus* in 56, and in 60 we find a church there with elders, and the epistle was sent to the church in 64.—This shews it was the care of the Apostles to gather the believers into churches, and maintain a constant care of them in that connexion, both while present with them and when absent from them, not only when they were first gathered, but on all occasions ever after, as *Paul* expresses it, That which cometh upon me daily, the care of all the churches. JESUS CHRIST was not only present with them therein in those days, but lo! he is with them alway, even unto the end of the world; therefore to despise them now, is as before, to despise JESUS CHRIST and him that sent him.

months; and upon the desputations of the unbelievers, he separated the Disciples, disputing daily in the school of *Tyraunus*: And this continued for the space of two years.

In *Acts* xxth we find a church at *Ephesus* with Elders; and we have an epistle wrote to that church: Thus a considerable part of the New-Testament is expresly directed to the disciples as thus connected together.

The *Revelation* is addressed to the seven churches in *Asia*; and each epistle is closed with—He that hath an ear let him hear what the Spirit saith unto the churches. And in chap. xxii. 16. I JESUS have sent mine Angel to testify these things in the churches.

These things being so, let the love of GOD our SAVIOUR, manifested in his will that all men should be saved and come to the knowledge of the truth, constrain the believers of it to consider what they are hereby called to, and to take heed lest they be led aside from the footsteps of the first flocks, by ignorance of, inattention unto, or *lukewarmness about what is plainly pointed out in the word: But that they search the scriptures till they are satisfied of the will of GOD in CHRIST JESUS concerning them, and attend thereunto. IIdly.

---

* It is said to the church of *Laodicea*, Because thou art lukewarm, and neither cold nor hot, I will spue thee out of my mouth. Lukewarmness in its own nature tends to such a disunion as consequently end in the loss of the appearance of the profession of the name of *Jesus*, in the places where it prevails, the Apostle to the Hebrews, to guard them against it, says, Take heed brethren, lest there be in any of you an evil heart of unbelief, in departing from the living GOD, but exhort one another daily, lest any of you be hardened through the deceitfulness of sin, for we are made partakers of CHRIST, if we *hold fast* the beginning of our confidence stedfast to the end. Let us *hold fast* the profession of our faith without wavering, and let us consider one another to provoke unto love and good works. Not forsaking the assembling of ourselves together, as is the manner of some, but exhorting one another; assembling to exhort one another is connected with *holding fast* the profession of our faith, and with watching against an evil heart of unbelief, in departing from the living GOD, in opposition to lukewarmness.

IIdly. It becomes the believers of the gospel, to consider wherein this salvation consists, as it respects our conduct one to another.

His name is JESUS, he shall save his people from their sins: Sin is a transgression of the law of love bound on the disciples of JESUS CHRIST: The second commandment is, Thou shalt love thy neighbour as thyself: Love worketh no ill to his neighbour; therefore love is the fulfilling of the law.

The works of the flesh are hatred, variance, wrath, strife: The fruit of the spirit is love. Now the salvation of the Gospel consists not only in a deliverance from the curse of the law, but also in a deliverance from sin, as it is a transgression of the law: From the works of the flesh, producing the fruits of the spirit; therefore, every thing contrary to the law of love in our conversation, deportment and dealing one with another is unbecoming the believers of the gospel salvation, who ought ever to consider themselves as under the highest obligation to love their neighbour as themselves, and ever be on their guard against every thing contrary thereto.

Can we believe that declaration, I, even I am he that blotteth out thy transgressions, *for my own Name's sake*, and will not remember thy sins, and indulge any thing contrary to the spirit of forgiveness taught by the precepts and example of *Jesus Christ* and his apostles?

Can we see our brother in need, and shut up our bowels of compassion from him, while we realize the grace of our Lord *Jesus Christ*, who, though he was rich for our sakes, became poor that we through his poverty might be rich; who remembered us in our low-estate, for his mercy forever?

Doth not the truth of the Gospel News constrain us with all our hearts to bless GOD, even the Father: How unbecoming is it then, with the same mouth, upon every provocation, to curse men, who are made after the similitude of GOD? Certainly these things ought not so to be.

How inconsistent for those who profess it their highest happiness to be forever freed from the inbeing of sin, and that the SAVIOUR is most inexpressibly indeared to them, in the view of his completing this work, to indulge in the practice of that, which we cannot be happy but in a freedom from ? Which indulgence tends to the unhappiness of all to whom we are known, and with whom we are connected, as far as its influence reacheth,

The certain ground of hope in the word, that JESUS CHRIST, who hath his fan in his hand will thoroughly purge his floor, consume the chaff, burn up the tares, destroy the works of the devil, take away the dross from the silver, that there shall come forth a vessel for the finer, and that he is not only faithful and just to forgive us our sins, but to cleanse us from all unrighteousness, ought to excite us to cleanse ourselves from all filthiness of flesh and spirit, to cleanse our way, by taking heed thereto according to the word.

And by taking heed to the word, we shall find directions for our conduct, in every relation and circumstance of life, brought up to one single point by our divine teacher: Therefore all things whatsoever ye would that men should do to you, do ye even so to them ; for this is the law and the prophets. This exhortation, like all others, is grounded on the manifestation of divine grace, as is evident by being ushered in by the word therefore : If we inquire wherefore ? the connection will shew : Therefore, because of the gracious readiness of your heavenly *Father* to give good things to them that ask him : And as the law and the prophets are all here drawn together by the *master of assemblies, the one shepherd*, so they are taken apart and parcelled out to us, in exhortations suited to every relation and circumstance of life, by his apostles, as is expressed by one of them. With whose words I close :—As ye know how we exhorted, and comforted, and charged every one of you, as a father doth his children, that ye would walk worthy of GOD, who hath called you to his kingdom and glory.

THE

The GOSPEL of PEACE, &c.

SECTION II.

The GOSPEL *of* PEACE *publiſhed among all nations: Or, an* INQUIRY *concerning* REPENTANCE *and* REMISSION *of* SINS. *From the* SCRIPTURES *of the* OLD *and* NEW-TESTAMENT: *Addreſſed,* Firſt, *To the* AUTHOR *of a* PAMPHLET, *entitled,* " Divine Glory in the Condemnation of the Ungodly." Secondly, To all for whom CHRIST died.

Hearken unto me ye ſtout-hearted that are far from Righteouſneſs. I bring near my righteouſneſs: It ſhall not be far off, and my ſalvation ſhall not tarry: And I will place Salvation in Zion, for Iſrael my Glory. ISAIAH xlvi. 12, 13.

Behold the man whoſe name is the Branch. He ſhall bear the Glory. ZECHARIAH vi. 12, 13.

But now commandeth all men every where to repent. ACTS xvii. 30.

FREQUENTLY obſerving the doctrine of repentance treated of in ſuch a manner as is difficult to underſtand, in conſiſtency with the goſpel of divine grace; it has often exerciſed my mind to enquire from the ſcriptures, after a ſatisfactory view of it; and finding that after our LORD's reſurrection, when that event took place which explained the ſcriptures, he opened the underſtanding of the diſciples that they might underſtand them, and ſaid unto them,—*Thus it is written, and thus it behoved Chriſt to ſuffer and to riſe again the third day;* as in Luke xxiv. 40. 46. It is added in Verſe 47, *and that repentance and remiſſion of ſins ſhould be preached in his name among all nations beginning at Jeruſalem.*

In inquiring into the nature or meaning of repentance, it may aſſiſt me to view every part of this paſſage. As,

What

What may I understand by repentance: What by remission of sins: What by its being preached in his name: How it concerns all nations; and, Why it was to begin at Jerusalem.

I. What may be understood by repentance.

Repentance is here brought in as that which the death and resurrection of CHRIST prepared a way for the proclamation of:—He said, *Thus it is written, and thus it behoved Christ to suffer and to rise from the dead the third day;* and that repentance, &c. here is a connexion between the sufferings and resurrection of CHRIST, and the proclamation of repentance as an act of grace founded thereupon, and issued for the encouragement of the rebel to return; who otherways could look for nothing but destruction. In this view it is the gracious call of the offended Sovereign to his revolted creatures, to return to him as their rightful owner and LORD.—Isaiah xxxi. 6. *Turn ye unto him, from whom the children of Israel have deeply revolted.*

II. What may be understood by remission of sins.

Sins or trespasses are called debts, *Matt.* vi. 12, 15. When a person is in debt, it is plain that law and justice demand remittance until full payment is made; the payment of the debt is its remission, and this remission satisfies the demands of law and justice, which were against the debtor: Here then remission is full satisfaction to that law, of which sin is a transgression, and to that justice which demands penalty of the transgressor; for unless law and justice be completely satisfied, there is no remission.

III. What by its being preached in his name.

Why, surely there is no other name under Heaven given among men, whereby we must be saved, either from the delusion, ignorance and darkness, whereby we have forsaken the right way, or whereby we may be returned to our rightful owner, or whereby law

and

and juftice are fatisfied. So then he himfelf is eminently the way in all thefe refpects. *Gallations* iv. 4, 5. GOD *fent forth his Son made of a woman, made under the law, to redeem them that were under the law*: The law had a demand of perfect obedience upon them that were under it, which to them was impoffible in their own perfons; he as their head, and in their ftead, is brought in; in the volume of the book faying, *Lo! I come to do thy will:* So that whatever the law required, was perfectly obeyed by him who did always the thing that pleafed the father, who delighted to do his will, and could not be convinced of fin, but could fay, *I was upright before him, I have glorified thee on earth, and finifhed the work thou gaveft me to do;* fo that he perfectly obeyed the law.

They that were under the law were under the curfe, he as the redeemer of them that were under the law, was made a curfe for us, fo fatisfied the penalty of the law; which is manifeft in his refurrection from the dead; for when law and juftice took hold of him as head of the human nature, (as if he were the only tranfgreffor) all being confidered in him; he became our furety, and the LORD laid the iniquities of us all upon him. Now unlefs law and juftice have full fatisfaction, the furety is not difcharged; but law and juftice being fully fatisfied, he *having made peace by the blood of his crofs; it was not poffible he fhould be holden of death.—Death hath no more dominion over him.*—Therefore the furety is legally difcharged.

Thus his refurrection from the dead evidences his accomplifhment of what he was made under the law, for *i. e.* To redeem them that were under the law; fo then the refurrection of JESUS CHRIST proves him our *Redeemer.*—Whofe Redeemer?—Them that were under the law. Then we belong to him by right

right of redemption, and ought to return to him as our rightful owner, repenting of our estrangement and alienation from him: But is there any encouragement hereunto: May we be received into favour? Yes!——Repentance and remission of sins. Repentance with remission of sins is preached in his name, and because there is full remission, there is the fullest encouragement to repentance. There is no other name that repentance will do to be preached in; call a man to repentance in the name of law and justice: Repent for the curses of the law, the wrath of God, the demands of justice are against you, and will surely and suddenly overtake you, except you repent; and it may drive him to endeavour to hide himself as Adam among the trees of the garden, and, when he finds he cannot, it may drive him to despair; for repentance cannot satisfy law or justice, or appease the divine anger: Neither is it in them to produce repentance, they may stir up enmity, and drive to despair, while the gospel is out of sight.—It is the prerogative of our Redeemer that has fully remitted our sins.——*He is exalted to give repentance and remission of sins.*

Among all nations this is to be preached, Jews and Gentiles. *For God hath shewed me* (saith Peter) *that I should call no man common or unclean; what God hath sanctified, that call thou not common.* There is neither Jew nor Greek, Barbarian, Cythian, bond or free, male or female, that is excluded. Repentance and remission of sins is to be preached among all nations: If there were not full remission, how could it be preached, or how could they be called to repentance? But there is. He that is truth has ordered it to be preached as a truth among all nations; but as he was rejected at Jerusalem, are not they excluded? No, *Verily: It is to be preached among all nations,* BEGINNING AT JERUSALEM. What, though they
like

like fishes, do all they can to escape the gospel net, will not he that made his Apostles fishers of men, so direct that net, as finally to take them in, with the fulness of the Gentiles, so that all Israel may be saved, as is written: It is written, therefore it shall be accomplished: Compare *Rom.* xi. 25, to 32, with the parallel passages in the prophet.

But we may enquire if this view of repentance be agreeable to the scriptures of the Old and New-Testament,

We find when *Solomon*, in 1st of *Kings*, viii. 47. praying for the children of *Israel* carried captive for their sins, says, if they shall bethink themselves, and repent, and make supplication, and return with all their heart, &c. then hear their prayer, &c. Verse 51 shews the ground of this prayer, *for they are thy people, and thine inheritance*—The idea of their being his people, and his inheritance, appears necessary to shew the aggravations of their folly in sinning against him, and the necessity of repenting and returning to their rightful owner.—*They are thine inheritance which thou hast redeemed,* Psalm lxxiv. 2. And when they are called to repentance in the prophet *Joel*, chap. ii. 13. it is *turn to the* LORD YOUR GOD. In *Jeremiah* xxvi 13. (though a time of the greatest degeneracy) they are thus called upon, *now amend your ways, and your doings, and obey the voice of the* LORD YOUR GOD: And in *Isaiah* lv. 7. *Let the wicked forsake his way, and the unrighteous his own imaginations, and return unto the* LORD, *and he will have mercy, and to* OUR GOD *he will abundantly pardon*: And in *Hosea* xiv. 1. *O Israel return unto the* LORD THY GOD. When GOD, by the prophet *Jeremiah* in his 3d chap. calls *Israel* and *Judah* to repentance verse 1, 7, 12. *Return again to me saith the* LORD. *Turn thou unto me. Return thou backsliding Israel saith the* LORD. In verses 14 and 22, their

their obligation thereto, and the ground of their encouragement is mentioned:—Verse 14, *Return for I am married unto* you:—Verse 22. *Return ye backsliding children, I will heal your backslidings*, not, *and I will*, as a condition (the *and* is there supplied by the translators) but I will heal your backslidings.—On this encouragement, which is the only all-sufficient one, they are brought in saying, *Behold we come unto thee, for thou art the* Lord our God. And in *Isaiah* xliv, 22, it is fully expressed in a similar manner to the passage in *Luke* xxiv. now before us.

| Luke xxiv. 47. *And that repentance and remission of sins should be preached in his name.* | Isaiah, xliv. 22. *I have blotted out as a thick cloud thy transgressions, and as a cloud thy sins: Return for I have redeemed thee.* |

But if it be said these passages of the Old-Testament respect ancient Israel, as God's peculiar people, not sinners of the Gentiles,—in answer it may be said, it has been shewn it was to be preached as a truth among all nations; and the Apostle's question is ready, Is he a God of the Jews only? Is he not of the Gentiles also? Yes, of the Gentiles also:—Are they blessed in *Abraham* so are all the nations of the earth—*in thy seed shall all the nations of the earth be blessed*:—Are they his inheritance,—his possession; so are the uttermost parts of the earth. It was the disposition that would confine the divine favour to the Jews, and to the most esteemed among them, that the preaching of *John* and of *Jesus*, under the law dispensation, called them to repentance from, or called them to repent of *Matt.* iii. 2.—*Repent for the kingdom of Heaven is at hand*: He preached thus in the wilderness of Judea, among those that supposed the Messiah would raise their nation to great worldly glory, and set them above other nations and that the most esteemed among them should be most promoted

moted therein: He calls them to repent of their worldly notions of CHRIST's kingdom: It was a kingdom of Heaven that was at hand, where every one was admitted and promoted according to the good pleasure of the King in virtue of his own righteousness, not according to their own supposed personal characters: So those that were exalted in their own and others apprehensions as mountains and hills, were brought low; and those depressed with a sense of their own vileness and unworthiness, and who were justly esteemed so by others low as vallies, without any encouragement in themselves, are exalted, agreeable to *Isaiah*'s prophesy, chap. xl. 4. *Every valley shall be exalted, and every mountain and hill shall be brought low, the crooked shall be made strait, and the rough places plain; and the glory of the Lord shall be revealed, and all flesh shall see together, for the mouth of the Lord hath spoken.*

Here we have a view of a perfect plain, where one should not obstruct or overtop another, in viewing the object to be revealed—*The glory of the Lord*: And as they all expected benefit in that kingdom from their own characters; some expected to be foremost on account of their own supposed good characters, and others depressed and despairing for want of such worthiness, they are called to repent of their error and mistake—it was a kingdom of Heaven that was at hand, where, none were admitted or excluded on account of their own personal character, but every one admitted on account of the perfect character of the Messiah.—*The glory of the Lord shall be revealed*—the glory of divine wisdom, justice, grace, and mercy—the glory of all the divine attributes and perfections, harmonizing in the method of salvation, by JESUS CHRIST, according to *Psalm* lxxxv. 10, 11. *Mercy and truth are met together, righteousness and peace have kissed: Truth shall spring out of*

K *the*

the earth, and righteousness shall look down from Heaven. Thus the glory of the LORD is revealed in him who is the brightness of his glory, the light of the knowledge of the glory of the LORD is in the face of JESUS CHRIST, in whom dwells the fullness of the God-head: In him, the glory of the LORD is revealed, and in his time and way all flesh shall see together, for the mouth of the LORD hath spoken.

If what has been said of *John's* preaching "*for the kingdom of Heaven is at hand,*" be agreeable to the scriptures, then we are to understand the preaching of JESUS in *Matt.* iv. 17. "*Repent for the kingdom of Heaven is at hand.*" And *Mark* i. 15, "*The time is fulfilled*: *The kingdom of Heaven is at hand: Repent ye and believe the gospel,* (*The glad tidings, the good news of salvation by* JESUS CHRIST,") and the preaching of the twelve that JESUS sent out two by two *Mark* vi. 12. Who *went out and preached that men should repent*, in the same view.

When JESUS arose from the dead, evidencing the perfection of his character, obedience and sacrifice; evidencing that justice was fully satisfied; then repentance and remission of sins are preached in his name: There can be no encouragement to repentance without remission of sins, if there be not full remission in the perfect work of CHRIST, all is terror, despair, alienation and enmity. *I said there is no hope, no, for I have loved strangers, and after them, will I go, Jeremiah* ii. 25. Let this truth, the doctrine of remission of sins, be clear, and there are the highest motives, encouragements and obligations to repentance; there is room for it to be preached in the name of JESUS among all nations, even beginning at Jerusalem: If we need any further, see *Acts* xvii. 20. *Though the times of ignorance* GOD *winked at, but now he hath commanded all men every where to repent.* Now since his resurrection hath he commanded. Consider

sider the dignity of the commander, and the authority of his commands, *Psalm* xxxiii. 9. *He spake, and it was: He commanded, and it stood.* The Apostle pursues the thought from his resurrection to his exaltation, as we read, *Acts* v. 30, 31. *The God of our fathers raised up* Jesus, *whom ye slew and hanged on a tree, him hath* God *exalted with his right hand, a Prince and a Saviour, to give repentance to Israel and forgiveness of sins:* And in *Acts* xi. 18. we have a specimen actually taking place: *Then hath* God *also to the Gentiles granted repentance unto life.* How is this evidenced? Why, they received or believed the Apostles testimony concerning the way of acceptance with God in every nation. It was according to *the word which* God *sent to the children of Israel, preaching peace by* Jesus Christ *who is* Lord *of all*, his being anointed with the Holy Ghost, going about doing good, his death and resurrection, and the evidences of it, together with the testimony of the Prophets concerning him, as we see in *Acts* x. 34 to 44. This preaching being accompanied with the Holy Ghost, gained full credit on the minds of the Gentiles, which when the church heard, they held their peace, and glorified God, saying, then hath God also to the Gentiles granted repentance unto life: So that as soon as they believed the report of the Gospel concerning the life, death and resurrection of Jesus Christ, by the first of which the precepts of the law are perfectly obeyed; by the next, the penalty of it is suffered, or the debt to it remitted; and by the third, viz. his resurrection, we have the full evidence thereof. As soon as this is believed, it is said, then hath God also granted repentance unto life, the immediate inseparable effect of believing the remission of sins in his name.

This is illustrated in the *Thessalonians*, when they believed the apostles testimony, in the 17th of *Acts*, he says, concerning them in his first Epistle, chap. i. 9. *What manner of entrance we had unto you, and how ye turned to* GOD *from idols, to serve the living and true* GOD, *and to wait for his Son from Heaven, whom he had raised from the dead.* To turn to GOD from idols is repentance. This was in consequence of the entrance of the apostles among them, or of the *Thessalonians* believing their report. What was their report among them? See *Acts* xvii. 2, 3. *Reasoning with them out of the scriptures, opening and alleging that Christ must needs have suffered and risen again from the dead, and that Jesus whom I preach unto you, is Christ,* verse 4. *Some of them believed.* Those believers composed the church of the *Thessalonians*, of whom it is shewn, how they turned to GOD from idols.

So in the 20th of *Acts*, 21, the apostle speaks of keeping back nothing that was profitable, but *testifying both to the Jews, and also to the Greeks repentance towards* GOD, *and (or * even) faith towards our* LORD JESUS CHRIST. His preaching the faith as has been above shewn, was virtually preaching repentance, as it immediately called and led thereto. Thus the Old and New-Testament jointly evidences the same truth, that *repentance and remission of sins is preached in the name of Jesus among all nations, beginning at Jerusalem.*

How can repentance be preached otherwise. If there be not remission in the perfect work of CHRIST, he is not our Redeemer, and WE cannot be called upon, when he says, *return for I have redeemed thee;* but be not deceived, *evil communications corrupt good manners.* He is risen from the dead, he is our Redeemer, we belong to him, and blessed be his name we are called to return, for he hath redeemed us. Who? Them that were under the law, all nations, even

---

* I am informed the same Greek word which is translated *and* is also translated *even*, as in the judgment of the translators was most suitable to the passage.

even beginning at *Jerusalem*. What were we redeemed for? That repentance might be preached to us in his name, that we might return to him, that we might receive the adoption of sons. Amazing grace indeed?

Objection.—But there are two passages in the New-Testament that seem at first view to mention repentance as a condition. The first is Acts ii. 38. *Then Peter said unto them, repent and be baptized every one of you, for the remission of sins, and ye shall receive the gift of the Holy Ghost.* But if it be safe to understand this *for*, &c. as the reason or ground of the call to repentance, *Repent, because of the remission of sins*, the difficulty will disappear, and the passage appear fully consistent with the other passages that have been brought to view; and this view I think may be fairly gathered from what the apostle had before been preaching of the death and resurrection of CHRIST, in which there is remission, and the evidence of it. But if it be still urged as a condition, it can be no otherways, than as it cannot otherwise take place in our minds, for though there is remission in the one sacrifice, and so no more offering for sin as the apostle expressed it, *Hebrews* x. 18, yet it cannot take place in the minds of any while they remain in unbelief and impenitence: Yet their unbelief cannot make the truth of GOD of none effect. While persons remain in unbelief they must remain in impenitence; for how can any repent of being in a wrong way until they know JESUS who is *the way*; of their being in error, until they know JESUS, who is *the truth*; and of their being in a state of death, and all their works, dead works, until they know JESUS, who is *the life*. Or how can any repent of their alienation and enmity until they know GOD in CHRIST, the just GOD and the Saviour—their rightful owner—their Lord Redeemer.

It

It may be what is above said, may help to illustrate the other passage in *Acts* iii. 19. *Repent ye therefore and be converted, that your sins may be blotted out, when the times of refreshing shall come, from the presence of the* LORD.

Repent ye therefore. Therefore refers to what went before; what the apostle had been preaching concerning the holy one, and the just, the prince of life, his death and resurrection, in which, as before, there was remission, and the evidence of it; in which there was enough to furnish even those that were charged with killing the prince of life with hope, with the " apprehension of the mercy of GOD in CHRIST," as even the Assembly's Catechism expresses it, so as to give them ground of encouragement to repentance.

Repent ye therefore and be converted ; be turned from your error, alienation and enmity, to allegiance to the prince of life, that your sins may be blotted out : For as infidelity and impenitence are inseparable ; so is faith, repentance and allegiance : While the former continues, guilt, distress, fear, horror and perplexity, remain on the mind.

When the knowledge of CHRIST, or faith, or the belief of the truth concerning JESUS CHRIST * take place

---

* It is the work of the spirit, for *no man can say that Jesus is the Lord, but by the Holy Ghost* ; and the Prophet *Zechariah*, chap. xii. 10. expresses it thus, *I will pour upon the house of David, and on the inhabitants of Jerusalem, the spirit of grace and supplications ; and they shall look on me whom they have pierced, and they shall mourn for him, as one mourneth for his only son, and be in bitterness as one is in bitterness for his first born.* But the spirit of God makes use of the truth of the gospel as a means hereunto ; is not this intimated in *Isaiah* xxx. 21. *Thine ears shall hear a word behind thee,* * *This is the way—walk ye in it.* Is not he the messenger, the interpreter, one of a thousand spoken of, *Job* xxxiii. 23. *To shew unto man his uprightness* ; the uprightness of Jesus Christ, through which, *he is gracious to him, and faith, deliver him, for I have found a ransom ; his flesh shall be fresher than childhood, he shall return to the days of his youth, he shall pray unto God, and he shall be favourable to him, and he shall see his face with joy.* Compare this with the description of the same person before he knew Jesus Christ as in the 19, 20, 21 and 22 verses.

* For we are always looking the wrong way for remission of sins until taught of God.

place in the mind, repentance and conversion take place there also; hereupon guilt, fear and terror are removed; that which was blotted out or remitted before, in the perfect work of Christ, is also blotted out of the mind and conscience; agreeable to *Romans* viii. 33, 34. *It is* God *that justifieth; Who is he that condemneth? It is* Christ *that died, yea, rather, that is risen again:* And instead of looking for the appearing of Jesus Christ with terror and amazement, it is waited for with hope, joy and consolation, in proportion, to the strength of faith, repentance and allegiance, agreeable to the forementioned, 1st of *Thessalonians* i. 9. 10. *They themselves shew of us what manner of entering in we had unto you: How ye turned unto* God *from idols, to serve the living and true* God, *and to wait for his son from Heaven, whom he raised from the dead, Jesus who delivereth us from the wrath to come.*

Thus have I pursued the inquiry concerning gospel repentance: And purpose to close with an address,

I. To the author of a pamphlet, entitled, " *The glory of* God *in the final condemnation of the ungodly.*" And,

II. To all for whom Christ died.

I. To the Author of the Pamphlet.

Dear Sir,

AS your pamphlet was probably the occasion of the foregoing reflections, I have taken the freedom to address you on the subject. When I read your work, if I recollect the idea the doctrine there advanced gave me, it was this, That Christ died for all, to bring them into a salvable state, yet all would not be saved, though they might, if they repented, consequently God's glory would finally illustriously appear in the everlasting condemnation of the finally impenitent.

And as the ear trieth words, as the mouth tasteth meats, I found it did not sound like the report of the gospel,

gospel, and on enquiring into the doctrine of repentance, I have collected the thoughts which are presented to you, I hope in love and faithfulness. The idea I received from the scriptures of the Old Testament is, that he should finish the transgression—make an end of sin—make reconciliation for iniquity—and bring in everlasting righteousness. The New Testament witnesses that he did.—The testator appeals to the father—*I have glorified thee on earth: I have finished the work thou gavest me to do,* and cries out on the cross, *It is finished,* and seals it with his blood, and witnesses it in his resurrection, when he shews himself alive to his chosen witnesses, who testified to the same truth.—One passage may suffice: In *Hebrews* x, 11th, the apostle speaking of the priesthood under the law, says, and every priest standeth daily ministering, and offering oftentimes the same sacrifices, which can never take away sin, but this man after he had offered one sacrifice for sins, forever sat down on the right hand of God. They stood as those that had not done—could not accomplish: But the High Priest JESUS after he had offered one sacrifice *sat down* as having finished his work, *finished transgression—made an end of sin—made reconciliation for iniquity—and brought in everlasting righteousness.* Verse 18th says, *Where remission of those is, there is no more sacrifice for sin.*

Thus the scripture leads to full remission, when he had by himself purged our sins, to a finished work.

But your doctrine appears to me to lead to an unfinished work, dependent on the exercises, the exertions, in short, the will of the creature, and because they will not come, that they might have life, he must glorify himself in the destruction of multitudes for whom he died.

Let me ask you, Sir, How? Is his mercy glorified? Is his justice satisfied? Is his power made manifest?

Is

Is he mighty to save? He will have all men to be saved, not he *would*, but he will. Who hath resisted his will? Is it the will of the creature?* Cannot he make them willing in the day of his power? His people shall be; and are not all his people for whom he died? But I forbear; wishing to say no more than is sufficient to discharge my conscience in love and faithfulness to you. But I cannot pass over your Essay without taking notice of the title, to compare it with the scriptures.

| Scripture text, *Romans* iv. 5. *He that justifieth the ungodly.* Rom. v. 6, *Christ died for the ungodly.* | Your Title. *Divine Glory brought to view, in the condemnation of the ungodly.* |

On enquiry, How can this be in consistence with those scriptures? I answer, it can be no otherways in a consistence with them, than in the fulfilment of *Isaiah's* prophecy, chap. liii. 4, 5, 6. *Surely he hath borne our griefs, and carried our sorrows: Yet we did esteem him stricken, smitten of God, and afflicted. But he was wounded for our transgressions, bruised for our iniquities: The chastisement of our peace was upon him, and with his stripes we are healed. All we like sheep have gone astray; we have turned every one to his own way, and the Lord hath laid on him the iniquity of us all.* So dying for the ungodly, he justifies the ungodly, and the divine glory is brought to view illustriously to eternity herein. For mercy is glorified; justice

---

* Two Clergymen, conversing together of the doctrine of the final Universal Salvation of all men, very much wondered at each other;—one held that all for whom Christ died should certainly be saved, but that he did not die for all;—The other that he died for all, but all would not be saved, because they would not come to him. Said the latter to the former, I'm very much astonished at you, that you do not embrace that doctrine—For if I believed as you, I should, for nothing is more clear from scripture, than that Christ died for all: The former answered, I as much wonder at you, that you do not embrace it, I am sure I should, if I believed as you, for if he died for all there is no power on earth or hell can hinder their salvation;—He cannot be disappointed.

justice is satisfied: and he speaks in righteousness, when he manifests himself mighty to save.

But view the title page as it appears intended, what consolation is there for a poor, destitute, ungodly creature? Suppose him on a death bed, agonizing with anguish of soul, nothing short of persuasion that there was an all-sufficient remedy for his deplorable condition, could afford him the least comfort or relief. Were you constrained in this sad hour to administer them from those texts, in the belief of your title, would he not say, I am mocked? But perhaps you might not offer them on such an occasion. Why? Are they not scripture truths? Did not CHRIST die for the ungodly, and in proof, his dying for our sins was accepted; he rose again for our justification, and is not the knowledge of this truth all-sufficient to quiet the most guilty conscience, and give hope towards GOD? Would it be safe to tell him the law of GOD stands in full force against him, when JESUS came to redeem them that were under the law? Would it not amount to denying that JESUS is come in the flesh? Would it be safe to tell such a man to exert himself in any way, however described, as if this was the last opportunity, and his all depended on it? It would indeed be to mock him! when his all depends on what JESUS CHRIST finished, and the relief of his mind on the knowledge of it.

Suffer me a little further, if in looking over this dreadful title, I express my surprise that to it should be added in the title page, *Search the scriptures;* when you attempt to illustrate it by reasoning, without producing one text to shew that the Ever-blessed speaks of condemnation as his glory. When the scriptures speak of the divine glory as manifest in his grace, mercy and forgiveness—when *Moses* said in *Exodus* xxxiii. 18. *I beseech thee shew me thy glory,* the answer is, *I will make all my goodness pass before thee,*

thee, and will be gracious to whom I will be gracious, and will shew mercy on whom I will shew mercy: Here goodness, grace and mercy is his glory. In *Proverbs* xix. 11, we read, *the discretion of a man deferreth his anger, and* HIS GLORY *to pass over a transgression.* If we understand the proverb, and its interpretation, it doubtless refers to the man CHRIST JESUS, in whom we have the light of the knowledge of the glory of GOD.

In *Psalm* cii. 16, it is said, *When the* LORD *shall build up Zion, he shall appear in* HIS GLORY.—How is this made manifest?—In regarding the prayer of the destitute; in hearing the groaning of the prisoner, and saving the sons of death—*To declare his name in Zion, and his praise in Jerusalem*—That is his name, *Forgiving iniquity, transgression and sins,* through the surety whom he would *by no means clear,* for *the Lord laid on him the iniquities of us all, and spared not his own son, but delivered him up for us all, in whom we have redemption through his blood, the forgiveness of sin, according to the riches of his grace:* Riches of his grace; is not this his glory? Yes, verily; the exceeding riches of his grace, in his kindness towards us through CHRIST JESUS.

The angel of the LORD came upon the shepherds, in *Luke* ii. 9. *And the Glory of the Lord shone round about them:* How is this made manifest? *Behold,* says the angel, *I bring you good tidings of great joy which shall be to all people, for unto you is born this day in the city of David, a Saviour, which is Christ the Lord: Glory to God in the highest, and on earth peace, good will towards men.*

I have briefly presented these few passages, wishing you to turn to the scriptures, to view the divine glory, and if these texts, with what has been brought to view (in page 73) of the glory of the LORD being revealed, was rightly understood by those that search

the

the scriptures, I doubt not it would lead into the understanding of many passages in the Old Testament, where the glory of the LORD appeared in the cloud, filled the tabernacle, filled the house, and the appearance of the likeness of the glory of the LORD, spoken of by Ezekiel, and many other passages, that speak of the Divine Glory, as they centre in JESUS the antitype, the brightness of glory; in whom the riches of his glory is made manifest, who came not to destroy men's lives, but to save them; not to condemn the world, but that the world through him might be saved. Indeed, Sir, if you think a few minutes, you cannot despise an invitation to this contemplation, for it is the final happiness of those given to JESUS CHRIST, to be with him, to behold his glory.

I would just take notice of what you say in page 50. "*I conceive therefore that every honest man that disbelieves the sentiment, will be free to declare it, and this plainly. I take liberty to add, that such a declaration will come with peculiar propriety and weight from the pulpit Watchman, what of the night, it is the language of the Almighty to gospel ministers.*"

"*With particular weight from the pulpit.*" I conceive the weight of any doctrine consists in the evidence of its truth and divinity, not in the place where, or from whence it is delivered. Suppose a pulpit ornamented to such an extravagant degree, that the first sight of it would strike, ii of *Chronicles* xxxiii. 7. immediately into the mind: Or suppose the preacher so distinguished in habit, as immediately to bring to view the warning of JESUS CHRIST to his disciples, in *Mark* xii. 38, and *Luke* xx. 46—would it not tend to a greater caution of mind about the doctrines they deliver, so that all hope of weight and importance must come from the clear evidence of the truth, that it is indeed the word of GOD which worketh effectually in them that believe, which is the word of the spirit, yea, quick and powerful—sharper han any two-edged sword. "*Watchman,*

"*Watchman, what of the night, it is the language of the Almighty to gospel ministers.*" However that may be, I am not able to say, but if it be so, gospel ministers are messengers of peace—good news—glad tidings: The founder of the gospel was so. *Isaiah* lxi. 1, *Luke* iv. 18, he was anointed *to preach the gospel to the poor; and how beautiful upon the mountains, are the feet of him that bringeth good tidings; that publisheth peace; that bringeth good tidings of good; that publisheth salvation; that saith to Zion, thy God reigneth*—not thy perverse will, nor thy adversary. The first preachers preached peace by JESUS CHRIST; he is Lord of all; and gospel ministers have now nothing else to bring to view but the preaching of JESUS and his apostles—If that was to publish peace and glad tidings of salvation, your doctrine of eternal condemnation is its opposite, and cannot possibly bring peace or glad tidings of salvation to any of the subjects of it: But seeing, *God was in Christ reconciling the world to himself, not imputing their trespasses unto them, may WE be reconciled unto God.*

II. To all for whom CHRIST died.

And blessed be GOD, he tasted death for every man. For if there be any for whom he did not die, it would be mocking them to preach the gospel to them, to tell them that the law is answered, that justice is satisfied, and mercy flows freely in a full consistency therewith, that the only living and true GOD is the just GOD, and the Saviour, and there is none else, to tell them of remission of sins, or call them to repentance, for certainly there could be no hope, if their sins were not remitted they never can be, for CHRIST dieth no more, there is no more sacrifice for sin; but seeing the righteousness of GOD, which is by faith, is unto all, as well as upon all that believe all may be called to repentance.

First,

First. Such as appear in a state of resolved infidelity and impenitence, and chose to live in profaneness and immorality, to such repentance and remission of sins, in the name of Jesus is preached: What though they deride the messengers, and the message, they shall be brought hereto, for *First*, Jesus Christ came to seek and save that which was lost; to call sinners to repentance. The several passages where this is mentioned. viz. *Matt*, ix. 13. *Mark* ii. 7. and *Luke* v. 32, have all referrence to publicans and sinners; the phrase for abandoned characters among the Jews at that day: And were not they, and are not the same characters now, though differently described, wrong; are they not alienated from their rightful owner, are they not lost; if so, Christ came to save them; are they not sinners—if so, he came to call them to repentance.

Secondly. Jesus sent his disciples to preach it in his name. *And as the rain cometh down, and the snow from heaven, and returneth not thither again, but watereth the earth, so shall my word be,* saith the Lord, by the prophet *Isaiah*, chap lv. 10, 11. *That goeth out of my mouth, it shall not return unto me void, but it shall accomplish what I please, and prosper in the thing whereto I sent it.*

Thirdly. *Now he hath commanded all men every where to repent* ; and his commands shall be obeyed, for *Psalm* cxlviii. *he commanded, and angels, sun, moon, and stars, the Heavens, and the waters above them were created.* 2 of *Corinth.* iv. 6.—*He commanded the light to shine out of darkness. Psalm* cvii. 25. *He commandeth and raiseth the stormy wind. Luke* viii. 25. *He commandeth even the winds and the waters, and they obey him.*

Fourthly. *He is exalted a prince and a Saviour, to give repentance to Israel, and remission of sins.* Prophesied of *Isaiah* xxx. 18. *Therefore will he be exalted that he may have mercy.* But it was to give repentance

tance *to Israel*. It was not then fully manifested that they were to go to the Gentiles: But from the time of *Peter*'s vision, he was taught to call no man common, or unclean; and the Gentiles appeared to be fellow-heirs, and of the same body; and that they were to preach among them the unsearchable riches of CHRIST.

Fifthly. The long suffering patience of GOD is extended for this end, 2d of *Peter*, iii. 9, the LORD is long suffering toward us, not willing that any should perish, but that all should come to repentance, agreeable to *Isaiah* xxx. 18, and therefore will the LORD wait that he may be gracious. Now put these things together, and shall the stout-heartedness and obstinacy of the unbelieving impenitent and profane children of men, disappoint him. What will they do? He is wise in heart and mighty in strength: None ever hardened himself against him and prospered; there is no wisdom, nor understanding, nor counsel against the LORD, who would set the briars and thorns against him in battle; he would go through them, and burn them together.

Perhaps they would fain flee out of his hand; but where will they flee from his presence? What the LORD saith by the prophet *Amos*, may be here brought to view, *Amos* ix. 2. *He that fleeth of them shall not flee away, and he that escapeth of them shall not be delivered; though they dig into hell, thence shall mine hand take them; though they climb up into Heaven, thence will I bring them down; and though they hide themselves in the top of Carmel, I will search and take them out thence; and though they be hid from my sight, in the bottom of the sea, thence will I command the serpent, and he shall bite them.* From hence it appears weak, fruitless and contemptible to set the obstinacy of man against the end of the coming, the call, the command, the design of the exaltation, and the long suffering

suffering patience of Jesus Christ; especially if we consider *Isaiah* xlv. 22, 23, where we have the divine oath that every knee shall bow; it may be added.

Sixthly. It is the design of the second coming of Jesus Christ to convince all that are ungodly, of all their ungodly deeds, and of all their hard speeches which ungodly sinners have spoken against him, *Jude* 14, 15. Then every eye shall see him, and they that pierced him and all kindred of the earth shall wail because of him, as we read *Rev.* i. 7. Compare this with *Zech.* xii. 10, and they shall look upon me, whom they have pierced, and they shall mourn for him as one mourneth for his only son, and be in bitterness for him as one is in bitterness for his first born. Here is wailing, mourning, and bitterness at the sight of Jesus Christ, in the most expressive language we can imagine. See *Jeremiah* ix. 10, 18, 19, which perhaps none can form an adequate idea of, but such as have been called into the described circumstances; which yet cannot be viewed as the language of despair; for how then can we understand the following words, *even so amen.* But if we may understand *John* as speaking of those who pierced him being brought every knee of them to bow to him, with the wailing of repentance, then the *even so amen* appears agreeable to the spirit of the gospel. Undoubtedly then every mouth will be stopped, and all the world guilty before God, which when the Apostle mentions, in *Rom.* iii. 19, he adds, in verse 21, *But now the righteousness of God without the law is manifest, being witnessed by the law, and the prophets, even the righteousness of God, which is by faith of Jesus Christ unto all, and upon all that believe: For there is no difference,* respecting the purchase of Christ, who died for all; and respecting the divine will, *who will have all men to be saved, and come to*

the

the knowledge of the truth, which agrees with *Romans* xi. 32, *he hath concluded them all in unbelief that he might have mercy on all*. This doctrine must be shocking to tradition, and no wonder, for *O ! the depth of the riches both of the wisdom and knowledge of* God, *how unsearchable his judgments, and his ways past finding out*. It appears to agree with the end and design of Christ's prayer, for his own immediate disciples, and for them that shall believe through their word, as expressed, *John* xvii. 21, 23. *That they all may be one as thou father in me, and I in thee ; that they also may be one in us, that the world may believe that thou hast sent me. I in them, and thou in me, that the world may know that thou hast sent me*. The very circumstance that the disciples were in, (verse 8), and have known surely, that I came out from thee, and they have believed that thou didst send me. The manifestation of this oneness I conceive to be what is called the manifestation of the sons of God, which the earnest expectation of the creature waiteth for. Every creature, both believers and unbelievers, are in some way groaning and traveling together for this, as we see in *Rom.* viii. 32. *For we know that the whole creation* (in the Bible margin it is every creature. I am informed it is the same word used in *Mark* xvi. 15, *Go preach the gospel to every creature)* the whole creation, or every creature, *groaneth and traveleth in pain together*. I know not of one of the human race that is not in some way groaning under the bondage of corruption. Verse 23. *And not only they, but ourselves also, which have the first fruits of the spirit, even we ourselves groan within ourselves, waiting for the adoption, the redemption of our body*—the whole body, of which Christ is the head.—This agrees with the design of Jesus being made under the law, that we might receive the adoption of sons.

II. Those of opposite character, that thank God they are not as other men, but pride themselves in their own religious characters, to the despising those abovementioned. To such repentence and remission of sins are preached in the name of JESUS. Alas, if they look for remission in their own name, or on account of any distinction in them, it will disappoint them; for, says the prophet, all our righteousness is as filthy rags: And *Paul,* speaking of his, says, what things I counted gain, those I count loss for CHRIST; but what has been already said on *John's* preaching, may suffice on this head.

III. Such as are distressed and perplexed for want of righteousness, wishing for some inherent qualifications, or to perform many external duties, to recommend them to the divine favour, or are ready to wish they were as such and such, who they apprehend to have high attainments, and great characters for piety; distressed with the anxious inquiry, wherewithall shall I come before the LORD? Will he be pleased with costly sacrifices—thousands of rams, or ten thousand rivers of oil, or my first born for my transgression;—the fruit of my body for the sin of my soul?— He hath shewed thee, O man, what good is the only all-sufficient one, to recommend thee to the divine favour, in the finished work of JESUS CHRIST, in which is full remission of sins, and a call to repent of seeking it any other where. *GOD is love, and in this was manifested the love of GOD towards us, because GOD sent his only beloved son, that we might live through him. GOD was in* CHRIST *reconciling the world unto himself, not imputing their trespasses unto them.* Only view the character of the true GOD as manifested in CHRIST. (Elsewhere we cannot see him, for no man hath seen GOD at any time; the only begotten son, who was in the bosom of the father, he hath declared him). Agreeable to *Zechariah* ix. 9. *He is just and having salvation.* Isaiah xlv. 21, *I the* LORD, *and none beside me, a just* GOD, *and a* SAVIOUR, *and none beside.* If justice

ice and salvation is united in the character of the only living and true GOD, and he calls to all the ends of the earth to look to him, and be saved, if it be rightly understood, it is enough to cheer the heart of the most forlorn and dejected in any corner of the earth.

IV. Those that believe that Jesus is the Christ, that he hath fully obeyed the precepts of the law in his life, and suffered the penalty in his death, to the satisfaction of justice, and thereby made full remission, as witnessed in his resurrection, so that their minds are at peace and rest in his finished work alone, as their only ground of hope—are hereby called to repentance, as those that are under the highest obligation thereunto, agreeable to *Ezek.* xvi. 63. *That thou mayst remember and be ashamed, and confounded, and never open thy mouth any more because of thy shame, when I am pacified towards thee for all that thou hast done, saith the Lord God.* Every view of every time, place and company, wherein they have spoken or done secretly or openly, those things that were contrary to the law of God, or whereby they have been going about to establish their own righteousness, in opposition to the righteousness of God, is ever matter of shame and abhorrence, and of admiration of the grace that appears in remission and reconciliation; and the law of love, that the gospel binds on Christ's disciples to love one another, as he hath loved them, must ever open a source of repentance when their conduct is counter thereto.

How unsuitable is it for CHRIST's disciples to practice upon that old *Pharasaick* tradition, *thou shalt love thy neighbor, and hate thine enemy*; when Jesus reconciled them when they were enemies, and taught them to love their enemies.

How unsuitable for those of them that have this world's goods, and see their brethren in need, to shut
up

up their bowels of compassion from them, when Jesus *though he was rich for our sakes became poor, that we through his poverty might be rich :* who has kindly told us, *the poor ye have always with you, and whensoever ye will ye may do them good :* Especially when he has said, *whosoever shall give you a cup of water, to drink in my name, because ye belong to Christ, verily I say unto you, he shall not lose his reward ; inasmuch as ye did it unto one of the least of these my brethren, ye did unto me.*

How unsuitable to the above-mentioned ground of satisfaction in the finished work of CHRIST, is every branch of conduct and conversation unbecoming the gospel, when it lays the believers of it under the most indispensible, eternal obligations to look upon themselves, their time, talents, interest and opportunities, as not their own, but belonging to their redeemer, and to be ever employed to his glory. If these things be duly considered, with the various thoughts they lead to, they will open up reasons for daily repentance to the believers of the gospel, with a full conviction they can have no confidence in the flesh, but their rejoicing must be in CHRIST JESUS alone, to whom be glory forever.

The Gospel thus Evidenced, preached to every creature.

SECTION III.

The GOSPEL CONSIDERED; *and the* MANNER *in which it should be* PREACHED; *with an* ENDEAVOUR *to shew from the* SCRIPTURES, *that* ELECTION *doth not* MILITATE *with preaching the* GOSPEL *to* EVERY CREATURE: *Several other objections considered.*

"Go ye therefore into all the world, and preach the gospel to every creature.

Not in words which man's wisdom teacheth, but which the Holy Ghost teacheth.

Not with wisdom of words, least the cross of CHRIST should be made of none effect.

IN attending to a sermon, some things occurred which brought a passage in the epistle to the Colossians, to remembrance, "*say to Archippus, take heed to the ministry, that thou hast received in the* LORD, *that thou fulfil it;* which produced an inquiry, who Archippus was; and comparing the epistle to the Colossians, with that to Philemon, it appeared probable, that Philemon, Epaphras and Archippus were ministers of the church of CHRIST, gathered from among the Colossians, which then met in Philemon's house; both epistles appear to be wrote and sent at the same time; however, Archippus was a minister of the church of CHRIST, who received his ministry in the LORD, and yet was the subject of this exhortation: Hence it was concluded that no minister of CHRIST is above receiving a similar exhortation from the brethren.

The next inquiry was, what was the ministry he received in the LORD, or which the ministers of
CHRIST

CHRIST receive in the LORD; supposing they receive the same now, as the ministers of the first churches did?

In answer, it may be said, that their commission was, "*to go into all the world, and preach the gospel to every creature.*" It is agreed that the word gospel, signifies good news, glad tidings: The prophets and apostles agree herein. The prophet *Isaiah* saith, "*O Zion that bringeth good tidings, get thee up into the high mountain; O Jerusalem, that bringeth good tidings, lift up thy voice with strength, lift up, be not afraid: Say to the cities of Judah, behold your* GOD. *How beautiful are the feet of him that bringeth good tidings, that publisheth peace, that bringeth good tidings of good: that publisheth salvation; that saith unto Zion, thy* GOD *reigneth.*" And similar is the word which GOD sent to the children of *Israel*; with which *Peter* was sent to the *Gentiles*, "*preaching peace*, by JESUS CHRIST, *he is* LORD *of all.*"

The scriptures do not leave us at a loss, respecting these glad tidings, "*for the scriptures foreseeing that* GOD *would justify the heathen* * *through faith, preached before the gospel unto Abraham, saying, in thy seed, shall all the nations of the earth be blessed;*" the same gospel is repeated to *Isaac*, and confirmed to *Jacob*, and is proclaimed from the top of *Jacob*'s ladder, where the LORD stood above it, and said, "*I am the* GOD *of Abraham, thy father, and the* GOD *of Isaac;*" this was also shown to *Moses* at the bush, and when he was sent to the children of *Israel*, he was directed to say unto them, "*I am the* GOD *of Abraham, the* GOD *of Isaac, and the* GOD *of Jacob; this is my name forever, and my memorial unto all generations.*" It is my unchangeable name, the unchangable name; of the unchangeable GOD; insuring blessedness in CHRIST JESUS, to all the nations, kindreds, and families

---

* The heathen that had no claim as being of the stock of *Israel* that had no worthiness, nothing to recommend them.

milies of the earth. And a believer of this gospel preached to *Abraham*, enters into rest; although he is in himself a poor, lost, wretched, miserable sinner, and understanding himself blessed in CHRIST JESUS, can rejoice in him, though he hath " no confidence in the flesh."

The prophet *Isaiah* speaking of the *Gentiles*, in his 54th chapter, says to them, " *fear not, for thou shall not be ashamed, neither be thou confounded, for thou shall not be put to shame, for thou shall forget the shame of thy youth, and shall not remember the reproach of thy widowhood any more: For thy maker is thy husband, and thy Redeemer the Holy One of Israel, the* GOD *of the whole earth shall he be called*." The prophet *Jeremiah*, in his 3d cahapter, speaking of Judah and Israel, saith, " *turn O backsliding children, saith the* LORD, *for I am married unto you.*" And the prophet *Isaiah*, appears to be speaking both of *Jews* and *Gentiles*, when he says, " *as the bridegroom rejoiceth over the bride, so shall thy* GOD *rejoice over thee.*"

If the nations, kindreds and families of the earth are blessed in CHRIST JESUS, and both *Jews* and *Gentiles* acknowledged as married unto him, then he is " the GOD of the whole earth."

Again, the whole earth are repeatedly called to sing a new song unto the LORD, as we see in *Psalm*, 96, 1, 98, 1, *Isaiah* 42, 10, 11. This new song is described, *Rev.* 5. 9. " *thou art worthy, for thou wast slain and hast redeemed us to God, by the blood, out of every nation, and kindred, and tongue, and people:*" If all the earth are called to sing this new song, surely all the earth are interested in the subject matter of it.

Again, the most opposed to the salvation of the gospel, and the preaching of it, are the subjects of prayer. The Psalmist, speaking in the person of
CHRIST,

Christ, in the 42d Psalm, where he complains of his reproachers, saying, "*my tears have been my meat, day and night, while they continually say unto me, where is thy God?*" And adds, "*when I remember these, I pour out my soul in me.*" This we see verified when they said, "he trusted in God, let him deliver him, if he will have him;" and hear Jesus Christ pour out his soul in him, in that prayer "*Father forgive them for they know not what they do;*" he also directs his disciples "*to love their enemies, and pray for them that despitefully use them.*" Did he direct them to love those whom he did not; did he not die that his enemies might be reconciled by his death; was not he always heard, and did he bid his disciples pray for what should not be granted?

Then surely the gospel also is to be preached to them, and this good news is to be published as a truth among such characters, "*That God was in Christ reconciling the world unto himself, not imputing their trespasses unto them;*" agreeable to the prophet Isaiah, "*I have blotted out thy transgressions as a cloud, and thine iniquities as a thick cloud, return unto me for I have redeemed thee.*"

Designed brevity, forbids the taking notice of many considerations that offer themselves, to prove and illustrate this truth, that Christ's ministers, commission is, "To preach the gospel to every creature." Two or three things offer themselves as inquiries or objections, as

1st. If the nations are blessed in Christ Jesus, both Jews and Gentiles, so that they are married unto him, and he is the God of the whole earth, whence is it such a place of sin and misery?

It may be said, if the woman interested in the estate and honours of her husband, treacherously depart from him, every step of her way, must be going further into the sink of sin and misery.

That

That this was the case with ancient Israel, is plain from Jeremiah, iii. 20. "*Surely as a wife treacherously departs from her husband, so have you dealt treacherously with me, O house of Israel,*" which will be evident to any one that reads the beginning of the chapter, to the 12 verse, and Ezekiel, xvi. 32, 45—and as this was the cause of the distress and misery, that befel ancient Israel, so it is the cause of all the calamities that befal us all, in copying after their wretched example. Certainly there is no want of blessedness in CHRIST JESUS; no want of power, riches, loving kindness, and mercy, in our Maker, our husband, the GOD of the whole earth; but all our unhappiness arises from our alienation from him, and the further we persue that path, the greater our misery and calamity, whether we know the cause or not.

Now if the husband of the treacherously departing wife, own her to be his wife, call after her to return, is willing and ready to receive her on her return, without upbraiding her, she is certainly blessed *in a husband* * though she forsakes her own mercies for lying

---

* The gospel, the Apostles preached was, 'that GOD was *in* CHRIST,' reconciling the world unto himself, not imputing their trespasses unto them, 1 Corinthians, v. 19. Agreeable to the gospel preached to Abraham, that '*in* thy seed shall all the nations of the earth be blessed,' Galations iii. 8, 16. The Psalmist saith, 'men shall be blessed *in* him,' Psalm lxxii. 17. The prophet saith, 'the nations shall bless themselves *in him*, and *in* him shall they glory,' Jeremiah, iv. 2. By the Apostle we are said to be ' chosen *in him*,' Ephesians i. 4. 'To be justified in him,' 1 Corinthians, vi. 11. 'To be gathered together *in him*,' Ephesians i. 10. ' To be rooted and built up *in him*,' Colossians, ii. 7. ' To be sanctified in CHRIST JESUS,' 1 Corinthians, i. 2. 'To be blessed with all spiritual blessings *in* CHRIST JESUS,' Ephesians, i. 3. 'To be made to sit together in heavenly places, *in* CHRIST JESUS,' Ephesians, ii. 6. ' All the promises of GOD are *in* him, yea, *in* him, Amen,' 2 Corinthians i. 20. ' And yea are complete *in* him,' Colossians, ii. 10. ' And we are *in* him, that is true *in* his son JESUS CHRIST,' 1 John, v. 20. Being blessed *in* him, denotes union as members to their head, ' all men being drawn to him when he was lifted up; and so one dying for all, all died; he tasting death for every man.' Therefore this gospel preached to Abraham, and preached by the Apostles is to be preached to those that are the most remote from blessedness in themselves, and when it is believed they are led to rejoice in CHRIST JESUS, though altogether destitute in themselves, unbelief and alienation, being the source of all our misery, believing the truth as it is in JESUS, we see our blessedness *in* him.

lying vanities, and is most forlorn and miserable in herself, while persisting in her alienation.

I need only repeat two passages of scripture, to lead our minds from the similitude just mentioned up to divine mercy. Jeremiah, iii. 1. "*But thou hast played the harlot many lovers, yet return unto me, saith the Lord*, verse 12, *return thou backsliding Israel, saith the Lord,* I will not cause mine anger to fall upon you*. Isaiah xlii. 22 ; *I have blotted out as a thick cloud thy transgressions, and as a cloud thy sins: return unto me, for I have redeemed thee*.' Thus Gospel Ministers have the testimony of God, by his Prophets, as well as the commission given to the Apostles, " to preach the Gospel to every creature."

2dly. It may be inquired, are not ministers to preach the law? Answer, " *by the law is the knowledge of sin, for what things the law saith, it saith to them that are under the law, that every mouth may be stopped, and all the world may become guilty before* God, having no hope but in *the righteousness of* God *by faith of* Jesus Christ, revealed in the Gospel."— The direction therefore, is "*to preach the Gospel to every creature.*"

There were some in the Apostles' day, that desired to be teachers of the law, understanding neither what they say, nor whereof they affirm. The Apostle says, "*the law was our school-master unto,* or until Christ," (to bring us, is supplied by the translators) " *that we may be justified by faith ; but when faith is come, we are no longer under a school-master.*" When faith is come, that is when Christ is come, who is the object of faith, and hath sent forth his servants to preach the Gospel, which is called the hearing of faith: " *Received ye the spirit by the works of the law,* or by the hearing of faith ? That is by the hearing of the Gospel preached." Objection.

* It is not return *and* I will not cause mine anger to fall upon you, as a condition ; the *and* is supplied by the translators, it is, return, I will not cause mine anger to fall upon you.

Objection. But doth not the scripture say, "*cursed is every one that continueth not in all things written in the book of the law to do them?*"

Answer. Yes, this is the language of the law, but the language of the gospel, is, "*Christ hath delivered us from the curse of the law, being made a curse for us,*" and CHRIST's ministers are to preach the gospel; perhaps some one will say, they are to preach it to the prepared subjects that are awakened by the terrors of the law, to seek salvation by CHRIST JESUS: They are to preach it to every creature, to tell every creature "*Christ hath delivered us from the curse of the law, being made a curse for us.*" To tell it as a truth; what! to unbelievers? Yes, to unbelievers; what constitutes a man an unbeliever, but not believing the report of the gospel. He that believeth this truth is saved from the tormenting fear of the curse of the law, believing the report of the gospel; while he that doth not believe this truth, remains under self condemnation or damnation, being in his own apprehension under the law, and under the curse: Man is denominated an unbeliever as not believing the truth.

If CHRIST's ministers wish to help unbelievers, let them keep close to their direction, tell the truth that is to be believed: Let them preach the "*ministry of reconciliation, that* GOD *was* in CHRIST *reconciling the world unto himself, not imputing unto them their trespasses: That he hath made him sin for us, who knew no sin, that we might be made the righteousness of* GOD *in him,*" and set forth the evidences of it in the resurrection of JESUS CHRIST, from the dead, that if GOD please to accompany the evidence to their minds, they may believe.

Earnest repeated exhortations to believe, are lost; only tending to confuse the mind that understands not what is to be believed, but when the truth to be believed

believed, is understood, and the evidences appears undeniable, it gains credit in the mind, and what we give full credit to is believed; therefore let the gospel be preached to every creature, tell the good news even to unbelievers, for " it is glad tidings of great joy to all people, tidings of a Saviour, which is CHRIST the LORD."

3dly. Doth not the doctrine of election, militate with the gospel's being preached to every creature? If the elect are only to obtain salvation to the rejection or reprobation of all others, how is it possible to preach the gospel to every creature?

For answer, it may be said, that this connecting of final rejection or reprobation with the doctrine of election, has no foundation in the scriptures. Election among men, chooses men to certain offices for the benefit of those that are not elected; and if we consider election in the sense of the scriptures, it will appear that it is designed for the benefit of others. If we turn our attention, first to JESUS CHRIST, it will lead our minds to *Isaiah* xlii. 1, ushered in with a note of attention, " behold ! *behold my servant whom I uphold, mine elect in whom my soul delighteth*," why is JESUS CHRIST called GOD's elect, see verses, 6, 7, " *I the* LORD *have called thee in righteousness, and will hold thine hand, and will keep thee and give thee for a covenant of the people, for a light of the Gentiles, to open the blind eyes, to bring out the prisoners from the prison, and them that sit in darkness out of the prison-house.*"

Question. But is it not said in the same prophesy, that he shall be a " *stone of stumbling and rock of offence to both houses of Israel* ;" and *Peter* " speaks of him *as a stone of stumbling and rock of offence, to them that stumble at the word, being disobedient, whereunto they were appointed.*" Surely, *Peter* doth not intend to militate with the doctrine of " *the restitu-*
tion

tution of all things, *spoken of by the mouth of all* God's *holy prophets since the world began*," their thus stumbling, is to fulfil the purpose of God, who hath concluded them all in unbelief that he may have mercy on all, and thus open the blind eyes, and bring the prisoners from the prison and those that sit in darkness, out of the prison-house." Agreeable to the prophesy of *Simeon*, in his address to *Mary*, " *behold this child is set for the fall and rising again of many in Israel, and for a sign that shall be spoken against.*" The apostles were chosen witnesses of the resurrection of Jesus Christ, and sent to the *Jews* ; the 70 disciples were chosen after, and sent to the Gentiles, to every place whether he himself should come. " The apostles were chosen to be Christ's witnesses," chosen to this end, *to go into all the world, and preach the gospel to every creature ;*" Jesus Christ tells them, " *ye are the lights of the world ;*" lights are to guide travellers in the way : for this end, the 70 were chosen and sent forth. "Tis expressly said of *Paul*, " *he is a chosen vessel unto me, to bear my name before gentiles and kings ; and the children of Israel ;*" and this chosen vessel was sent unto the gentiles, to open their eyes and to turn them from darkness to light, and from the power of satan unto God."

Which evidences that their election was for the benefit of others. Even in the xi of *Romans*, where the apostle speaking of the *Israelites*, says, " *the election hath obtained, and the rest were blinded,*" and speaking of the stumbling of the blinded, saith, " *have they stumbled, that they might fall*; God *forbid !* and shews it was to bring about the purposes of God, respecting the gentiles, which being accomplished, " *all Israel shall be saved as it is written ;*" and speaking of these stumbling *Jews*, he saith, " as concerning the gospel, they are enemies for your sakes, but as touching the election, they are beloved for the father's sakes

for

for the gifts and calling of GOD are without repentance;" *shews them,* " *concluded in unbelief, that* GOD *may have mercy on all.*"

So when the apostle, to the *Ephesians,* speaks of their being predestinated to the adoption of children by JESUS CHRIST, according to the good pleasure of his will, to the praise of his glory, he shews the divine design herein, that in the dispensation of the fulness of time, he might gather together in one, all things in CHRIST, both which are in Heaven and on earth in him.*

It is said by the apostle *James,* " *of his own will begat he us, by the word of truth that we might be a kind of first fruits of his creatures;*" now the first fruits are not the whole harvest, only an earnest of it, as we see by " the hundred forty and four thousand, that are sealed in the *Revelations,* and stand with the Lamb on the mount Zion, with the harps of GOD ;" these first fruits are the " elect redeemed from among men, that follow the lamb, whithersoever he goeth.

Now it is observable both in the 7th and 14th chapters, that the sealed, the first fruits, or the elect, were not the whole of the saved, for the hundred forty-four thousand sealed, being mentioned, we read in the 9th

---

* The view that has been taken of election, being for the benefit of others, and not for their destruction, might be illustrated from the old testament scriptures. When it pleased God to select Abraham from among those that served other gods, and bless him, others were not excluded, for his blessing shines most illustriously in that part of it thus expressed, in thy seed shall all the nations of the earth be blessed. The choice of Moses and Aaron, the Levites, the 70 Elders and the 12 princes, were all for the benefit of all Israel, and the blessings they enjoyed were conveyed to them, through the faithful attention of those various characters and officers, to their appointments, by whom they were led forward to the typical rest, or land of Canaan. So are God's elect under the gospel dispensation, chosen as instruments, in their places, to bring to view from the scriptures, the glad tidings of the gospel; shewing Jesus as the way to the heavenly Canaan, the rest that remains to the people of God, where the leaves of the tree of life shall heal the nations, and there shall be no more curse, but the throne of God and the Lamb, shall be in it, and his servants shall serve him, and they shall see his face agreeable to the prayer of Jesus Christ, John, xvii. 24, " father, I will, that they also whom thou hast given me, be with me where I am ; that they may behold my glory."

9th verse, "*after this I beheld, and lo a great multitude which no man could number, of all nations and kindreds, and people, and tongues, stood before the Throne, and before the Lamb, cloathed with white robes, and palms in their hands, and cried, salvation to our* GOD, *and to the* LAMB.

This was so wonderful, to see this innumerable multitude, beside the sealed, the elect, the first fruits, that the inquiry is, what are these, and whence come they? The answer is, "*these are they that come out of great tribulation, and have washed their robes, and made them white in the blood of the Lamb,*" therefore are they before the throne, &c. These are they that came out of great tribulation: What greater tribulation can we suppose, can befal the children of men, than what arises from an apprehension of a possibility of being reprobated to eternal damnation? And being on this account, all their lifetime subject to bondage through fear or death; for such to find themselves before the throne, in virtue of the blood of the Lamb, no wonder they cry with a loud voice, salvation, &c. no wonder they feel their obligations to serve him day and night in his temple, " having him that sitteth on the throne, to dwell among them, delivered from hungering or thirsting any more, and having GOD to wipe away all tears from their eyes." If we look into the 14th capter, after the description of the hundred forty-four thousand, standing with the Lamb, on the mount Zion, with the harps of GOD, and singing the new song, we find, verse 6, another angel "*fly in the midst of Heaven, having the everlasting gospel to preach unto them that dwell in the earth; even to every nation, tongue, and people:*" Thus I think if the doctrine of election were rightly understood, it can be no objection to preaching the gospel to every creature.

The

The Apostle *Paul* gives the sum of the gospel which he preached in the beginning of the 15th chapter of the first epistle to the *Corinthians*, contained in the death and resurrection of CHRIST with the evidences of it, and speaking of the other Apostles, he saith, verse 11, " *whether I or they, so we preach and so ye believed.*

Not so we preached, but so we preach, they continue to preach the same doctrine, in their writings handed down to us, and blessed be GOD, we have the fulfilment of that prophecy, (in that we have the free use of the scriptures of truth) recorded in *Isaiah* xxx, 20, " *yet shall not thy teachers be driven into a corner any more, but thine eyes shall see thy teachers, and thine ear shall hear a word behind thee, saying this is the way ;*" the gospel always finds us with our backs to it, pursuing another way, and points out the way into which we are to return, is not this turning, repentance unto life ? Is not the preaching the gospel, included in Paul's exhortation to Timothy, " *my son be strong in the grace, that is in Christ Jesus ;*" the same Apostle tells us what this grace is, " *ye know the grace of our Lord Jesus Christ, who, though he was rich for our sakes, became poor, that we through his poverty might be rich* ; this is the grace made manifest in the gospel, the tidings of it are to be told to every creature; this is the grace whereby we serve God acceptably, which our Apostle exhorts to hold fast, we receiving a kingdom which cannot be moved; we read it, let us have grace, but the margin reads it agreeable to the original, " let us hold fast the grace whereby we may serve GOD acceptably with reverence and godly fear," for our GOD is a consuming fire ; every thing in the service of GOD, that hath not respect to the grace that is in CHRIST JESUS, is wood, hay, stubble, and must be burnt up.

The apostle Peter drawing to a close in his first Epistle, speaking of what he had been writing, says, "*I have written briefly, exhorting and testifying that this is the true grace of God, wherein ye stand;*" if we look back into the Epistle, we find him writing of the grace, that is in CHRIST JESUS, who his ownself bear our sins in his own body on the tree, for CHRIST hath once suffered the just for the unjust, that he might bring us to GOD, by whose stripes ye were healed. Much hath been said about marks and evidences of true grace, in the hearts of men; but the voice behind us, reminds us of the true grace of GOD, and the evidences of it manifested in CHRIST JESUS, this is the grace, the Apostle exhorts the Hebrews to look diligently, least they fall from, we read it " looking diligently, least any man fail of the grace of GOD," but according to the margin, agreeable to the original, it is, least any man fall from the grace of GOD. From the grace of GOD to the grace of man; from the grace that is in CHRIST JESUS, by which alone, we are accepted to grace, in our own hearts, which cannot procure our acceptance with GOD: Can any one in the exercise of reverence and godly fear, approach the divine presence, in his own name, making mention of the grace, that is in his own heart, as that whereby he may serve GOD acceptably, it brings to mind, Isaiah, xxvii. 4. "*Who would set the briers and thorns against me in battle, I would go through them, I would burn them together, or let him take hold of my strength, he may make peace with me, he shall make peace with me;*" peace is preached by JESUS CHRIST.

The scriptures testify of Christ, both in the law of *Moses*, the Prophets, and the Psalms: The great error of many preachers, has centered in their apprehension, that the scriptures testified of good men, and in proportion as this error has prevailed, we have

have heard of the virtue and piety of *Abraham, David*, the Prophets, and other pious men, whom we have been excited to follow, in hope of divine favor, if we could come to their attainments; but the light discovers this to be a species of idolatry, putting the Creature in the place of JESUS CHRIST, or at least between us and him, while the gospel calls us " *to behold the lamb of God, that taketh away the sin of the world.*" The light discovering this error, in the place of it, there has crept in, perhaps a more undiscernable one, when preachers have been led to speak excellently of the character and finished work of CHRIST, they have known something else besides JESUS CHRIST, and him crucified, having a great part of their discourses, taken up about the excellency of believers, their experiences, attainments, devotions in their closets and families, and at public worship, and in their conduct in moral civil life, to the flattering of their pride and importance, causing them to conceive themselves the chief of saints, to the abasement of those that have not these attainments. But let it be considered whether it would not be more advantageous to the believers of the gospel, as well as nearer their pattern, if they were put in mind of the various apostolic exhortations to them, and put upon inquiring how much cause they have for shame and humiliation, that these exhortations have so little influence on their minds and conduct, which if attended to with sobriety of mind, would tend to excite them, to take rank with the chief of sinners, and to glorify GOD, for mercy, upon a level with the vilest. Such preachers as are above described, draw the minds of their hearers from the one object, having two to present before them; whereas the Prophet Isaiah, proposes one object, " *The glory of the Lord shall be revealed, and all flesh shall see together. Look unto me and be saved, all the ends of the earth.*" John says,

says, "*Behold the Lamb of God that taketh away the sin of the world;*" and Paul determins *to know nothing among them, save Jesus Christ and him crucified.* Let Peter close with his testimony of CHRIST, as recorded in his 1st Epistle, 2d chapter, 24 verse, "*Who his ownself, bear our sins in his own body on the tree, that we being dead to sin, might live to righteousness, by whose stripes ye were healed.*"

Should the mind of any, suggest the old objection, to preaching the gospel to every creature, that was brought in the apostle's days and is kept up, down to our day, that it endangers morality, and will excite to continue in sin, that grace may abound.

It may be answered, that the morality of the gospel is founded on divine love, both by JESUS CHRIST and his apostles; when JESUS CHRIST gave the golden rule, as it is deservedly called, it was founded on the love of GOD, set forth in a most striking figure, "*what man is there of you, who if his son ask bread, will he give him a stone?*" Is there such a man among you that are evil, prone to covetousness, anger and various other evils? Is there one among you, who, if his son ask bread, will he give him a stone, and thus mock his hunger? What heart, among you that are evil, can do this? *If ye then being evil, know how to give good gifts to your children, how much more shall your father who is in Heaven, give good things to them that ask him? Therefore all things whatsoever ye would, that men should do to you, do ye even so to them;* you never need defraud or over-reach one another, to obtain any good you may think you want, because your heavenly father is more ready to give good things to them that ask him, than the best of you are to give bread to your children, let his love constrain you in all things, to do one to another, as ye would they should do to you: when JESUS bid his disciples love their enemies, he gave the example in his love to them.

When

When he bid them pray for them that said all manner of evil of them falsly for his name fake, he gave his example on the cross, " *Father forgive them, for they know not what they do.*"

He faith to his disciples, a new commandment I give unto you, " *That ye love one another, as I have loved you,*" mark that, and consider, how did he love his disciples? Let one of them answer, " *herein is love, not that we loved God, but he loved us, and sent his son the—propitiation for our sin,*" (he adds) " *beloved, if God so loved us, we ought to love one another,*" the love of God and our neighbour, contains all morality, and we love him because he first loved us, and when we believe the love of GOD to our neighbour, as well as to ourselves, we shall see the only foundation of loving our neighbour as ourselves.

The morality of the gospel is founded on divine love by the Apostles; they preached the gospel to every creature, those who were gathered to the faith of the gospel, they collected into churches, and taught them to observe all things whatsoever JESUS CHRIST commanded; they exhorted, comforted, and charged every one of them, as a father doth his children, that they would walk worthy of GOD, who hath called them to his kingdom and glory. Let any one whose mind is concerned about the preaching of the gospel to every creature, endangering morality, look over the epistles, wrote to the churches, collected by preaching the gospel, and they will see in the former parts of those epistles, the riches of divine grace, contained in the doctrine of CHRIST, then, the obligations the disciples are under to adorn this doctrine, in their lives and conversations in the various places and relations that they sustain; that they which have believed in GOD, be careful to maintain good works, not merely to talk of them, with approbation, but be at the cost of maintaining them. If these things be

soberly

soberly attended to, it will appear to any impartial inquirer, that the interest of morality is not endangered by preaching the gospel to every creature.

Having inquired who *Archippus* was, and what was the ministry he received in the LORD; the next inquiry is, in what manner is this ministry thus received of the LORD, to be delivered to the people? The answer to this inquiry is given by the apostle. "*Not with wisdom of words least the cross of Christ should be made of none effect,*" 1st of Corinthians, xvii. to the end. "*And I brethren, when I came to you, came not with excellency of speech or of wisdom, declaring unto you the testimony of God, for I determined not to know any thing among you, save Jesus Christ, and him crucified,*" 1st of Corinthians ii. 1 to 5. "*And my speech and my preaching was not with enticing words of man's wisdom, but in demonstration of the spirit and of power, now we have received not the spirit of the word, but the spirit which is of God, that we may know the things that are freely given us of God, which things we speak, not in the words which man's wisdom teacheth, but which the Holy Ghost teacheth, comparing spiritual things with spiritual.*" Verses 12, 13. That is, I conceive comparing the types and prophesies of the Old Testament, with their fulfilment in the antitype, as recorded in the new.

If it should be inquired, why were the apostles of CHRIST thus cautious to shun the enticing words of man's wisdom? the two reasons the apostle gives, may be brought as an answer;—First, the corruption of the doctrine of CHRIST, in these words, "*not with wisdom of words, least the cross of* CHRIST, *should be of none effect,* the preaching of the cross, or of CHRIST crucified, is to the *Jew* a stumbling-block, and to the *Greek* foolishness," now there have not been wanting those who sought by wisdom of words, to make the offence of the cross cease from the apostles days, down

down to our own. The false teachers in the apostles days, laboured to reconcile the stumbling *Jew* to the gospel, by adding the ceremonies of the law, teaching the Gentile believers, " *except they be circumcised after the manner of Moses, they cannot be saved*, making by their wisdom, the cross of Christ, of none effect," for saith the apostle, " *whosoever is circumcised, he is a debtor to do the whole law, Christ is become of none effect*," seeking thus to be justified by the law, they fall from the grace of the gospel. The false teachers from the apostles days to our own, have in like manner studied by wisdom of words, to reconcile the doctrine of Christ to the wise *Greek*, who held it foolish to build the hope of salvation on Christ crucified, as the only exclusive foundation; saying it is foolish for an ungodly sinner, to look for justification by the work of Christ, unless he have repentance, faith, obedience, &c. which are brought in as props to the work of Christ, as though it were not alone all-sufficient; faith, as it is thus considered, is not the belief of the gospel, which reports our blessedness in Christ Jesus, but is something we must have wrought in us, or exercised by us, in order to our being interested therein. Repentance as it is thus considered, is not a turning from ourselves, and all creature dependence, where we have been seeking life, to Christ, who is our life; but is a certain sorrow, for our open heinous, and even secret sins, to qualify us for obtaining forgiveness by Christ Jesus. Obedience is likewise considered a necessary qualification for our acceptance; not as a testimony of our gratitude, that he hath made us accepted in the beloved.

And in this mistaken view, faith, repentance and obedience, being added to the work of Christ, are calculated to bring the doctrine to the wisdom of the Greek, who always suppose God will be propitious

to

to the believing penitent and obedient. Every species of false religion, of what ever name or denomination, will agree here, while every true christian will agree with the apostle, that it is * a faithful saying, and worthy of all acceptation, that JESUS came to save sinners, of whom I am chief; but that CHRIST came to seek and save that which was lost, died for the ungodly, came to save sinners, even the chief, will not do to mention alone, it is too weak and foolish.

It is true, say they, that CHRIST came to save that which was lost, and no sinner will miscarry, who seek him sincerely, earnestly and perseveringly; but the text says, "*he came to seek and to save that which was lost,*" 'tis true say they, " CHRIST *died for the ungodly,*" and all of that discription shall be benefited thereby, that will come to him; but they will not come that they may have life; but read the text, "*my people shall be willing in the day of my power.*"

Yes, say they, but who are his people, who are given to him? Let the scriptures answer, " *the father loveth the son, and hath given all things into his hands, he hath given the heathen his inheritance, and the utmost parts of the earth, his possession,* and all that the father giveth, shall come."

Thus we have contemplated how the wisdom of words, is employed, to endeavor to take away the stumbling block from the *Jew,* and the imputation of foolishness from the *Greek;* and that every attempt of this kind, is making the cross of CHRIST of none effect. The second reason, the apostle draws from the effects on the hearers; where the doctrine of CHRIST is maintained, there should be a constant care to use great plainness of speech, because the poor have the gospel preached to them, and if it is preached in language above their capacity, although it may be very good, and easy to be understood by the learned, yet

if

---

* And will break out with the prophet Micah, who is a God like unto thee that pardoneth iniquity.

if there come in one that is unlearned, how shall he Amen, at thy giving thanks, seeing he understandeth what thou sayest ; except (says the apostle) *ye utter the tongue, words easy to be understood, how shall it known what is spoken; for ye shall speak unto the ai and he says, I had rather speak five words with my derstanding, that I might teach others also, than thousand words in an unknown tongue.*

Although tongues have ceased, yet these expr fions of the apostle, may at this day be improved a guard against language above common capacities, a when such language is familiar by use, to any of t preachers of the gospel, such would do well to atter the exhortation of the apostle, let him that speaks an unknown tongue, pray that he may interpret? him pray that he may be able to come to the capaci of the most unlearned of his hearers, when preachi the gospel of CHRIST; it seems as if this was what t apostle meant, by saying, " *brethren be not childr in understanding, in understanding be men,*" as it ii mediately follows his saying, he had rather speak fi words with his understanding, that he might tea others, than ten thousand that could not be unde stood ; for saith he, *if I know not the meaning of t voice, I shall be to him that speaketh, a barbarian, a he that speaketh a barbarian unto me.*

Upon the whole, the apostle appears to aim at i culcating the delivering of the gospel with plainness speech for the above reasons, which appear weight and worthy of attention ; and says, " *seeing then have such hope we use great plainness of speech, and n as Moses, who put a veil over his face ;*" and in anothe place *neither of men sought we glory, neither of you no of others.*

Let gospel ministers imitate the apostle herein, le them attend the express declaration of scripture, bot of the Old and New Testament, that unite to publis salvation, to the ends of the earth, and to the evidences of the truth of these glad tidings, of great joy to all people; that being convinced of the truth of this good news, they may tell it as a truth to their hearers, even to unbelievers, in as plain, intelligible a manner as may be, that if it please God to accompany the truth with divine evidence, they may believe, and believing have life through his name.

Let the hearers, whose minds are at a loss about the truth of the Gospel, bend their attention to the search of the scriptures after the example of the *Bereans*, to see if these things are so.

And those that are satisfied of the truth, from scripture evidence, abound in thanksgiving for the manifestation of the exceeding riches of the grace appearing therein, and make it their constant study to live as the grace of God, which hath appeared, which bringeth salvation to all men, teacheth, viz. " denying ungodliness and worldly lusts, and to live soberly, righteously and godly in the world, looking for the blessed hope, and the glorious appearing of the great God and our Saviour Jesus Christ, who gave himself for our sins, that he might redeem us from all iniquity, and purify unto himself a peculiar people zealous of good works."

Let the words of the apostle *Peter* close, " *If any man speak, let him speak as the oracles of God, if any man minister, let him do it as of the ability, that God giveth; that* God *in all things may be glorified thro'* Jesus Christ, *to whom be praise and dominion for ever,* AMEN.

A Sober Attention to the Scriptures of Truth, &c.

SECTION IV.

A Sober Attention *to the* Scriptures *of* Truth, *for a* Satisfactory Answer *to the Most* Important Question *that ever* Exercised *the* Minds *of* Men.

To the Law and to the Testimony.   Isaiah.
If Baal be a God let him plead for himself.   Judges.

My respected and beloved Friend,

IT appears very unsuitable to the spirit of the gospel to engage in any religious controversy in a way of striving for the mastery, therefore when you pointed me to the 330th page of the 2d volume of letters on Theron and Aspasio, the 3d edition; where the author speaks of two worlds, Christ 'hath his world, and Satan hath his world, &c. Were it not for an apprehension that the glory of him who has said the world is mine and the fulness thereof; and that the peace and comfort of every creature, and their obligation to their rightful owner, is concerned in knowing whose they are, and whom they should serve; I should pass it over unnoticed; but, persuaded that this is the case, and that you yourself have much perplexity of mind on this subject, and have made me acquainted with a repeated wish, that I would give you my thoughts upon it; I have been excited to read the passage and the scripture text alluded to in support of that opinion: And sat down to collect a plain simple view of the scriptures, in order to get a just idea from them on the subject. When I recollect-

ed

ed that I had already done it several years ago, at the desire of a female friend, who requested me to look into a pamphlet she had lately read, in opposition to the doctrine of Universal Salvation, under the signature of Adelos, in which there appeared to her some arguments unanswerable. This anonymous writer may be supposed to take his sentiment on this subject by tradition from the passage you pointed me to, in the aforementioned author: Therefore, I concluded it would comport with your request, to shew you a copy of that letter, which I now send you as follows:

Copy of a Letter sent to a Gentlewoman at Halifax, December 9, 1787.

MADAM,

YOU requested me to look into a pamphlet you have been reading, in opposition to the doctrine of Universal Salvation, under the signature of Adelos, in which you think are some arguments unanswerable; and to give you my opinion, I have at length found and read it. It is introduced with a preface, in which he speaks of Truth as a pearl of inestimable worth; or a chaste virgin of heavenly birth, and immortal charms; and in the first chapter, shews that men are generally uncertain where to look for it, and have a false direction given to their minds, by their wish, by parents, teachers, the public, the great, the ancient fathers, &c.

Now, endeavoring as much as may be to avoid these false directions, and attend to the infallible standard, I shall proceed to say that which strikes my mind, and which, I mean chiefly to attend to is page 42, margin, " *Out of all nations, and kindred, and people, and tongues, and so are part of the nations only, and yet are* GOD's *whole world, of the redeemed, distinguished from Satan's world, for which* JESUS *neither prayed nor died.*" The whole discourse turns
upon

upon this as its main hinge; let us look into the scriptures and see if these things are so : If we begin to look for *Satan*'s world, although he told our LORD JESUS, Mark, iv. 5, 6. after shewing him all the kingdoms of the world in, and saying, all this power will I give thee, and the glory of them, if thou wilt fall down and worship me, all shall be thine : And although he is called, 1st of Corinthians, iv. 4. *The God of this world*, and it is said, 1st John, v. 19. *the whole world lieth in wickedness*, or in the wicked one ; yet I know of no text of scripture that speaks of any part of the world as his, by creation, or by purchase, or by gift, or in any other way, that makes him their rightful owner, or makes them his, or leaves them without rebuke in obedience to him, which they would be if he were their rightful LORD.

He is represented as their deceiver, 1st Tim. ii, 14. *the woman being deceived, was in the transgression*. Deut. xi. 16. shews that the heart must be deceived, to turn aside from the true GOD. In Rev. xx. 10, we read of *the Devil that deceived them*, and in Rev. xviii. 23. we read of the means made use of to this end : *For by thy sorceries were all nations deceived*; and as their deceiver, he leads them captive, 2d Tim. 2, 26. *who are taken captive by him at his will*; having deceived them into his snare, and led them captive, he exercises an usurped dominion over them, and is called, *the spirit that now worketh in the children of disobedience*. Being deceived and insnared, they have fallen from obedience to their rightful owner and LORD, so are denominated children of disobedience, while they follow the dictates of Satan, the ruler of the *darkness* of this world. But if they were his property, if he were their creator, preserver, or redeemer, they would owe obedience to him, and not be stiled children of disobedience in their subjection to him, the Devil with the principalities and

powers

powers in his confederacy, are called, Ephesians, vi. 11, 12. *the rulers of the darkness of this world*, and Satan, who is called the GOD of this world, is said *to blind the minds of them that believe not*, 2d Corin. iv. 4. yea, they are represented as delirious, distracted, mad. See the man among the tombs, Mark, v. 15. Luke viii. 35.

But this is not confined to an individual; it will be found universal, not only in the spiritual whoredom of the house of Israel, but of all nations. 'Tis said of Babylon (that is the abomination of the whole earth, Rev. xvii. 5.) *That all nations have drunk of the wine of the wrath of her fornications*, Rev. xviii. 3. and Jeremiah saith, *the nations have drunken of her wine, therefore the nations are mad*.

Thus we find Satan's world a deceived, deluded, ensnared, captivated, enslaved, distracted, mad world. That he usurps a dominion over, who are absolutely wrong in their obedience to him, acting against their rightful owner, so as to deny his right to them, and his dominion over them; described by the Apostle Peter, *as denying the Lord that bought them; and bringing upon themselves swift destruction*; and by Jude, *as turning the grace of our God into lasciviousness, and denying the only Lord God, and our Lord and Saviour Jesus Christ*. This is a brief scriptural description of what is called Satan's world. But does this description of them alienate them from being the property of their rightful owner?

If GOD's chosen people should vaunt themselves that they were his exclusively, and the rest were Satan's world, would they not embolden and encourage the deceived captives of Satan, to continue in his service as their rightful owner and LORD? Would they not join with them in denying them to be the property of the Lord that bought them, in denying the only LORD GOD our Lord and Saviour JESUS CHRIST?

and

and shew that they themselves were so far under the power of the deceiver.

When God spake to the children of *Israel*, whom he selected from all other nations as his peculiar people in *Exodus* xix. 5. He says, *now therefore, if ye will obey my voice indeed, and keep my covenant, ye shall be a peculiar treasure unto me above all people, For all the earth is mine,* Psalm xxiv. 1. *the earth is the Lord's, and the fulness thereof, the world and they that dwell therein, Ezekiel* xviii. 14, *all souls are mine,* hence he is called the God of the spirits of *all flesh, Numbers* xvi. 22, repeated, chap. xxvii. 16, and he saith by the prophet *Jeremiah, behold, I the* Lord *the* God *of all flesh, Jeremiah* xxxii. 27, *The* God, *of the whole earth shall he be called,* saith the prophet *Isaiah,* chap. liv. 5. (if so, what world belongs to Satan of right, so as to be called his world?) and yet, notwithstanding a great part of the world are in the before-described bondage, and slavery to Satan. *But* God *so loved the world that he gave his only begotten Son, that whosoever believeth in him should not perish, but have everlasting life; for* God *sent not his Son into the world to condemn the world, but that the world, through him might be saved, John* iii. 16, 17, hence we read *the Father loveth the Son, and hath given all things into his hand,* verse 35, agreeable to what was said in the second Psalm, ask of me and I shall give the heathen thine inheritance, *and the uttermost part of the earth thy possession.*

Hence Jesus Christ says, *all that the Father hath is mine,* but why was this? The answer, is, *John* xvii. 2, *that he should give eternal life, to as many as thou hast given him,* consequently Jesus Christ saith, *John* vi. 37, 38, 39. *all that the Father giveth me, shall come unto me, and him that cometh unto me, I will in no wise cast out; for I came down from Heaven not to do mine own will, but the will of*

him

him that sent me : and this is the Father's will who hath sent me, that of all that he hath given me, I should lose nothing, but should raise it up at the last day.

Thus we see divine love hath given the world a Saviour, and hath given all things into his hand, that by his saving power, he many give eternal life, to all that are given to him.

Now if we review the state of mankind under the power of Satan, and view the character of the Saviour, we shall see their salvation in him. Have they lost the way of life, being deceived by falshood, into the way of death? *He is the way, the truth, and the life.* When he is made manifest, truth scatters deceit and falshood, reveals the way to the lost, and shews life to them that sit down discouraged in the region and shadow of death; he sent his apostles *to turn from darkness to light, and from the power of Satan to* God.

And as all the Father hath is given to him, the heathen his inheritance, and the utmost part of the earth his possession, those chosen out of the world appear in character as his, while the world in distinction from them are lying in the wicked one; yet being his inheritance and possession. *He shall break them with a rod of iron and dash them in pieces, as a potter's vessel.* Their union in following the usurper in opposition to Christ, shall be broken by his irresistible power, who is their rightful owner. *For this purpose was the son of* God *manifested, that he might destroy the works of the Devil.* In the passage mentioned in the 2d Psalm, their appears an allusion to an inheritance, that as we say, is all wild, uncultivated, and inhabited by wild beasts, taken in hand by the owner, broken up with instruments of iron, which the more speedily and effectually it is done, redounds to the honor of the owner.

There

There is another allusion to an husbandman, who when he had sowed good seed in his field, and the enemy sowed tares among the wheat, which sprung up and grew, that was able to separate them in the time of the harvest, so as not to lose the least grain of wheat, which was wheat when sowed, and when it grew, and when it was harvested, though the tares grew with it twined about it and entangled it; yet had them all separated and burnt up, while the wheat was gathered into his barn.

Similar to this, is what we hope for from the Great Husbandman: To be finally freed from the power and tyranny of Satan; and from every thing that offends and works iniquity. But it is said, the field, is the world, not the Church; but it is his field for the world saith the owner, and blessed be his name, mine, and the fulness thereof.

Stain, the enemy who sowed the tares, has no right to the field in any part of it; he owneth no world. That world that lieth in him, is led captive by him, yet belongeth to him who is mighty to save: who prayed for those who were thus drawn into disobedience, and enmity against him, on the cross, *Father, forgive them, for they know not what they do,* and directed his disciples to imitate him, in praying for those that despitefully use and persecute them.

This direction being put in their mouths by him, and exactly agreeable to his prayer on the cross, undoubtedly will be answered; as well as that put into the mouths of the disciples by the Apostle, that prayer, supplication, and intercession be made for all men, because he will have all men to be saved, and come to the knowledge of the truth.

Adelos says, " *That it means only all sorts of men, is confirmed by this, that his will is as much that they should come to the knowledge of the truth, as that they should*

should be saved ; and it is plain he does not will every individual should come to the knowledge of the truth, facts shew the contrary."

His reasoning is contrary to the faith of *Abraham,* who against hope, believed in hope, knowing what GOD had promised he was able to perform: And to the apostle *Paul,* who in the 2d of *Hebrews,* quotes a passage from the 8th Psalm, thou hast put all things under his feet, and to shew that *all,* in this place indisputably means *all,* he adds, in that he put all things under him, he left nothing not put under him. But now we see not yet all things put under him, but we have the assurance of the accomplishment of it, in the following words. But we see JESUS who was made a little lower than the Angels, for the sufferings of death, crowned with glory and honor, that he by the grace of GOD, should taste death for every man.

And, although *Adelos* repeats in another passage, " *facts shew the contrary,*" as if a repetition of the expression, would shew the thing true ; yet it appears contrary to *Isaiah* xi. 9. *The earth shall be full of the knowledge of the* LORD, *as the waters cover the sea,* Knowing him, consequently *all nations shall serve him,* as, *Psalm.* lxxii. 11. Agreeing with *Psalm* lxxxvi. 9. *All nations whom thou hast made, shall come and worship before thee, and glorify thy name.* Daniel says, chap. vii, 14, *and there was given him, dominion and glory, and a kingdom ; that all nations, people and tongues, should serve and obey him.*

And though we see not yet their accomplishment, we know he is faithful that has promised, who also will do it. Therefore, let not *Adelos* be so sanguine in his conclusion, but if the vision tarry, wait for it, it will surely come, it will not tarry : Wait for *the times of the restitution of all things, spoken of by the mouth of* GOD'S *holy prophets, since the world began.*

Adelos

Adelos says, page 60th, " *as to the nations, they may be compared to vast columns of water, moving a steady course down their channel, they cannot be diverted or turned back.* I wish him to remember the red sea, the river Jordan, and the power of him *that sayeth to the deep be dry, Isaiah* xliii. 27, *and I will dry up thy rivers,* I wish him to read the cxivth Psalm, with the cxxvi. And because *Simeon* hath declared how God at the first, visited the nations, to take out of them a people for his name, let him not say, as at page x, " *it was not the intent of* Jesus *to do more than to collect out of the nations a people for his name.*"

I shall take notice of one text that *Adelos* mentions, as coming from the whore of Babylon, *Rev.* xviii. 7, 6. *I sit a queen, and am no widow, and shall see no sorrow, therefore shall her plagues come in one day; death and mourning, and famine; and she shall be utterly burnt with fire,* &c. And compare it with *Isaiah* xlvii. 8, 9. *Thou sayest in thine heart, I shall not sit a widow, neither shall I know the loss of children; but these two things shall come on thee in a moment, in one day: The loss of children and widowhood, they shall come on thee in their perfection.* Have not all nations drank of the wine of her fornication, and the kings of the earth committed fornication with her? and shall they not be turned to hate the whore, and make her desolate, and naked, and eat her flesh, and burn her with fire? And if the nations that have drunk the wine of her fornication, may be looked upon as her children, in whatever capacity, either as national churches, or any of the various denominations called christian, or antichristian, or what or whoever may be looked upon as her children, she shall be bereaved of them, so as to have no single individual left, else the loss of children and widowhood come not in their perfection: And this, says the text, shall come on her in a moment, in one day: She shall

shall be destroyed with the brightness of Christ's coming; the kingdom of Satan and Antichrist, is a kingdom of darkness, which the light of the word consumes, by turning the slaves in that kingdom *from darkness unto light, and from the power of Satan unto* God. When the knowledge of the Lord shall fill the earth, as the waters cover the sea, or when the brightness of Christ's coming is made manifest, antichrist shall be destroyed. This is what we hope for, from him, who hath delivered us from the curse, being made a curse for us, that he will save us from the in-being of sin; his name is Jesus, he shall save his people from their sins.

Further, as the Great Owner says, the world is mine, and the fulness thereof; and the usurper owneth no world, but the Saviour and his Apostles, have directed the Disciples, to pray for those he has deceived, and led captive at his will, even the worst of them, Doth he not greatly err, to say, " *that there is a world for which he neither prayed, nor died?*"

The passage in the 17th of John, I think, if rightly understood, will not warrant his assertion in the beginning of the Chapter, he speaks of the Father's giving him *power over all flesh, that he should give eternal life to as many as he had given him.*

Then he speaks of his immediate Disciples, to whom he had manifested the Father's name, and prays for those things for them, of which they stood in need of, as his witnesses, that he did not pray for, for the rest of the world.

Afterward he prays for those that should believe on him through their word, then comes in the design of this prayer; verse 21, that they all may be one, as thou Father art in me, and I in thee; that they also may be one in us, *That the world may believe, that thou hast sent me.* Verse 23, *that the world may know that thou hast sent me.* In which Jesus prays that the

the world may know and believe that he is the sent of God; the same that distinguished the Disciples from the rest of the world, in verse 8th, *the world hath not known me, but these have known me, and they have believed that thou hast sent me.*

Thus Jesus prays that the world may be brought into the same circumstances, that distinguished the disciples from the world. We read in verse 24, *Father I will, that they also, whom thou hast given me, be with me to behold my glory.*

What is the meaning of *also*? Is it not generally under stood to bring in something that had not before been particularly noticed, or discovered? As if Jesus had said, I not only pray for my immediate disciples, and those that shall believe on me through their word, that they may be one, that the world may know and believe: But adds, Father I will that they *also* whom thou hast given me, be with me, where I am, to behold my glory. Any one that believes this to be true, may say, Am I given to Christ! What a heathen! The most contemned: What, one in the utmost parts of the earth, the most neglected: And doth he will that those given to him be with him, to behold his glory. Oh! Language fails, to express the gratitude, and joy and obligation to obedience, that I, and every heathen, and every creature in the utmost parts of the earth, are hereby called to exercise.

We were given to him that he might give eternal life to as many as were given to him; verse 2d, and is it not the beginning of life eternal, to know the love of God in Christ thus made manifest?

And as Jesus prayed for the world, so he died for them; when he was lifted up, he drew all men unto him; and one dying for all, all died, as the Apostles judge, *if one died for all, then were all dead*: 2d Corinthians i. 14. And thus saith the gospel of reconciliation,

ciliation, *God was in Chrift reconciling the world to himfelf, not imputing their trefpaffes unto them.* He died for the ungodly, and tafted death for every man.

I thought to proceed to take notice of feveral truths which Adelos fpeaks, which his fentiments lead him to confine, but having exceeded the bounds of a letter, fhall leave it to another opportunity.

Yours, &c.

SHIPPIE TOWNSEND.

Bofton, Dec. 9, 1787.

THUS, my friend, I have fhewn you the fcope and fubftance (not having an exact copy) of a letter that was written fometime paft, on the fame fubject, judge for yourfelf if it is not agreeable to the fcriptures of truth. If I have not already wearied you, I will fubjoin fome further thoughts that were then written concerning the truth he fpeaks, which his fentiments lead him to confine.

Adelos fpeaks the truth " concerning the appearance of primitive chriftianity, and the diftinction of the Difciples from the reft of the world."

But why they were thus diftinguifhed, but to be his chofen witneffes, to bear teftimony againft the corruption of Antichrift, and bear witnefs to the truth and ways of Christ, amidft a crooked and perverfe generation, among whom they were to fhine as lights in the world ? lights are not to hinder travellers from feeing, but to fhew them the way in which they may walk with fafety. The appearance of primitive chriftianity, and the firft Difciples, were lit up to turn the attention of loft and bewildered travellers, to the new and living way, hear one of the primitive preachers exprefs himfelf on this head, *unto me who am lefs than the leaft of all faints, is this grace given, that I fhould preach among the Gentiles, the unfearchable riches of* Christ : *And to make all men fee what is the fellowfhip of the myftery,* &c. Ephefians iii. 8. 9.

Again,

Again, it is a truth which he takes notice of, that "*Aaron* as a type bears the names of the children of *Israel* on his breast plate, and on his heart, and not the names of the Egyptians, &c." But it is as true, that the Egyptians are included in the promise, as well as *Israel*; read, *Isaiah* xix. from 13 to the end, and you will see that though they were deceived and seduced, and were caused to err in every work of theirs, as a drunken man staggereth in his vomit. Yet in that day, verse 19, *shall there be an altar to the Lord in the land of Egypt*, verse 21, *and the Lord shall be known to Egypt, and the Egyptians shall know the* LORD *in that day*, &c. verse 22, *and the* LORD *shall smite Egypt, he shall smite and heal, and they shall return to the* LORD, *and he shall be intreated of them, and shall heal them;* verse 24, *in that day shall Israel be the third with Egypt, and with Assyria, even a blessing in the midst of the land;* verse 25, *whom the* LORD *of* HOSTS *shall bless, saying, Blessed be Egypt my people, and Assyria the work of my hands, and Israel mine inheritance.* The gospel corresponding with the prophecy shews, that he is the GOD of the *Gentiles* as well as the *Jews*: That the *Gentiles* are fellow-heirs, that as the name of *Israel* was on the breast plate of *Aaron*, the type and the children of *Israel* came to GOD, by the typical high-priest, so the Egyptians, the *Gentiles* come to GOD, by the great high priest of our profession; *for all nations whom thou hast made shall come and worship before thee, and glorify thy name*, Psalm xxvi. 9, so, however true *Adelos*'s remark is, that grand kingdoms at this present time are destitute of the words of eternal life, yet we are not at liberty with him to conclude that GOD has not a people among them, least we should deny the heathens were his inheritance, and the uttermost parts of the earth his possession. Among men, that part of their inheritance that is not culti-
vated

vated is as much their own as the fenced pasture and plough-land, or even the garden.

Again, it is a truth, *that the epistles of the Apostles were written to believers, that composed the churches of the Saints.* Yet it is true, that in them the Apostle wrote to the Disciples, of that salvation that respected the rest of the world. To the church in *Rome,* whom he addresses as beloved of God, called saints, he says, chap. v. 18, *as by the offence of one, upon all men to condemnation : Even so by the righteousness of one, upon all men to justification of life.* Verse 21, *that as sin reigned unto death, even so might grace reign through righteousness unto eternal life, by* Jesus Christ our Lord. If sin reigned unto death over the posterity of *Adam*, it cannot be *even so* respecting grace reigning through righteousness to eternal life, except it extend as far as the reign of sin. *Adam* is called a figure of him that is to come; now if their be more in the figure than in the substance, it is not a figure of that substance.

To the church at *Corinth*, sanctified in Christ Jesus, called Saints, with all that in every place call on the name of Jesus Christ our Lord, both theirs and ours, he says, 1 Epistle xv, 22, *as in Adam all die, so in* Christ *shall all be made alive.* Verse 49, *as we have borne the image of the earthly, we shall also bear the image of the heavenly,* and 2d Epistle, 5th chapter, 14, *for the love of* Christ *constraineth us, because we thus judge if one died for all then were all dead :* Hence verse 19, God *was in* Christ *reconciling the world unto himself, not imputing their trespasses unto them.*

To the churches in Galatia, he says, in chapter iv. 4, *in the fulness of time* God *sent forth his son, made of a woman, made under the law, to redeem them that were under the law*; if we believe Jesus Christ is come in the flesh, we believe he accomplished what

he

he came for; and as he came to redeem them that were under the law, we believe his redemption as extensive as that description; and believing, may exult with the Apostle, in Chapter iii. 13, CHRIST *hath deliverd us from the curse of the law, being made a curse for us.* To the Saints at Ephesus, and to the faithful in CHRIST JESUS, he says, Chap. i. 9, 10, Having made known to us the mystery of his will, according to his good pleasure, which he purposed in himself; *that in the dispensation of the fulness of time he might gather together all things in* CHRIST, *both which are in heaven, and which are in earth in him,* chapter iii. 8 9, unto me, who am less than the least of all saints, is this grace given, that I should preach among the *Gentiles*, the unsearchable riches of CHRIST: And to make *all men see* what is the fellowship of the mystery, &c. To the Saints in CHRIST JESUS at *Philippi.* He brings to view the humiliation and exaltation of JESUS CHRIST, and his name above every name, *that in the name of* JESUS *every knee should bow,* not at the name, but in the name, which denotes true worship, 'tis agreeable to the exhortation of the Apostle to the *Colossians,* iii. 17, and is the same word that is there used, *whatsover ye do in word or deed, do all in the name of the* LORD JESUS: And here we may take notice, that the Apostle, speaking to them, says, chapter i. 20, *and by him to reconcile all things to himself, by him, whether things in heaven, or things on earth.* When the Apostle writes to the Evangelist *Timothy,* the same truths are inculcated, 1st of *Timothy,* 2, from one to the 6th verse; and *Titus* ii, 11, *the grace of* GOD, *which bringeth salvation to all men hath appeared*: We have already had occasion to mention, what he says to the *Hebrews,* in chapter ii, 8, 9, *James* is so far from supposing the begotten by the word of truth, are GOD's whole world, that he calls them first-fruits:—

Of

Of his own will begat he us, by the word of truth, that we should be a kind of first-fruits of his creatures. And Peter speaks of *false teachers, who shall privily bring in damnable errors, even denying the Lord that bought them, and bring on themselves swift destruction;* for destruction and misery are in their ways, who deny the Lord that bought them, who is the way of peace; but hath the Lord bought them? Then they are his, according to Isaiah xliii. 1, *I have redeemed thee, thou art mine,* and he will not lose the purchase of his blood; though they have destroyed themselves, in him, is their help. John, you know speaks of Jesus, *as the propitiation for our sins, and not for ours only, but for the whole world,* and in the Revelations, he says, *and every creature in Heaven, on earth, and in the sea, heard I, say blessing, and honour, and glory, and power, unto him that sitteth on the throne, and unto the Lamb for ever and ever.* Saw he not then in vision, every knee bow in the name of Jesus? Now when we consider the Apostles and first disciples, the first churches, and those in after ages who followed the footsteps of the first flocks elected, chosen or predestinated, hereunto by Jesus Christ, according to the good pleasure of his will, to whom the mystery of his will is made known, according to the good pleasure which he hath purposed in himself. Ephesians, i. 5. 9, We find it was *that in the dispensation of the fulness of time, he might gather together in one, all things in Christ, verse* 10, *and to make all men see what is the fellowship of the mystery.* (Think of the expression) Jesus Christ, says Matthew, xi. 25, *I thank thee, O Father, Lord of Heaven and earth, that thou hast hid these things from the wise and prudent, and hast revealed them unto babes, even so Father, for so it seemed good in thy sight:* 'Tis revealed to make all men see, not for those to whom it is revealed, to glory over their fellow men, from whom it seems good in the sight of GOD, it should yet be hidden, by telling them they shall never see, *" There are multitudes of them that belong to Satan's world, for whom Jesus neither prayed nor died ?* If he that hath mercy on whom he will, of his own will hath begotten them by the word of truth, that they should be a kind of first-fruits of his creatures, let them remember, that the whole harvest, even the latest part of it belongs to the same owner, and not be so ready to assert that a part belongs to his enemy, whom the Great Owner has cast out, and drawn all men unto himself, John xii. 31, 32.

Now my beloved friend, let me ask myself and you a plain question, which, perhaps we have been often asked in our childhood: Who made you? Who preserves you? Who redeemed you? The answer will determine whose we are, and whom we should serve, for our Creator, Preserver, and Redeemer, is our Owner and LORD. To him we look to safeguard, and defend his own property, to provide for them, in sickness and health, to be with them in life and death; for even death itself cannot alienate his property; for living and dying, we are the LORD's. The Apostle in Romans viii. 38, says, *I am persuaded, that neither death nor life, nor Angels, nor principalities, nor powers, nor things present, nor things to come, shall be able to separate us from the love of God which is in Christ Jesus our Lord.* So that death can neither destroy the Divine propriety in us, nor his love to us. Glory be to his name.

THESE things being so, it is evident that obedience is due to our Rightful Master and LORD: And any man that acts under the Prince of darkness, the Prince of the power of the air, the Spirit that now worketh in the children of disobedience, in opposition to CHRIST JESUS, must be self condemned, as in rebellion to his Rightful Sovereign: But if the

contrary

contrary were true, and any part of the world belong to Satan, as their rightful owner and Lord; they have to look to him for protection, and owe their obedience to him, and cannot be deemed rebels in their subjection to him; shocking consequences of attempting to prove that any part of mankind belong to Satan, see how it opens the flood-gates to all impiety and wickedness. And as we are every one of us under every possible obligation of obedience to him, so we are to consider ourselves members of his Great Family; and to love one another, as he has given commandment, and as we have opportunity, do good to all men, especially unto them who are of the household of faith.

To what hath been said, there arises the following objections; namely, Jesus Christ says, of the Jews, *ye are not of my sheep, as I said unto you.* In answer, it may be said, the Prophet Isaiah saith, all we like sheep, have gone astray: And the Apostle Peter, describing the disciples to whom he wrote, says, *ye were as sheep going astray, but now are returned to the shepherd and bishop of your souls:* But those Jews that rejected him, did not yet appear in that character, therefore he saith, ye are not of my sheep; *my sheep hear my voice, and they follow me;* as if he had said, they believe me to be their shepherd; you are not of that character, and do not appear as my sheep; yet he saith in the same Chapter, *other sheep I have that are not of this fold,* in which expression he appears to describe those that are yet in unbelief, and do not appear in character as his sheep, are not yet brought into the fold. *Them also I must bring, and they shall hear my voice, and there shall be one fold and one shepherd.* Mark the expression, *I must, they shall*, I must bring, they shall hear my voice.

Again Jesus Christ saith to the unbelieving Jews, that sought to kill him, John viii. 44, ye are of
your

your father the Devil. In this passage, JESUS CHRIST appears to denominate them, by the influence they were then under, as when he called Peter Satan; when speaking under his influence, we read, Matthew xvi. 21, JESUS began to shew his disciples, how that he *must* go into Jerusalem, and suffer many things of the elders and chief priests, and scribes, and be killed, and be raised again, the third day: Peter took him, and began to rebuke him, saying, that be far from thee, LORD: This shall not be unto thee: *But he turned, and said to Peter, get thee behind me Satan;* take notice, it follows in the forementioned, John viii. 44, *and the lust of your father ye will do, he was a murderer, and abode not in the truth, when he speaketh a lie, he speaketh of his own, for he is a liar and the father of it.* As though he had said, while you refuse to admit the truth, testified of me, you cherish a lie, and that lie thus cherished, prompts you to seek to kill me. Thus you appear in character as the children of the Devil, as being influenced by him, to lying and murder. Agreeable to 1st of John iii. 8, *he that committeth sin is of the Devil,* influenced by him thereunto; but this notwithstanding, there is this consolation, that JESUS CHRIST prayed for those thus influenced; even for his crucifiers; Father forgive them, for they know not what they do. And John saith for this purpose, the Son of GOD was manifested, that he might destroy the works of the Devil.

Again it is said, 2d Thessalonians, i. 6, to the 10th, *seeing it is a righteous thing with God, to recompence tribulation, to them that trouble you; and to you that are troubled, rest with us, when the Lord Jesus shall be revealed from heaven, in flaming fire, with his mighty Angels, taking vengeance of them that know not God, and that obey not the gospel of our Lord Jesus Christ: Who shall be punished with everlasting destruction,*

destruction, from the presence of the Lord, and from the glory of his power. Hence the inquiry is, doth not this text militate with what has been said. For answer, let it be considered, the LORD JESUS CHRIST shall be revealed in flaming fire, doth not that manifest his Deity? For our GOD, is a consuming fire. With sobriety and reverence let it be considered, what this everlasting consuming fire destroys: The foregoing words in Hebrews, xii. 28, 29, are: Wherefore, we receiving a kingdom that cannot be moved, let us hold fast the grace whereby we may serve God acceptably, with reverence and godly fear, *for our God is a consuming fire*: the grace whereby we may serve GOD acceptably, is the grace that is in CHRIST JESUS. Every thing aside from this, offered as an attempt to serve God acceptably, will not abide the fire, will be consumed and destroyed, agreeable to 1st Corinthians iii. from 11, to 16, for other foundation can no man lay, than that which is laid; which is JESUS CHRIST. Now if any man build upon this foundation, gold, silver, precious stones, wood, hay, stubble: Every man's work shall be made manifest, for the day shall declare it, *because it shall be revealed by fire; and the fire shall try every man's work: of what sort it is.* If any man's work abide which he has built thereon, he shall receive reward. If any man's works shall be burnt, he shall suffer loss; *but he himself shall be saved: Yet so, as by fire.* Gold, silver, and precious stones will abide the fire, like the grace whereby we may serve GOD acceptably; but wood, hay, stubble, is fuel of fire, and must be burnt up, agreeable to Isaiah ix. 5, where every battle of the warrior is contrasted with this: for every battle of the warrior is with confused noise, and garments rolled in blood; sometimes one prevailing, and sometimes the other; but it doth not destroy the enmity: But this shall be with burning fuel of fire (not burning *and fuel*

fuel of fire: the *and* is supplied) for unto us a child is born. The prince of peace, and the government shall be on his shoulders.

Thus we see what the flaming fire is to consume, when the Lord Jesus shall be revealed in flaming fire, taking vengeance on them that know not God, and obey not the gospel of our Lord Jesus Christ, who shall be punished with the everlasting destruction, of all their hopes and prospects of standing in disobedience to the gospel: and of all the wood, hay, and stubble, that foolish builders have built on the foundation: Of all the tares that entangle the wheat, and the chaff that cleaves to it, of every thing that is fuel of fire. Of every thing aside from the grace that is in Christ Jesus, the grace whereby we serve God acceptably: While blessed be his name, even the foolish builder himself shall be saved yet so as by fire. This view of taking vengeance appears agreeable to Isaiah xxxiv. 4, *say to them of a fearful heart, fear not, behold your* God *will come with vengeance, even* God *with a recompence, he will come and save you.* And Psalm xcviii. 8, *thou wast a* God *that forgavest them, though thou tookest vengeance on their inventions,* which last passage, I suppose, refers to those who came out of Egypt and did not enter into the earthly Canaan, for whom *Moses* prayed, Numbers xiv. 19, and was answered, *I have pardoned according to thy word.* * Who though they were cut off from entering into the earthly Canaan, were not cut off from pardoning mercy.

This brief view of these three texts, is brought to shew that no divine dispensations in reproof, or correction, dissolve the relation of the Father of the family of the whole creation: His name is unchangable, according to Mica iii. 6, *For I thee* Lord, *I change not; therefore ye sons of Jacob are not consumed*

---

* Note. According to thy word, what word did Moses use, or what name did he pray in. See verses 17, 18, 19, according to the greatness of thy mercy, and as thou hast done from Egypt until now.

fumed. He is still the just GOD, and the SAVIOUR, Father and REDEEMER is his name, from everlasting, and will remain so to everlasting. Therefore, see the prophet Isaiah, chap. xlii. 10, 11, 12, sing unto the LORD a new song, his praise from the ends of the earth! Ye that go down to the sea, and all that is herein; the isles and the inhabitants thereof. Let the wilderness and the cities thereof, lift up their voice, the villages that Kedar doth inhabit: Let the inhabitants of the rock sing: Let them shout from the top of the mountains. Let them give glory to the LORD, and declare his praise in the islands. Let us look over the various expressions, and find any if we can, that are excluded from joining herein; and if there should still remain a doubt, let us turn to Psalm xcviii. from 1, to 4, O sing unto the LORD a new song, * for he hath done marvellous things: his right hand and his holy arm hath gotten him the victory. The LORD hath made known his salvation; his righteousness hath he openly shewed in the sight of the Heathen: He hath remembered his mercy and his truth towards the house of Israel; all the ends of the earth have seen the salvation of our GOD. (In his mercy and truth towards the house of Israel expressed in his promise to Abraham, all the ends of the earth are included) make a joyful noise unto the LORD, all the earth: Make a loud noise, and rejoice and sing praise. Let the prophet Isaiah, close the subject, see chap, xliv. 22, 23, I have blotted out as a thick cloud thy transgressions, and as a cloud thy sins: Return unto me, for I have redeemed thee. Sing, O ye heavens; for the LORD hath done it: Shout ye *lower parts* of the earth: Break forth into singing, ye mountains, O forest, and every tree therein: For the LORD hath redeemed Jacob, and glorified himself in Israel.

Several

* See what the new song is, Revelations, v, 9.

Several Objections against the Extent of the Gospel Salvation considered.

SECTION V.

Some REMARKS *on a* PAMPHLET, *entitled,* ALL MEN WILL NOT BE SAVED FOREVER: *Wrote by* SAMUEL MATHER, *Pastor of a Church in* AMERICAN BOSTON, *in answer to one, entitled,* SALVATION FOR ALL MEN ; *in which there is an endeavour to clear several passages of Scripture, which appear very much darkened by the Writer, and the several Authors referred to in that performance : By comparing Scripture with Scripture, or attending to the Scripture as its own interpreter. Addressed to Mr.* MATHER: *Together with some Remark on the* insidious PAMPHLET *(so called, by him.) To which is annexed* FOUR INFERENCES *from the above* REMARKS.

To the law and to the testimony, if they speak not according to this word, it is because there is no morning in them.—*Prophet* ISAIAH.

For I determine to know nothing among you, save Jesus Christ and him crucified ; for though we walk in the flesh, we do not war after the flesh, for the weapons of our warfare are not carnal, but mighty through God, to the pulling down of strong holds, casting down imaginations, and every high thing that exalts itself against the knowledge of God, and bringing into captivity every thought to the obedience of Jesus Christ, which things also we speak, not in the words, that man's wisdom teacheth, but which the Holy Ghost teacheth, comparing spiritual things with spiritual.—*Paul to the* CORINTHIANS.

To Mr. MATHER.

SIR,

AS the subject before us is the common salvation, I take liberty to lay aside your addition, as that which no way belongs to the point in controversy, and consider myself as on a perfect level with you,

(your

(your superiority in years excepted, to which I mean ever to have a due regard) that I may write with that freedom and plainness, that becomes one, contending for a truth, which I judge, of equal importance to all the descendants from apostate Adam. I remember to have heard this observation, that while we are attempting to pull down our neighbour's one idol, we are in danger of setting up two of our own; but I hope I am not so ignorant of the pride of the human heart, and the devices of the grand adversary, as to think myself not equally liable with others engaged in controversal writings, to contend for victory and triumph, rather than truth; and of being influenced by the vanity of my carnal mind, rather than the meekness and gentleness of CHRIST. To him who is able to keep me from falling into the condemnation of the devil, I now commit myself, and proceed to the remarks proposed; may they be made with that meekness that becomes the man who fears GOD, loves his truth, doth not despise, but love his neighbour.

Notwithstanding the many objections I have against your performance, I must acknowledge there are some things in it that justly demands one's attention, in the premonition to the reader; your bringing up to view, *Matthew* vii, 13, 14, the exhortation to enter into the straight gate—and to beware of false prophets; was very agreeable as you present it to view— "*as coming from the great light of the world, the only and true way to* GOD *and happiness;*" and it fixed my thoughts the more, as it is a passage of scripture, that has many years engaged me in the inquiring what is the true import of it, as not knowing but that I might profit by your interpretations thereof, which indeed did not appear satisfactory to my mind, more than any thing that I had been before acquainted with; therefore I set myself to inquire into the meanng of those words of the LORD and SAVIOUR, with other parts of the divine word, by compairing scripture with scripture, as it is undoubtedly the best, and is its own interpreter.—When I consider JESUS CHRIST, as made under the law, and speaking as under the law to those that were also under it, and that it was his design to manifest himself as the true Messiah, the antitype of what took place under that dispensation, I apprehend in this exhortation he has the same thing in view, and speaks of himself as the antitype of what was said of the gate in the Old Testament scriptures; perhaps in *Ezekiel*, chap. xliii. 4, and 4, 2, 3, and 45, 19, which passages were they well understood, perhaps would illustrate this matter; but I shall only take notice of what is said in Psalm cxviii. 19, 20, where the Messiah is brought in, saying, *open to me the gates of righteousness; I will go in to them and praise the* LORD; *this gate of the* LORD, *into which the righteous shall enter.*—Here we have the mediator in virtue of his own righteousness, calling for the opening the gates of righteousness, which may be illustrated by *John* x. 2, *he that entereth by the door is the shepherd of the sheep, and he enters the gate of righteousness as head of his body.* By his own righteousness, his perfect obedience to the law, and his full satisfaction to divine justice, in which the father is well pleased: So entering by him, is entering into the straight gate, into the narrow way, the only way leading to life; JESUS CHRIST admits no competitor, no rival with him; nothing to be made mention of but his righteousness and his only; not merely for the entrance into the gate; but all along the narrow way, and so jealous is he of his honor, that he allows of no subjection to any other Lord;—this appears to me, the most likely meaning of the straight gate and narrow way, which it is manifest, there be but few that find; as it is natural for us all in some way or other, besides him, to go about to establish our own righteousness

righteousness and seek to ennter in thereby, which though many seek thus to enter, they never shall be able; for eminently he is the way, the truth and the life; whilst the body of the Jewish nation were seeking righteousness by the works of the law, the LORD lets them know the master of the house was about to rise up and shut the door of that dispensation; and when he shall have so done, their knocking and pleading, what they had been done, and the many advantages they had enjoyed, would not avail them, while they rejected the straight gate and narrow way, and they with their pleas utterly rejected; while he should say to them, I know ye not, while others, i. e. the *Gentiles*, should come from the east and west, north and south, and sit down with the patriarchs, and thus it would appear that the great saviour according to the good pleasure of his will, was found of them that sought him not, thus *Israel* that followed after the law of righteousness hath not attained to the law of righteousness; wherefore, because they sought it not by faith, but as it were by the works of the law; if the two passages that speak of the straight gate be considered and compared, I think these thoughts must appear agreeable to the scope of them. *Matt.* vii. 13, and *Luke* xiii. 13, 24—and it must be acknowledged that it was not more the error of the people under the old dispensation by many deceitful ways, to be endeavouring to establish their own righteousness, than it is for those who call themselves christians, and the uncertainty and perplexity which arises from that painful question, What lack I yet, will forever torment them, till the straight gate and narrow way is wide opened to them; wherefore, woe to them who pretend to another gate or way beside JESUS CHRIST, the true way; he warns against false prophets, that come in sheeps cloathing, but inwardly they are ravening wolves, and says, by their fruits ye shall know them;

do men gather grapes of thorns, or figs of thistles; the fruits by which Mr. *Mather* judges of them " is their own irregular, worldly and sensual lives and conversations;" and the same fruits of their doctrine, but as this is not a satisfactory discovery, because men of such lives and doctrines don't come in sheeps cloathing, but appear outwardly and inwardly alike, and there does not seem much danger of their deceiving; it may then be inquired, who are the false prophets? I answer, our Lord who hath warned us against them, has not left us without their distinguishing marks, by which to know them, therefore looking for the meaning of Jesus Christ, let us compare the passage with the apostle *Peter*, 2d epist, ii. chap. beginning who says, *there were false prophets among the people, even as there shall be false teachers among you, who privily shall bring in damnable errors, even denying the Lord that bought them, and bring upon themselves swift destruction, &c.* Denying the Lord that bought them; as in the straight gate and narrow way: the gospel admits of no competitor, no rival with Jesus Christ, nothing to be made mention of but his righteousness, no subjection to any foreign lord; so the false teachers are those that privily bring in something besides, and cannot trust the finished work of Christ alone, as the exclusive ground of hope towards God, without something wrought in us, or done by us to recommend us to the divine favour; and though these teachers will with much plausible language speak honourable of Jesus Christ; yet will warn of the danger of holding his character and finished work as witnessed in his resurrection, as the sole foundation of hoping for divine mercy to eternal life; is not this privily denying the Lord that bought them.—Again, when the scriptures assert, *that he gave himself a ransom for all; that he tasted death for every man; that he is the propitiation for the whole world;*

world; that he will have all men to be saved, and come to the knowledge of the truth: (or even as some read, coming to the knowledge of the truth, and being saved) the love of CHRIST constrained the Apostle thus to judge; *that if one died for all, then were all dead; and that he died for all, that they which live should not henceforth live to themselves, but unto him that died for them and rose again; that as sin reigned to death, even so might grace reign through righteousness to eternal life, by Jesus Christ our Lord.* Is it not denying the LORD that bought them, to assert this cannot be scripture doctrine, because is leads to licentiousness; when the Apostle truly says, *he died for all, that those that live should not henceforth live to themselves, but to him that died for them and rose again:* and another Apostle tells us—*we love him because he first loved us; and this is the love of God that we keep his commandments;* let God be true, and every man a liar.

The doctrine of CHRIST leads to himself as the true vine, the cause of all fruitfulness; the root of the righteous that yieldeth fruit agreeable to *Hosea* xiv. 8, *from me is thy fruit found;*—and to *John* xv. beginning; *as the branch cannot bear fruit except it abide in the vine, no more can ye, except ye abide in me;—I am the vine, ye are the branches, he that abideth in me and I in him, the same bringeth forth much fruit, for without me ye can do nothing.* Now when obedience is urged from other motives, and to other ends by false teachers, we may as well gather grapes of thorns, or figs of thistles. I must here make a pause, that I may acknowledge the great satisfaction you gave me in your remarks upon Mr. *White*, the full testimony you have given to the doctrine of the great GOD and SAVIOUR.

I mean to credit you for the whole of what you have written from page twelve, line eleven from the bottom—

bottom—" *but you say there is one thing that follows, that is quite inexcusable;*"—" mark says, he who is this saviour, i. e. of all men; it is GOD, not CHRIST." " Let us look into the 1st of *Timothy*, 2. 3, and we shall see who is GOD our Saviour, and we shall see that in the Greek it runs, *in the sight of the Saviour our God, and servants are enjoined to shew all good fidelity that they may adorn the doctrine of God our Saviour in all things,* in *Titus* ii. 10, but it is in the Greek, *that they may adorn the doctrine of the Saviour our God in all things;* and how contrary is this to the interpretation of Mr. *White*, as well as other Arians. However, it is the truth as it is in JESUS the Saviour our GOD, and worthy of all acceptation." And in page 14, line 8 from the top, you say, " if the words be justly translated, the sense will be, there is one GOD and one mediator of God and man, the man CHRIST JESUS, and so it signifies that the mediator is both GOD and man; but we note, that the learned *Bitterfield*, has proposed this translation of the words, which it must be owned answers word for word to the Greek; the one GOD, the one who is also mediator of GOD and man, is the man CHRIST JESUS; so then the man CHRIST JESUS, who is the mediator, is GOD as well as man, so that he is GOD and man united." The above quotation is what strikes my mind with satisfaction, as the truth, as it is in JESUS the Saviour our GOD; and were I capacitated to recommend them to every ones consideration, I would do it; though I cannot, I dare not, for any other paragraph in your whole performance; and what follows immediately hereupon, is as shocking as that quotation was pleasing; to which you add, " *but although this mediator has given himself a ransom for all; for it must be granted that he has given a sufficient ransom and propitiation for all; and he will not cast abroad any, who penitently come to him as he re-*
quire

quires, to gain and enjoy the benefit of it ; yet it is no where said, that they who will not come to him for life and happiness, shall enjoy the benefit of his ransom and propitiation ;" the sum of which is, that though our Saviour be GOD, and has given himself a ransom, a sufficient ransom and propitiation for all, yet it depends upon the will of man, whether any shall enjoy the benefits of it ; I would ask you, sir, Did you ever read *Jeremiah* 31, 31, 34, and chap. 32, 38, 40, and chap. 33, 8, with the *Hebrews* 8, from 8 to the end, and *Hebrews* 10, 16, 17, 18 ? You seem, indeed, Sir, as if you thought the new covenant might be broken as the old one was ; but it must be from your inattention to the Scriptures, *I will be their* GOD, *and they shall be my people ; I will cleanse them from all their iniquities whereby they have sinned against me, and I will pardon all their iniquities whereby they have sinned, and whereby they have transgressed against me* ; the ground of which is the sufficiency of the ransom and propitiation—*I will forgive their iniquities and remember their sins no more ;* alluding to the sacrifice of CHRIST, where the remission of them was, *Hebrews* 10, 17, 18, and the Apostle says, *Having therefore brethren, boldness to enter into the holiest by the blood of* JESUS—their boldness did not arise from their own repentance; their own good dispositions ; but came in by the blood of JESUS.— Would it have been possible for you to have expressed yourself as you have done, if you had attended to *Isaiah* 45, 22, 3, 4, *Look unto me and be ye saved all the ends of the earth, for I* GOD *and none else ; I have sworn by myself, the word is gone out of my mouth in righteousness, and shall not return, that unto me every knee shall bow, and every tongue shall swear, surely shall say, in the* LORD *have I righteousness and strength, to him shall come, and all that are incensed against him shall be ashamed ; in the* LORD *shall all the seed of Israel be justified and shall glory.*   Sir,

Sir, if you could accept advice from one, but a few years younger than yourself, it would be to lay aside your numerous train of commentators and ancient fathers, (about five and twenty of which have been called in to your aid in your little piece) and leave the scriptures to speak for themselves; for instance, suppose we should lay aside Messrs. *White, Austin, Beza* and *Grotius*, upon 1st of Timothy, ii. 3, 4, and betake ourselves to the scriptures for to find the meaning. *I exhort therefore that first of all, supplication, prayer, intercession, and giving of thanks, be made for all men, for kings and even all in authority, that we may lead a quiet and peaceable life, in all godliness, and honesty;* and the ground and reason upon which the Apostle founds his exhortation is as follows ; *for this is good and acceptable in the sight of God our Saviour, who will have all men to be saved and come to the knowledge of the truth* ; for the one GOD, the one who is also mediator of GOD and man, (as you say it is in the Greek) *gave himself a ransom for all.* Here we see the prayer of faith in the public assembly was to be made for all, according to the will of GOD, and to which the people of God could heartily say, Amen—for there is ground of faith, in prayer for all men.

For kings, it is said ; *Psalm* lxxii. 10, 11, *the kings of Tarshish and the Isles shall bring presents ; the kings of Sheba and Seba, shall offer gifts ; yea, all kings shall fall down before him : All nations shall serve him. Psalm* cii. 15, *So the heathen shall fear the name of the Lord, and all the kings of the earth thy glory. Psalm* cxxxviii. 4, *All the kings of the earth shall praise thee, when they shall hear the words of thy mouth* (or come to the knowledge of the truth) —but doth not the kings of the earth set themselves, and their rulers take council together, against the Lord and against his anointed ? and have not many of them

them been the bafeſt of men? Yes, verily: How then ſhall it be accompliſhed? becauſe he has ſaid it it in his word, and he has given himſelf a ranſom for them; it is he that giveth ſalvation to kings;—hence there is ground to pray for kings, ground of faith in prayer for them, becauſe it is good and acceptable in the ſight of God our Saviour, who will have them to be ſaved;—and is there not the ſame ground of faith in prayer for all men? Was there not an original bleſſing pronounced upon them all in their head their firſt parents, in the day they were created? When GOD bleſſed them; Geneſis v. 2, And though the bleſſing was forfeited, it was not revoked or recalled, for the gifts and callings of GOD are without repentance; if he gives commandment to bleſs it cannot be reverſed, Numbers, xxiii. 19, *God is not a man that he ſhould lie, neither the ſon of man that he ſhould repent; hath he ſaid it, and ſhall he not do; or hath he ſpoken, and ſhall he not make it good? behold! I have received to bleſs, and he hath bleſſed, and I cannot reverſe it*:—Therefore on the fall of our firſt parents the ſerpent was curſed, and the way in which the pronounced bleſſing ſhould take place, is revealed in the promiſed ſeed of the woman, and afterwards to *Abraham*—*In thy ſeed ſhall all the nations of the earth be bleſſed;* and afterwards in the prieſthood, ſacrifices, types and ſhadows of the Jewiſh diſpenſation—in the *Prophets* and in the *Pſalms; concerning him who is mighty to ſave, God over all, bleſſed forever*: When I conſider that for the accompliſhment of this great and comprehenſive truth full of bleſſing—*God was manifeſt in the fleſh, the one God, the mediator of God and man, the man Chriſt Jeſus: the brightneſs of the divine glory, and the expreſs image of his perſon, in whom the fulneſs of the godhead dwelt*: I inquire, did not the fulneſs of the human as well as the divine nature, dwell in him alſo? Is he

not

not the head of the whole human nature as extensively as *Adam* was? I think it is impossible to conceive the Apostles meaning in *Romans* v. from 14 to the end, in any other light: Indeed, Sir, I am at a loss for what purpose you bring this passage into view in page 15, and filling a paragraph with it, and then saying nothing about it; let it be attended to with sobriety; and it will prove that CHRIST is the head of every man, in which *Adam* was a figure of him; and that as head of every man he gave himself a ransom for all, therefore to pray for all men, is good and acceptable in the sight of GOD our saviour, who will have all men to be saved and come to the knowledge of the truth;—but you say, page 13, " *May they expect to be brought to this saving knowledge in a land of darkness and misery; we have no warrant for thinking any such thing from the word of God.*" How shocking is this, where GOD hath said by his messenger, he will have all men to come to the knowledge of the truth;—it favours of the same impious infidelity that the people of ancient Israel were chargeable with; *Psalm* lxxviii. 19, *yea they spake against God; they said, can God prepare a table in the wilderness?* verse 20, *Can he give bread also; can he provide flesh for his people; hath he said and shall he not do it? hath he spoken, and shall he not bring it to pass? The Lord gave the word, and great was the company of those that published it, for with God all things are possible.*

Now as CHRIST was the head of every man, when he was lift up, he drew all men unto him; and so when one died for all, then were all dead—Please, sir, to look into the text in 1st of *Corinthians*, v. 14, in your Greek testament, and see if it is not there, *if one died for all, then all died.*

Is not Paul to be thus understood, when he says, *I was crucified with Christ?* Was it his privilege* only, or did CHRIST by the grace of GOD taste death for every man? Agreeing with 1st of *John,* ii. 2, *And he is the propitiation for our sins; and not for ours only, but for the whole world;* which is agreeable to his *giving himself a ransom for all;* and therefore, *will have all men to be saved and come to the knowledge of the truth;*—therefore, there is ground of faith in prayer for all men.

There is another text mentioned, (which though my mind has been much exercised, and it may be, have not yet, that understanding of, as I could wish) your illustration thereof, not being satisfactory upon it by any means. Let us look for the meaning of it by comparing it with other scriptures;—but first I would take leave to lay aside Messrs. *Joseph, Nicol Scot, Samuel Clark* and *Lebnitz,* with the other learned men mentioned.—2d. I would read both verses, the text is *Isaiah* lxvi. 23, 24, *And it shall come to pass from one new moon to another, and from one sabbath to another shall all flesh come to worship before me saith the Lord, and they shall go forth and look on the carcasses of the men that have transgressed against me, for their worm shall not die, neither shall their fire be quenched, and they shall be an abhorring to all flesh.* You mention *Isaiah* lxvi. 24, and say, " *Allowing the words of our Lord in Mark* ix, *to be taken from them, this interpreter does not appear to have observed, that just before this passage, it is written of the eight worshippers of*

---

* It was Paul's privilege indeed to be acquainted with this grace, to enjoy the comfort of it, and to be influenced to fruitfulness by it; while it was not the divine good pleasure to manifest himself to the world; but *John* xvii. 21, 22, 23, informs us, *There is a time coming, when the world shall know and believe that Jesus Christ is the sent of God; know and believe the same truth that the disciples know and believed,* verse 8, *Which then, distinguished them from the world, and this is what Jesus had in view in praying for his immediate disciples, and those that should believe through their word.*

of God our saviour, and they shall go forth and look on the carcasses of the men that have transgressed against me." I suppose the eight worshippers to be an error of the press, putting *eight* for *right*; but if so, then the right worshippers are all flesh, *for all flesh shall worship*—but as this was not your design, here is an evident error, that when you appear to endeavour to correct another with the scripture, you do not cite the text as it stands.

3dly. Having read the text, would proceed to look for the meaning of it by comparing it with other scriptures; here we shall agree that all flesh have transgressed; and the text says, *all flesh shall worship, and the carcasses of the transgressors shall be an abhoring to all flesh.* Now the inquiry is, what is meant by the carcasses of the men that have transgressed; if we compare some other scripture prophesies, particularly *Jeremiah* xvi. 18, *And first I will recompence their iniquity and their sin double, because they have defiled my land and filled mine inheritance with the carcasses of their detestable and abominable things.* Ezekiel xliii. 7, 8, 9, *And he said unto me, son of man, the place of my throne and the place of the soles of my feet where I will dwell in the midst of the children of Israel forever, and my holy name shall the house of Israel no more defile; they nor their kings by their whoredoms, nor by the carcasses of their kings in their high places, in their setting their threshold by my threshold, and their post by my post;—they have even defiled my holy name by their abominations, wherefore I consumed them in mine anger; now let them put away their whoredom and the carcasses of their kings far from me, and I will dwell in the midst of them forever.*—What is here called carcasses, is their whoredom, their going aside from the straight and narrow way he had prescribed, and worshipping in ways of their own or others devising, which is spiritual whoredom, and abomination

tion to him, and when these abominations so prevailed, as to be established by the kings, as the form of worship ordered to be observed as the religion of the kingdom, they are called the carcasses of their kings, and as this profane worship was paid in high places, it was called the carcasses of their kings, in their high places, and as it took the place of the worship of the true God, it is called their threshold, by my threshold, and their post, by my post, by which they profane his holy name;—Now as this is very evident, if we look over the history of the kingdoms of Judah and Israel, so a little attention would shew that this is applicable to all flesh who have corrupted their way, all agreeing in going astray; though every one turns to his own way, every one's own way in this view, is the carcase of his abomination, and when ever any are turned from idols, to the living God, their way of going astray from him, becomes to them an abhorrence, because it is an abomination to the Lord, against which our God, who is a consuming fire, a jealous God, has declared, and will eternally manifest his displeasure. When all flesh shall come to worship before the Lord, the carcasses of the men that have transgressed, will be abhorrent to them.

I offer these my thoughts freely, if any one upon comparing these scriptures, shall give a more probable meaning of them, than I have advanced, I hope it will be candidly received, if I was to inquire into the meaning of what God our saviour says, when referring to this passage in the 9th of *Mark*, I should take notice of the occasion of his writing these words, in order to understand them, and if I mistake not, they are addressed to his immediate disciples, who had been disputing which should be greatest; from the 33d, to the end of the 37th verse; then in verse 38, *John* answered him (as not yet cured of this fondness for pre-eminence) saying, *master we saw one casting out*

out devils in thy name, and we forbad him, because he followed not us.—Now the whole from the 39th verse, to the end, appears addressed to the disciples upon the very subject in answer to *John,* who spake in behalf of himself, and his fellow disciples, *master we saw one, &c.* Omitting what might be observed in the preceding verses, I shall take notice of the 43d verse, If thy hand, thy foot, thine eye offend thee, if you find a disposition to despise one of these little ones and to prefer yourselves above them, because your eyes have discovered truth and duty beyond them, or because your feet have carried you further in your master's cause than they are able to go, or because your hands have laboured therein, or have dealt out to the poor and necessitous beyond what they ever were, or are ever like to be able; this pride of heart is aside from the narrow way, it is taking a step into the broad way, it leads to destruction; in the narrow way, CHRIST is all, his wisdom guides, his power supplies, his feet was ever employed in going about doing good; were it not better you had no foot, nor hand, nor eye, to enter into life, halt or maimed, being wholly hopeless, helpless, and destitute in yourself, nothing to hope for but mere mercy as manifest in CHRIST JESUS; than having two feet, hands, and eyes, to abuse these gifts to the purposes of your own pride, and so to fall under the divine displeasure, who scorneth the scorner, resisteth the proud, and knoweth them afar off; for what can strike the mind of any person with more darkness, perplexity, and distress, than to have the apprehension that our GOD who is a consuming fire, a jealous GOD, is displeased with him.

When pride of heart and despising little ones, take place, the favor of the knowledge of JESUS CHRIST, the salt of the covenant of GOD, is lacking; for every one shall be salted with fire;—may not this receive
illustration

illustration from Matthew, iii. 11. *He shall baptize with the Holy Ghost and with fire*—Is it not the fire of love, love to him and to the least of these little ones for his sake; and every sacrifice shall be salted with salt, that you now offer; looking for pre-eminence, one above another has no favor in it; it doth not favor of the knowledge of myself, and therefore it is not accepted; every sacrifice shall be salted with salt—have salt in yourselves, and peace one with another. I am satisfied that these thoughts are agreeable to the scope of the passage; though being but an inquirer, am not able to comprehend the full meaning of them, or to speak of every sentence in them; but this seems evident that those things that Jesus Christ meant for the instruction and warning of his disciples, are now made use of as though they were only intended for the profane and openly vicious among mankind.

In taking notice of the title page, you say, "*Even the title page is not without its errors; it is this, salvation for all men illustrated and vindicated as a scripture doctrine; had the writer intended, and said, salvation for all men revealed and offered in the gospel; this would have passed well enough for a scripture doctrine; but that all men shall actually obtain salvation sooner or later, which is the intent and meaning of this writer, this cannot be fairly illustrated from the sacred writings, nor can it be fairly and honestly vindicated as a scripture doctrine.*" Let us look of this a little: "Salvation for all men revealed a scripture doctrine;" then it is a truth, a revealed truth it could not be, if it were not an original, eternal truth, I think I need say no more on this. "Salvation for all men revealed and offered in the gospel;" that Jesus Christ or his salvation are offered in the gospel, is without any foundation in the scriptures, and conveys an idea very dishonourable to him, and very exalting

to

to human pride; if any thing be offered to me I am at once in some respects upon a level with the offerer, and may receive or not as I please; the gospel reveals JESUS CHRIST and his salvation, and where the evidence of the truth strikes the conscience, the light discovers that however incensed against him, I have been, I must be entirely beholden to him for salvation, and must be subject to his authority, or fall under his displeasure, I cannot quit his dominions.— *Acts* iv. 11, 12, The various passages, where the call and invitation of the gospel are spoken of, such as, *look to me and be ye saved all the ends of the earth, come unto me all ye that labour and are heavy laden, and I will give you rest*, calls the attention of the lost bewildered children of men that are grouping in the dark after salvation and rest, to the object where salvation and rest is to be found; for as *Moses lift up the serpent in the wilderness, so must the son of man be lifted up, that whosoever believeth on him should not perish but have everlasting life;* he is brought to view that whosoever believeth the truth concerning him that has his mind satisfied on divine evidence of the truth, testified of CHRIST and his salvation, should not perish, but have eternal life, the faith of the gospel is the belief of the truth, not the accepting of an offer: But were it that salvation was offered to all, it could not be sincere if it was not for all; *but God sent not his son into the world to condemn the world, but that the world through him might be saved.*

Sir, one thing more I would take notice of, is this, that as the title of your piece is, " *All men will not be saved,*" the design of your piece is to prove the title; and the reason is given in page 25, line 7, from the top—" *On the other hand, it is plain and evident to all sound and considerate minds, that the broaching of it* (viz. the doctrine of universal salvation) *has a very dangerous tendency: and hence it should not be admitted*

admitted for a scripture truth." When at the same time you say, page 24, line 9 from the bottom, *" Nor is there the least reason to believe, that their sufferings will make them the willing people of God, as the sufferings of punishment naturally excites an aversion in the sufferer, to the inflictor of the punishment ; and as the sufferings and torments increase and go forward, the enmity and rage of those that endure them, proceed and encrease against their punisher."* If this be true (as undoubtedly it is) it is easy to see the dreadful tendency of your endeavours, through your whole performance. Indeed, Sir, you have here out-done me, for I want words to express the inconsistency and impiety, appearing in the passages put together, especially when I take into view the last sentence—*" And let all the human race, as we are required, serve Jehovah, our Lord and Judge, with fear and trembling before him, from consideration of his holiness and righteousness, his terrible majesty, and consummate truth and faithfulness ; and let us seasonably repent and give glory to God in Christ Jesus that we may not be vexed in his sore and perpetual displeasure, but that we may be blessed in him and with him compleatly and forever."* Such an affront upon the human race, at least on that part of them that will not be saved, according to your title (such an affront on Jehovah our LORD our GOD, and Judge, GOD our Saviour, is here offered, that repentance is here put in his place, as that which will go beyond the ransom he paid, so that though all men will not be saved thereby, yet if they repent and give glory to GOD in CHRIST, they may) that though they will not be saved, they are called to repent, that they may. Was poor creatures ever more tantalized.

But that I may not indulge myself too far, I will sum up what I have to say in the language of scripture. You seem to me to appear here, as the Jews, who

who being ignorant of God's righteousness, and going about to establish their own, have not submitted to the righteousness of God.

One would think both your extractor and yourself, were better acquainted with the weapons that are carnal, and not mighty thro' God, by your opposing learned and pious men, to learned and pious men, and fitting imaginations, and high things, that exalt themselves against the knowledge of God; and had the extractor been led by the spirit of the truth, he would appear to vindicate, he would have seen himself upon a perfect level with his fellow-sinners, beholden to mere mercy with the vilest, and not, in confidence of his own superiority, set at nought a stranger, by ignorantly endeavouring to slur his doctrine, which he himself, as yet, appears unacquainted with: But he makes himself a preacher—is not made so as we are—he followeth not us.

When John in the name of the rest of the disciples, said to Jesus, *we saw one casting out devils in thy name, and we forbade him, because he followed us not,* he knew they were set apart to their work by Jesus Christ himself, yet he was rebuked, and got the repeated warning against offences that we have taken notice of in the 9th of *Mark*, from the 43d.

How unbecoming then must it be for those who have any ground to question the truth of their being taught of God to know Jesus Christ, and of their being divinely called to preach him, to treat those that preach Jesus Christ in such a manner, because they followed not them.

It would become us whenever we find ourselves disposed to offend any of those little ones that believe in Jesus, or at least for whom he died, to attend soberly to the above-mentioned 9th of *Mark*, and when we come to understand and practice the exhortation in the 50th verse, *have salt in yourselves,* it will lead us to peace one with another. I would

I would also take notice of the extractor's endeavouring to distinguish himself, by bringing in the state of unutterable misery that many of the sons and daughters of Adam will pass through, before they are prepared for, and admitted to, the joys of God's presence in heaven.

If he intends this as the legal penalty they are to suffer for sin, he sets aside the atonement, and puts sufferings in its room, as you appear to put repentance in the place of the great propitiation, in your last paragraph; I think there is an obvious distinction between the punishment *of* sin and the punishment *for* sin, held up in the scriptures.

When they speak of the punishment FOR sin, it is thus:	When they speak of the punishment OF sin, it is thus:
Isaiah liii. 5, He was wounded FOR our transgressions, bruised FOR our iniquities. Verse 8, FOR the transgressions of my people, was he stricken.	*Leviticus* xxvi. 41, 43, If then their uncircumcised hearts be humbled, and they accept the punishment OF their iniquities. And they shall accept the punishment OF their iniquities.
Romans iv. 25, He was delivered FOR our offences.	*Lamentations* iii. 39, Why doth a living man complain, a man for the punishment OF his sins.
Rom. v. 6, Christ died FOR the ungodly.	Chap iv. 6, For the punishment OF the iniquity of the daughter of my people is greater than the punishment OF the sin of Sodom.

The punishment *for* sin, is what the law demands of the transgressor, *for* the satisfaction of law and justice; *the soul that sinneth shall die, every man shall die*

die for his iniquity. Now Jesus Christ being made under the law, was to redeem them that were under the law, he took the fullness of the human nature in its fallen state, and became its universal head in as extensive a sense as the first *Adam, Romans* v. 14, to the end. The Prophet *Isaiah* says, *All we like sheep have gone astray—And the* Lord *laid on him the iniquity of us all—And he bear our sins in his own body to the tree.—When he was lift up he drew all men unto him;* so that they were all considered in him, and as the head of every man, *the sword of justice awoke against the man,* God's *fellow,* and he died for our offences; and by his death finished transgression and made an end of sin, *and brought in everlasting righteousness, and made full reconciliation for iniquity,* which is abundantly witnessed in his resurrection, *for he rose again for our justification;* his resurrection is the evidence and assurance, that law and justice is satisfied, *that the father is well pleased for his righteousness sake.*

We may then adopt that language; he bore our griefs and carried our sorrows; was wounded *for* our transgressions, he was bruised *for* our iniquities, the chastisement of our peace was upon him, and by his stripes we are healed. Is not this the scripture view of punishment *for* sin?

The punishment *of* sin, is that which is inseparably connected with it, and consequent upon it: Darkness, distress, perplexity and misery, is ever attendant upon transgression, and forever follows upon it.

To illustrate my meaning, let us view any person led by his lusts, by the God of this world, to the grossest acts of abomination.

Suppose a man led by the lusts of the flesh to fornication, then to hatred of the person seduced and abused by him; then to neglect and despise the fruit of his body, to take no care for its support, maintenance

ance or education, unless by compulsion of the law, and then to wish it dead: Here we see the punishment of sin inseparably connected with it. *Proverbs* vi. 33, *A wound and dishonor shall he get, and his reproach shall not be wiped away.* There we see the transgressor, not only bearing the contempt and scorn of the world, painful enough to a tender mind, but smarting under those wounds of the spirit which are intolerable in those horrors of mind, from the fearful apprehension of the displeasure of him, who has said, *fornicators shall not inherit the kingdom of God;* and he has reason to fear his being among those that shall rise to shame and everlasting contempt. Here we see something of the punishment *of* sin, but it has nothing of the nature of the punishment *for* sin, it doth not satisfy justice, it doth not make atonement. If this man be relieved from the fear of everlasting punishment, it must be the knowledge of CHRIST, the lamb of GOD, who taketh away the sin of the world, who died for our offences, and rose again for our justification; that must give him a living hope towards GOD; it is not his sufferings, his sense of guilt, his present or dreaded future misery, while he expects that justice will seek satisfaction from him in his own person. But the knowledge of the truth concerning JESUS CHRIST, is his exclusive, all sufficient relief.

The same might be observed of pride, and a haughty contempt of such as the scripture calls little ones; the scripture says, *Prov.* 29, 23, *A man's pride shall bring him low;* so low as that nothing can cheer and raise the spirit to consolation and peace, but the hope that arises from the abasement and humiliation of JESUS CHRIST;—and, indeed in the view we have of our own vileness, or the sins of others, we shall see that sin naturally, as well as by the righteous judgment of GOD, brings us low, and leads to darkness, confusion, perplexity

perplexity and misery; and it would be profitable for us all to reflect on our own ways of transgressing, and judge ourselves, to the humbling of the pride of our own uncircumcised hearts, and except the punishment of our own iniquity, with our months stopped, guilty before God, nothing to encourage or give us hope, but the gospel report concerning Jesus Christ —this would be more decent, becoming and profitable, than to exercise ourselves about the theory of the eternal punishment of some vile men much more wicked than ourselves; alas! where would such be found, if our consciences faithfully laid before us the aggravations of the guilt we are chargeable with; besides if we view the state a man is in before the knowledge of Jesus Christ, under the fearful apprehensions of suffering in his own person, the demerit of his crimes, it is ever accompanied with hatred of God, till his true character which is love, is made manifest, and we love him, because he first loved us; and what atonement can that make for past offences.

I would further take notice, that the extractor appears as one ashamed of the doctrine of the common salvation as revealed in the scriptures, and therefore chose to venture an acknowledgment of it, in company with eminent divines; and so not the authority of scripture testimony held up; but the scriptures as held and explained by eminent men, is by him brought to view, that our faith might stand in the wisdom of men, not in the word of God, and thus has cause of shame, especially that he should extract the one thing that you justly say is quite inexcusable— " and mark you, who is this Savior, it is God, not Christ." But why is this distinction, we know nothing of God, but as he manifests himself in Christ? When *Philip* said to Jesus, *Lord shew us the Father and it sufficeth us: Jesus saith unto him, have I been so long time with you, and yet hast thou not known me, Philip?*

Philip? *He that hath seen me, hath seen the father; and how sayest thou, shew us the Father; believest thou not that I am in the Father and the Father in me; and no man knoweth the Son but the Father, neither knoweth any man the Father but the Son, and he to whomsoever the Son will, revealeth him;* and JESUS CHRIST says, *I have manifested thy name to the men which thou gavest me out of the world, and I have declared unto them thy name, and will declare it, that the love wherewith thou hast loved me, may be in them, and I in them.*

I do not conceive how men can have a satisfactory apprehension that they worship one GOD, that make such distinctions, unless they mean to set aside JESUS CHRIST as the object of worship, if he be not GOD our Saviour; if GOD, not CHRIST is this Saviour; then JESUS CHRIST is not the object of worship; and if this be the real sentiment, I need no longer wonder to hear men pray to GOD, without any mention of the name of JESUS CHRIST, till they are one quarter or one third through their prayer, or in some instances, not till the close of their prayer: it is enough to draw forth the lamentation of Mary from the worshippers of JESUS, or them that call on that name: They have taken away my LORD, and I know not where they have laid him. JESUS CHRIST says, *John* x. 9, *I am the door, by me, if any man enter in he shall be saved, and go in and out, and find pasture. John* xiv. 6, *I am the way, and the truth, and the life, no man cometh to the father, but by me*: But these seem to have access without the door; by some other way.

I know nothing of GOD, but as he reveals himself in CHRIST JESUS. If I view the creator, I must view him in CHRIST, for all things were created by him, and without him was not any thing made, that was made. If I view the preserver, I must view him in CHRIST; for by him all things consist, upholding all things

things by the word of his power. If I view the redeemer, the saviour, I must view him in CHRIST; for as much as ye were not redeemed, but by the precious blood of CHRIST, as of a lamb, without blemish and without spot, GOD was in CHRIST reconciling the world. There is not any one thing in all the scriptures, that is mentioned as an attribute perfection or operation of GOD, but the same is manifest in CHRIST JESUS. If I had capacity and opportunity, this might be illustrated from all the works of JESUS CHRIST, when he was upon earth, and from his doctrines; for instance, is it the peculiar prerogative of GOD to forgive sins, and to heal diseases, as attributed to him in *Psalm* ciii. 3, This we see thus manifested in JESUS CHRIST. *Matthew* ix. 2d, to the 8th. *Mark* ii. from 5th to the 12th. *Luke* v. 18th, to the 25th, He said, *thy sins are forgiven thee*: And to prove he had power on earth to forgive sins, he saith to the sick of the palsy: *Arise, take up thy couch, and go into thy house, and he arose immediately, &c.* For my part I cannot conceive of any relation that GOD stands in to us, as our GOD, but in CHRIST; if JESUS CHRIST bids his disciples when they pray, say, *Our Father*, it is as considered in him, by whom we have the adoption of children; JESUS, after his resurrection, bid Mary Magdalen, in *John* xx. 17, *Go to my brethren, and say unto them, I ascend to my Father and your Father, and to my God and your God*: And as the elder brother, not ashamed to call them brethren, he says, in verse 21, *Peace unto you, as* Father *hath sent me, so send I you.* To add no more, the true character of GOD, or the character of the true GOD, is, Isaiah xlv. 21, *I the* Lord? *and no God else beside me; a just* God *and a saviour. : none beside me.* This is the character of JESUS CHRIST. Zechariah ix. 9, *He is just and having salvation,* Isaiah lxiii. 1, *I that speak in righteousness, mighty to save:* And no where else is

the

the juſt God and ſaviour made manifeſt ; how then could one, profeſſedly pleading for the ſalvation of all men, extract ſuch a paſſage, as if he would plead for ſalvation, and ſet aſide the ſaviour ? But I am perſuaded, that every one, that have their minds led into the ſpirit of the doctrine of univerſal ſalvation, will rejoice in that explanation of *Iſaiah* vii. 14, which we have in *Matthew* i. 23, *His name ſhall be called Emanuel, which being interpreted, is* God *with us.*

I would add the quotation, from the 1ſt of *Corinth.* xv. from the 24th, to 25th verſe, has rather excited my attention, than ſatisfied my mind, from all that hath been ſaid in both pieces, by the various authors. Therefore as an inquirer, I would attend to the chapter, if perhaps, it may pleaſe him, from whom comes wiſdom and underſtanding, to enlighten my mind to underſtand a paſſage, which through my life has been among the things, hard to be underſtood ; the firſt part from the beginning, to the 11th verſe, is clear and plain, and holds forth the death and reſurrection of Jesus Christ as the goſpel of ſalvation, that all the apoſtles united in, that the firſt diſciples believed, and by which they were ſaved with the evidences of it : From the 12th, to the end of the 19th verſe, he inquires, *if Chriſt be riſen from the dead, how ſay ſome, there is no reſurrection,* and argues in a manner, that ſhews the union of Jesus Christ with the human nature, as members of his body ;—*If the dead riſe not, then is Chriſt not raiſed*—if the body riſe not, then is not the head raiſed—*and if Chriſt is not raiſed, then is our preaching, and your faith vain*—and we falſe witneſſes, and you in your ſins. From verſe 20th, he ſays, *But now is Chriſt riſen from the dead, and become the firſt fruits of them that ſlept* : The firſt fruits is the joy, the glory, the foretaſte, the earneſt of the harveſt and ſanctified the whole. *Since by man, death, by man, the reſurrection from the dead;*

—For

—For as in Adam all die, even so *in Christ, shall all be made alive*. How came death by Adam? Because he was head and representative of his offspring, and they considered in him, and so universally in him all die: *Even so in* Christ, *shall all be* made alive, because he is head, as universally as Adam; and all are made alive as extensively, else, it could not be *even so*. But every man in his own order, *Christ the first fruits;* the head, the first born among the many brethren, that in all things he might have the pre-eminence, the first begotten from the dead; the prince of the kings of the earth, unto him that loved us, &c. After that, they that are Christ's at his coming.

If we inquire who are they? it may be answered, there are many among those that are Christ's, who are called the first fruits unto God and the lamb, as we read in the Revelations, a kind of first fruits of his creatures, as *James* expresses it, such as have been set apart by Jesus Christ according to the good pleasure of his will, to bear witness to his name, truth and ways before the world, to whom it hath been given in behalf of Christ, not only to believe on him, but also to suffer for his sake; and the Apostle says, if we suffer we shall also reign with him. And we read of those that had not worshipped the beast, nor his image, nor received his mark in their forehead, nor in their hands, and they lived and reigned with Christ a thousand years. These are those spoken of in *Rev.* xiv. Beginning the hundred forty and four thousand, that *John* beheld standing with the lamb on the mount Zion, who are expressly called the redeemed *from among men*, the first fruits unto God and the lamb. If the apostle is supposed to speak of them as they that are Christ's at his coming, yet not to the exclusion of those that are Christ's, according to other scripture texts, for certainly he knows how to fulfil his promises to his faithful witnesses, without excluding

cluding the rest of the purchased possession, for we find in the 6th verse of the xivth of *Revelations*, after the mention and description of the first fruits, the hundred forty and four thousand: Another angel fly through the midst of Heaven, having the everlasting Gospel to preach unto them that dwell on the earth, even to every nation, and kindred and tongue and people, agreeable to what we read in the seventh chapter, where the hundred forty and four thousand that were sealed, are spoken of: We read in the 9th verse, after this I beheld, and lo a great multitude, which no man could number, of all nations and kindred, and people, and tongues, stood before the throne, and before the lamb, cloathed with white robes and psalms in their hands, and cried with a loud voice, saying, salvation, to our GOD, &c.

So then if we inquire who are CHRIST's in a more extensive sense, it may be answered, those the father gave him: The *Jews*, the *Gentiles*, the ends of the earth, *Isaiah* xlix. 5, 6, the heathen his inheritance, the utmost parts of the earth his possession. Those he came to save, *John* iii. 17, Those for whom he tasted death, *Heb.* ii. 9, Those for whom he gave himself a ransom, 1st of *Tim.* ii. 6, Those for whom he is the propitiation, *John* ii. 2.

They are CHRIST's. Yes, they are, even when deluded by satan, and led away by their own lusts, to prodigality and disobedience: The prodigal was a son when dead and lost; he will not leave them there, if they are CHRIST's, they will rise in their order after him.

Then the end: What end? The end divine wisdom had in view, through the whole of satan's reign as the god of this world: That JESUS CHRIST should destroy the works of the devil, and put down all rule, all authority and power; all the rule, authority and power in the kingdoms of this world, and in the hearts of men that have been in opposition to him, under the

the god of this world, the spirit that now worketh in the children of disobedience: For he must reign till all his enemies be made his foot-stool.—*The last enemy shall be destroyed—Death.* Death is the last enemy, and it shall be destroyed; it is a conquered enemy —*For he hath put all things under his feet.* The Apostle in *Hebrews* ii. 8, says, *Thou hast put all things in subjection under his feet. For in that he put all in subjection under him, he left nothing not put under him. But now we see not yet all things put under him. But we see Jesus, who was made a little lower than the angels, for the sufferings of death, crowned with glory and honour, that he, by the grace of God, should taste death for every man.*

And when all things shall be subdued unto him; when this shall take place, then shall the son also himself, be subject to him that put all things under him, that GOD may be all in all. By the Son, I understand, the one new man; that JESUS CHRIST makes in himself of all nations, kindreds, people and tongues; that in Adam, their first head had been in a state of rebellion, and were never as one in subjection before; never unitedly called GOD, Father: It seems to be that state, that every creature groans and travels in pain together for; and not only they, but those that have the first fruits of the spirit, groan within themselves, waiting for the adoption; *viz.* the redemption of our body. *Romans* viii. 23, When the whole body of which CHRIST is the head, are subject to him, are redeemed from sin and satan; it is called the adoption. When Adam, who was the son of GOD; called the son of GOD in his relative capacity, as head of the human nature, turned prodigal with all the disobedience, shame, sorrow, guilt and misery attendant thereupon, is recovered by the second Adam to favour, to subjection, and to the adoption; the son himself is subject to him that put all things under him. It cannot

not mean JESUS CHRIST, confidered in himfelf; he ever did the things that pleafed the Father, never was in a ftate of rebellion and difobedience; befides, JESUS CHRIST fays, *John* x. 30, *I and the Father are one;* and when he fays, *all things are put under him,* it is manifeft that he is excepted, *which did put all things under him:* But the Son in the above fenfe, was never in fubjection before.

That God may be all in all: While the rebellious fon plays the prodigal, captivated by Satan, his will, his various lufts, whether it be in a way of profanenefs, uncleannefs, religious pride, or covetoufnefs, he is purfuing not the will of GOD in CHRIST JESUS, concerning him, but appears to be purfuing his lufts as if they were his all; but when brought home to fubjection, GOD is all in all: Not GOD as diftinct from CHRIST, but GOD in CHRIST, EMANUEL, GOD with us, the juft GOD and the Saviour, there is none elfe:—This view, is confiftent with JESUS, the fame yefterday, to day, and forever: And with what the Apoftle in *Heb.* i. 10, 11, 12, quotes from *Pfalm* cii. 25, 26, 27, and applies to JESUS CHRIST; *And thou Lord in the beginning, laid the foundation of the earth: and the heavens are the work of thy hands. They fhall perifh; but thou remaineft; and they fhall wax old, as a garment; and as a vefture, fhalt thou fold them up; and they fhall be changed. But thou art the fame, and thy years fhall not fail.*—And with *Ifaiah,* ix. 6, and *Luke* i. 33, *And, he fhall reign over the houfe of Ifrael for ever, And of his kingdom there fhall be no end.* To which the worfhippers of the one, only living, and true GOD, manifeft in CHRIST JESUS; will unitedly add their *Amen,* and here find a fource of eternal fecurity and joy.

But to draw to a clofe—I would take notice of your laft page; but indeed it puts me in mind of the repeated direction in the 8th of Ezekiel. *Turn thee yet*

yet again; thou shalt see greater abominations. You say, "*If it be inquired, why God should continue any to be the instances of his extreme and perpetual vengeance.*" In reply you say, "*That the just Judge of all the earth, has an undoubted right to support the dignity of his government.*" And is not the dignity of his government effectually supported by the obedience and sacrifice of JESUS CHRIST, who died for the ungodly. You add, "*And not suffer any contempt to be cast upon him, by the bold transgressors against his holy will and laws:*—How is that to be prevented according to you? It is by making them examples of his extreme displeasure, and perpetual vengeance; that is, according to your own words, page 24, line 9th from the bottom, "*As the suffering of punishment naturally excites an aversion in the sufferer, to the inflictor of the punishment; and as the sufferings and torments increase, and go forward, the enmity and rage of those that undergo them, proceed and increase against their punisher.*" To put them in a state, where they will eternally be increasing their enmity and rage against GOD!—Indeed, Sir, I want words to express the horridness of your evil communications. What! A great part of the dominions of the King, the LORD of hosts, to be in eternal rebellion, in increasing enmity and rage against him, as the only way to prevent contempt to be cast upon him, by bold transgressors of his laws. I believe it is the divine design, not to suffer any contempt to be cast upon him by the bold transgressors against his holy will and laws; but how? I shall endeavour from the prophet *Isaiah*, to shew unto you a more excellent way; he lets us know, *that every knee shall bow to him.*

Thus I believe the contempt of bold transgressors will cease, being brought to bow to him. See an example of a bold transgressor being thus brought to bow in Saul, of Tarsus, who went to bind all that call

on

on that Name; but behold he prayeth—he calleth on the Name he persecuted before: There can be no acceptable prayer but in that worthy name.

But I suppose it will be objected, that this bowing will be the bowing of an overcome victim of justice, in order to his confinement, trial and execution. In answer to this, I would beg your patience, till I again repeat the passage in the 45th of *Isaiah*, from the latter part of the 21st verse, just as it stands, without the italick word, supplied by the translators, and make some observations upon them. *I the Lord, and no God else beside me, the just God and the saviour, none beside me: Look unto me, and be ye saved, all the ends of the earth; for I God, and none else, I have sworn by myself—the word is gone out of my mouth in righteousness, and shall not return that every knee shall bow,* and every tongue shall swear, surely shall say, in the Lord, have I righteousness and strength—unto him shall come,*

---

* It is said, that the true reading of the Apostles quotation of this text in Philippians ii. 10, is, that *in* the name of Jesus, not *at* the name, (as it is said) that is the true reading, and that it is the same with Colossians iii. 17. *Do all* in *the name of the Lord Jesus.* If you please, you may look in your Greek Testament, and see if it is not so. Now when we consider this, it obviates the objection that has been raised, after this manner: Yes, every knee shall bow at the name of Jesus; One day they shall all be brought to own him Lord; to their eternal confusion, they shall bow at his name, as a poor criminal at the name of the Judge, that is just going to pronounce a sentence of death, from which there is no appeal, nor escape.

But the text says, *That in the name of Jesus, every knee shall bow, and every tongue confess that Jesus Christ is Lord, to the glory of God the Father.* As when a poor woman, who hath no riches, no worthiness, nothing by which she can attain any thing in her own name, is married to a Prince, she is intitled to his name, his person, his riches, his honour, and now appearing in his name, she is regarded as him. So when in the name of Jesus, every knee shall bow, it is in this view, exactly similiar to the Prophet Isaiah, to which the Apostle here alludes; the very matter of what every tongue shall swear, is, *Surely shall say, in the Lord have I righteousness and strength, to him shall come*; Surely shall say, the mind shall be as satisfied of this truth, as ever any person was of any thing to which he was called to swear; these things being so, we have the joint evidence of both Testaments to this truth, confirmed by the blood of the New Testament, by the death of the testator, and witness in his resurrection: So however dark, ignorant, miserable, we are in ourselves; when we come to the knowledge of Jesus Christ, to bow in his name, we may sing;

Thou

come, and all that are incensed against him, shall be ashamed: In the Lord shall all the seed of Israel be justified, and shall glory.

I the Lord, and no God beside me; the just God, and the saviour, none beside me. The character of the true GOD, is the just GOD and the saviour, there is none else; no GOD beside; then certainly, the just GOD, that is not the saviour, is not the only, living and true GOD; but is such a one as is spoken of in verse 20, *A graven image, a God that cannot save:*—No matter whether graven on wood, or in the imagination of those that pray unto a GOD that cannot save; and as he is the same yesterday, to day and forever; with whom there is no variableness, neither shadow of turning; consequently, whenever any come to the knowledge of him; they know the just GOD and the saviour, there is none else, no GOD beside; and this is his true character, whether we know it or not:—So then, when the earth shall be filled with the knowledge of GOD, as we are assured it shall, it will be with knowledge of the just GOD and the saviour.

Look unto me, and be ye saved, all the ends of the earth.—Here is a call or command, to all the ends of the earth, it is his pleasure that it should be so; and what the LORD pleaseth, that he doth: *For I, God, and none else, I have sworn by myself, the word is gone out of my mouth in righteousness*—*That unto me, every knee shall bow, and every tongue shall swear.*—Then follows

> Thou art our wisdom, Thou our guide,
>   Thou art our righteousness;
> We're blind and guilty, thee besides,
>   Thou art our holiness.
>
> From slavery and bonds to sin,
>   Thou us, alone can'st free;
> From captive state, where we have been,
>   Redemption we shall see.

For he is made to us, of God, wisdom, righteousness, sanctification and redemption: He hath a name above every name, *That in the name of Jesus, every knee shall bow, every tongue surely shall say; In the Lord have I righteousness and strength; to him shall come.* So be it, the Lord hasten it, in his time.

follows the matter of the oath, that every tongue shall swear, *Surely shall say, in the Lord have I righteousness and strength*: This being considered, will invalidate the objection; for if every tongue shall surely say, in the LORD have I righteousness and strength, they shall surely be saved by him, they shall have no lack of righteousness nor strength.—*Unto him shall come*—And surely the comers, are the true worshippers, they are so described, under the Old Testament dispensation, as *Hebrews* x. 1, Could never make the comers hereunto perfect; that is the worshippers under that dispensation, and under the New-Testament dispensation. In 1st of *Peter*, ii. 4, the worshippers are described by coming to JESUS CHRIST, who has promised rest to the weary and heavy laden, on their coming to him, *Matthew* xi. 28, Coming is also synonymous to believing: *He that cometh unto me, shall never hunger, and he that believeth on me, shall never thirst.* So then, in this view, when it is said, *unto him shall come*, it intends they shall be worshippers of him, believing on his name.

And all that are incensed against him, shall be ashamed—Who have been incensed against him? Surely all, *Isaiah* liii. 3, *He was not despised and rejected of men; He was despised, and we esteemed him not*—Surely, you and I have been incensed against him, and it is high time for us to be ashamed of the carcasses of our whoredoms and detestable things—it is time for us, with our sisters, *Sodom, Samariah* and *Jerusalem,* to be ashamed and confounded, and never open our mouths any more, because of our shame; when he hath revealed himself in CHRIST, pacified towards us for all that we have done.

In the Lord shall all the seed of Israel be justified, and shall glory. By Israel I understand JESUS CHRIST. Who are his seed? Those that are blessed in him; that is all the nations of the earth. *Gen.* xxii. 18,—

Pfalm xxii. 27, *All the ends of the world shall remember and turn unto the Lord; and all the kindreds of the nations shall worship before thee; for the kingdom is the Lord's; and he the governor among the nations: A seed shall serve him; it shall be accounted to the Lord for a generation: they shall come and declare his righteousness unto a people that shall be born, that he hath done.* The chosen seed that in every age are brought to the knowledge of him, are a specimen, an earnest, the first fruits unto GOD and the lamb, and are chosen for this end, as we may see in the first of *Ephesians,* from the beginning to the 10th verse: See verse 5th, *Having predestinated us unto the adoption of children by Jesus Christ, to himself, according to the good pleasure of his will, to the praise of the glory of his grace.* Verse 9th, *Having made known unto us the mystery of his will according to his good pleasure, which he hath purposed in himself;* For this end, verse 10th, *That in the dispensation of the fullness of times, he might gather together in one, all things in Christ, both which are in Heaven, and which are on earth in him.*

This being the case, way is made to call upon "all the human race, as we are required, to serve Jehovah our LORD, our GOD and judge, with fear, and rejoice with trembling, and seasonably repent and give glory to GOD in CHRIST JESUS;" not as you express it, "that we may not be vexed with his sore and perpetual displeasure," but because he has blotted out, as a thick cloud, our transgressions, and as a cloud, our sins, we are called to return, for I have redeemed thee. *Isaiah* xliv. 22.

But I would further take notice of another particular you mention.

You say, that the same epithet is used for the punishment of the wicked, as for the life of the righteous, and why must a two-fold meaning be given to it?" Page 22, line 14 from the top.   The

The reason I would offer, is in the words of the Apostle, *Sin reigns to death, but grace reigns through righteousness to eternal life by Jesus Christ,* who say, *because I live, ye shall live also:* But death, which is the wages of sin, and the extent of its reign is to be destroyed and swallowed up in victory, when the Lord God, with his own benign hand shall wipe tears from all faces.

Now, Sir, keeping in view, *James* v, 19, 20, *If any of you do err from the truth, and one convert him, let him know that he that converteth a sinner from the error of his ways, shall save a soul from death, and hide a multitude of sins.* As the only way to this end, I have endeavoured faithfully to discover some of your errors, from the word of GOD; and as I have no design to offend you, I am not conscious of any thing to that end; I rest in the truth of that word, *he that rebuketh a man, afterward shall find more favour than he that flattereth with his tongue.* So devoting my labour to the honor and glory of GOD, our Saviour, to whom be glory and majesty, dominion and power, both now and ever.—AMEN.

I subscribe myself,
your Servant, for JESUS sake,
SHIPPIE TOWNSEND.

Boston, January 1, 1783.

INFERENCES.

UPON reflecting on the truth contained in the foregoing letter, there arises to view these reflections, as resulting therefrom, viz. 1st, The obligations to love: 2dly, Submission; 3dly, Gratitude and obedience; and 4thly, Thanksgiving.

1st. Love to him who hath thus loved us. *We love him because he first loved us: God is love, and he that dwelleth*

dwelleth in love, dwelleth in God, and God in him; and this commandment have we from him, that he that loveth God, love his brother also; if God so loved us, we ought to love one another. How? Jesus Christ told his disciples, *John* xiii. 34, *that ye love one another as I have loved you*: How doth he manifest and we perceive his love to us? *John* iii. 16. *Hereby perceive we the love of God, because he laid down his life for us, and we ought to lay down lives for the brethren; but whoso hath this world's goods, and seeth his brother have need, and shutteth up his bowels from him, how dwelleth the love of God in him?* — When we see him, *who was rich, for our sakes become poor, that we through his poverty, might be rich*, it ought to excite us to lay aside prospects and endeavours to lay up treasure on earth, and to engage us to lay down these gay prospects of life, for the brethren to minister with liberality to them; to the necessities of the poor that are always left with us, to prove the sincerity of our love: *The poor ye have always with you; and whensoever ye will, ye may do them good;* and if our means are small, we ought to ply the greater diligence in our callings. For this very end, the gospel motives are, 1st of *Thessalonians*, iv. 11, 12, *That ye study to be quiet, and to do your own business, and work with your own hands; that ye may walk honestly towards them that are without, and that ye may have lack of no man.* — 2d epistle, 3d ch. p. 11, 12, *For we hear there are some which walk disorderly, working not at all; now such we command and exhort by our Lord Jesus Christ, that with quietness they work, and eat their own bread.* — *Ephesians* iv. 28, *But rather let him labour, working with his hands, the thing which is good, that he may have to give him that needeth.* These are gospel motives.

Next the gospel examples. We have already hinted at the example of Jesus Christ, who went about

about doing good, healing the sick, relieving the afflicted, feeding the hungry; came not to be ministered unto, but to minister, and give his life a ransom for many. We have the example of Paul, *Acts* xx. 34, *Yea, yourselves know that these hands have ministered to my necessities, and to them that are with me.* Then the example of Paul and his companions, 1st of *Thessalonians,* ii. 9, *For ye remember, brethren, our labour and travel; for labouring night and day, because we would not be chargeable to any of you, we preached unto you the gospel of God.* And his exhortation to the Ephesian elders, *Acts* xx. 35, *I have shewed you all things, how that so labouring you ought to support the weak, and to remember the words of the Lord Jesus, how he said it is more blessed to give than to receive.*

For shame let none under such obligations as divine love lays, with such examples, motives, precepts and exhortations, excuse themselves for want of ability, while they live in idleness; and let every one thus obligated, directed and exhorted, remember we are to love one another, saith Jesus, *as I have loved you.* His love sought us as well as saved us: Our duty then is to seek out the objects of distress, agreeable to the character of the virtuous woman, the spouse of Christ, *Prov.* xxxi. 20, *She spreadeth out her hand to the poor,: Yea, she reacheth forth her hands to the needy.*

Again: Jesus Christ loved us when enemies— *Rom.* v. 10. Then 'tis our duty to love our enemies, and to do good to them that hate us, and pray for them that despitefully use us. *Prov.* xxiv. 21, *If thine enemy be hungry, give him bread to eat; and if he be thirsty, give him water to drink.* Again: Jesus Christ having loved his own, *which were in the world,* needing the constant exercise of his love, in his care of and kindness to them, *he loved them to the end.* And would we love one another according to his rule,

rule, *as I have loved you*, we must attend to the exhortation—*Gal.* vi. 9. 2d of *Theff.* iii. 13, *But ye, brethren, be not weary in well doing.*

2dly. Our obligations of submission to the will of God our Saviour in what he alots to us in his providence. When we consider God is love, and has a design of love in all his dispensations towards us; if in his providence, vanity is wrote on our outward estate we can't be brought so low, as he who was rich and became poor in love to us for our sakes; and it is ordered by his wisdom, who knows what is most needful to subdue our covetousness and fondness for a hope in this life, and our pride of living independent, &c.

If we imagine our honour is struck at, in some things, that we say, flesh and blood cannot bear, we cannot be so abased, as he, who being in the form of God, and thought it not robbery to be equal with God, but made himself of no reputation, was despised and rejected, derided, blindfolded, buffetted, spit upon, and suffered ignominy, till he could say, as Psalm 69, 20, *Reproach hath broken my heart*—yet he failed not, nor was discouraged, but went through his undertaking till he could say, *it is finished*; and hath in his wisdom and love, ordered this very circumstance to subdue our pride, and teach us our honor lies in denying ourselves and following him, in conformity to his example of meekness, who when he was reviled, reviled not again. And to his precepts, and to the precepts of his Apostles: *But I say unto you that ye resist not evil: but if any man smite thee on the one cheek turn to him the other also: Recompence to no man evil for evil; be not overcome of evil, but overcome evil with good.*

If he is pleased to bereave us of relations, even those that had the chief place in our affections, it is ordered in wisdom and love by him, who gave his own

own life a ranfom for us, and knows what we need to cure us of idolizing them, and to fhew us that he alone is our chief good—(a perfon who had repeatedly been bereaved, upon inquiring what have I done, that I muft be fo afflicted, had his mouth ftopped by this reply—what have you not done?) for every Babel tower we build upon our children, *to make us a name;* every fpreading gourd, that our imaginations bring up in a night, of which we are exceeding glad—our towering imaginations of future greatnefs, and worldly happinefs in our relations, are all known to him, and he fees when it is neceffary to take them from us; who corrects us for our profit, that we might be partakers of his holinefs. If our troubles were greater than thefe, and we have living afflictions, and of long continuance in our relations, there is a hiftory in *Mark* 5th, from 1ft to the 19th, defigned for the confolation of fuch relations. *Go home to thy friends, and tell them how great things* JESUS *hath done for thee, and had compaffion on thee.* He is the fame, and has the fame defigns in view in his difpenfations.

The ficknefs of Lazarus was for the glory of GOD, that the fon of GOD might be glorified thereby—This man was born blind, that the works of GOD fhould be made manifeft in him; yea, a tribute of glory is raifing to him who caft out feven Devils from Mary Magdalen, and fet the adulterefs free, with direction to go and fin no more. If I could paint out greater affliction than any I have mentioned, it muft be the diftreffed cafe of poor prodigal children, from their father's houfes, ladened with guilt, oppreffed with fhame, afflicted with a ftubborn loathnefs to return, pinched with hunger, going with reluctant fteps towards the place where the fwine are fed, to look for relief from thence—Even this painting hath a bright fide, when we confider that in all the diftrefs into which their

wilful

wilful, shameful folly hath plunged them; there is a design of love in over-ruling all this misery, as a means to bring them to themselves and return them to their father's house: What, though they may not yet have come to this length, and are resolvedly guarding against this depth of distress and poverty, that hath been described;—though they choose to continue in the way leading thereunto; there is this consolation, that every knee shall bow, *and the loftiness of man shall be bowed down, and the haughtiness of man shall be made low, and the* LORD *alone shall be exalted, and the idols he shall utterly abolish.*

I would further say, we are the property of our Creator, Preserver and Redeemer, and obliged to glorify him in our spirits, and bodies, which are his; then surely, we are not our own, nor at our own disposal, and it is our indispensible duty to keep the place he allots, and do what he bids us, till he calls us away. To suppose our lives at our own disposal, is a strong delusion to believe a lye; and as this delusion has obtained in the minds of those that have professed a high sense of honour and honesty in their dealings, among men, I would endeavour to shew, 1st. that it is the most contemptible sentiment that can be embraced—2d. it is the most knavish and dishonest, beyond high-way robbery—3dly. it is the most ungrateful:

1st. The most contemptible, not only as it tends to brand the name and memory of a man from age to age, among men, but first, as it is the evidence of murmuring and discontent with the allotments of a wise and kind providence, it is a delusion that has its rise from enmity to GOD.—2dly. As it tends to a foolish, fruitless atttempt to run away from our rightful owner; I say, fruitless because it is impossible, for *If I ascend unto heaven, thou art there: If I make my bed in hell, behold thou art there: If I say, the darkness*

darkness shall cover me, even the night shall be light about me: yea, the darkness hideth not from thee, but the night shineth as the day; the darkness and the light both alike to thee—And what is more foolish, and contemptible than a runaway, who finally runs right into the hands of his master.

2dly. It is the most knavish, as it tends to an attempt to rob GOD at once of all his property that is in our power.

3dly. It is the most ungrateful, as it is directly contrary to all that love, grace and mercy that is made manifest in the gospel, and to our duty consequent thereupon: *For the grace of* GOD, *which bringeth salvation unto all men, hath appeared; teaching us, that denying ungodliness and wordly lusts, we should live soberly, righteously and godly in this present world—looking for that blessed hope, even the glorious appearing of the Great* GOD, *even our Saviour* JESUS CHRIST, *who gave himself for us, that he might redeem us from all iniquity, and purify unto himself, a peculiar people, zealous of good works.*

3dly. A sense of obligation to gratitude and obedience, results from the belief of this truth; whoever knows it, knows they are not their own, but bought with a price, and under undisputable, indispensable, eternal obligations, to glorify GOD in their spirit and bodies which are his. Then surely we ought always to keep our eye on his will, as our rule in all our actions, and look on our interest, our time, and all our talents as his, and at his service, and be frequently inquiring of ourselves, whether what we speak and do, is agreeable to the will of GOD in CHRIST JESUS, concerning us, agreeable to the exhortation, *Colossians*, iii. 17, *Whatsoever ye do in word or deed, do all in the name of the Lord Jesus.* And when we act contrary thereto, we are guilty of base ingratitude.

What is worse than to call a man ungrateful? Yet, black as it is, we are guilty of it every time we hearken to the temptations of Satan, and walk after our own lusts. What can be conceived of, so ungrateful, as when the grace of GOD, that bringeth salvation to all men, hath appeared, instead of hearkening to what it teaches, men curse, and damn one another, bite and devour one another?

When he feeds and clothes us, the tendency of our hearts is, *to make empty the soul of the hungry, and cause the drink of the thirsty to fail, devising wicked devices, with lying words, even when the needy speaketh right.* Isaiah, xxxii. 6, 7. O our ingratitude! *The ox knoweth his owner, and the ass his master's crib; but my people doth not know, Israel doth not consider.* Isaiah, i. 3. But is there hope for us? Yes; 1st of John, iii. 5. *And ye know that he was manifest to take away our sins.* 1st of John, iii. 8. *For this purpose the son of God was manifested, that he might destroy the works of the Devil.* Well may we cry out with the prophet *Micah*, vii. 18, 19. *Who is a God like unto thee, that pardoneth iniquity, and passeth by the transgression of the remnant of his heritage? he retaineth not his anger forever, because he delighteth in mercy: He will turn again, he will have compassion upon us; he will subdue our iniquities; and thou wilt cast all their sins into the depths of the sea.* Yea, saith GOD, by the prophet *Isaiah*, chap. xliv. 22, *I have blotted out as a thick cloud, thy transgressions, and as a cloud thy sins,* and calls upon us to *return, for I have redeemed thee.*

Surely then we are called, 4thly, to thanksgiving. Isaiah, xliv. 23. *Sing, O ye heavens, for the Lord hath done it: Shout ye lower parts of the earth: Break forth into singing ye mountains, O forest, and every tree therein: For the Lord hath redeemed Jacob, and glorified himself in Israel.*

This

This is a subject that would lead our minds from eternity, to eternity, back to the source and fountain of mercy, which the Apostle John speaks of, when he says, *God is love;* and forward to the fruit of the purchase of JESUS CHRIST, the reward of his righteousness, to *the hope laid up in heaven,* to what *eye hath not seen, nor ear hath heard, nor hath entered into the heart of man to conceive:* For which all the dispensations of providence are over-ruled in the present life; which, if rightly understood, would lead the mind to an understanding of that exhortation to the disciples, 1st of *Thessalonians,* v. 19, *In every thing give thanks, for this is the will of God in Christ Jesus, concerning you.* But as this opens a large field, and I have already been more lengthy than I intended, I shall close with that short, comprehensive exhortation, we have in Psalm, cxvii, *O praise the Lord all ye nations; Praise him all ye people, for his merciful kindness is great towards us, and the truth of the Lord for ever: Praise ye the Lord.*

SECTION

SECTION VI.

To the SINGING CHOIR, *by whom I have been several times entertained as an hearer.*

BELOVED YOUNG MEN,

WHEN we take a view of what we are in ourselves, in our fallen nature, and of the darkness, distress and misery we are exposed to from the dread apprehension of the execution of the curse of the law upon us as breakers of it, that we can have no gleam of hope from ourselves; and are enabled to see our deliverance in CHRIST JESUS, who took our nature into union with himself, as our head, our second Adam; and being made a curse for us, hath delivered us from the curse of the law, hath sought and saved our lost nature, and sent the glad tidings to every creature. So that though we have not any ground of hope in or from ourselves, the scriptures set before us the LORD JESUS CHRIST, who is our hope, as absolutely all-sufficient for us in our character as lost, destitute, ungodly sinners; for when we were without strength, CHRIST died for the ungodly. When this is understood as the only, and at the same time as the all-sufficient hope, how must our minds filled with gratitude burst forth into songs of praise! How calculated is it to ravish our hearts, to hear the gracious calls to all the earth, and every part of it, with such as go to sea, and all that are therein, to celebrate his praise. What a divine claim is hereby laid upon every one of us, to love him who first loved us, and to love one another as he hath given commandment. That a sense of these things may abide on our minds whenever we join to sing the praises of GOD, and that it may excite us steadily to aim at a conversation becoming the gospel, is the hearty wish of your very obliged friend, who presents you the following view of a most august Singing-Choir.

Boston, May 10, 1793.   A VIEW

A UNIVERSAL CALL to THANKSGIVING.

A universal Call to THANKSGIVING *for the glad tidings of the* GOSPEL *thus evidenced and promulgated in a* VIEW *of a most* MAGNIFICENT SINGING-CHOIR, *presented to the* SINGING SOCIETIES *of every denomination, and to all lovers of* MUSIC.

Psalm xlvii. 7, *Sing ye praises with understanding.*
Solomon Song, ii. 12, *The time of singing is come.*
Psalm cxlviii. 11, 12, 13, *Kings of the earth and all people, princes and all judges of the earth, both young men and maidens, old men and children—let them praise the name of the* LORD.

HAVING been sundry times admitted to a Singing-Choir as a hearer, my thoughts extend beyond the bounds of that small society, to view a more extensive one. This turned my thoughts to the Psalms, to find the chief musician; and finding above forty of them dedicated to the chief musician, I found in a translation printed in 1613, they were inscribed to him that excelleth.

A learned writer endeavours to show from the Hebrew words, that these Psalms are dedicated to JESUS CHRIST. It is he that excelleth, or is most excellent. *O Lord, our Lord, how excellent is thy name in all the earth!* In him I find the head, the director and preceptor of the Choir of musick I was looking after.

I would next endeavour to find of whom it is composed, and here it may be said none are to join therein but such as he calls; and all that he calls are made welcome, and cannot be excluded. Who then doth he call?

Answer.

Answer. All the earth, Psalm, lxvi. 1, 4, *Make a joyful noise unto the Lord, all the earth, all the earth shall worship thee, and sing unto thee, they shall sing unto thy name.* Psalm xcviii. 4. *Make a joyful noise unto the Lord, all the earth; make a loud noise, and rejoice and sing praise.* Psalm c. 1, *Make a joyful noise unto the Lord all ye lands. Come before his presence with singing.*

But not the earth alone, he calls Heaven and earth, saying, Psalm lxix. 34, *Let the Heavens and earth praise him.* Isaiah, xliv. 23, *Sing, O heavens, for the Lord hath done it. Shout ye lower parts of the earth, break forth into singing ye mountains;* O forest, and every tree therein.* So that all the earth is not only called, but left any from their local situation, or particular circumstances, should imagine themselves not included, it is said, Isaiah xlii. 10, 11, 12, *Sing unto the Lord a new song, his praise to the end of the earth. Ye that go down to the sea, and all that is therein, the isles, and the inhabitants thereof. Let the wilderness and the cities thereof, the villages that Kedar doth inhabit. Let the inhabitants of the rock sing, let them shout from the top of the mountains, let them give glory to God, and declare his praise in the islands.*

When we view the various expressions here used, can we find one exception? And if all without exception are thus called upon to praise GOD for the redemption by JESUS CHRIST, included in the new song all are included in that redemption that JESUS hath obtained as *the head of every man*, who *when he was lift up drew all men unto him; and tasted death for*

---

* *O forest, and every tree therein.* The fruit trees are not mentioned; the forest trees are unfruitful. If the design of the Holy Spirit is to call on every destitute creature that hath no ground of encouragement in himself, to sing the praises of him who hath said, *Hosea,* xiv. 8, From me is thy fruit found. The grace appears how great. Which shews our obligations to shew forth his praise by our speech, our songs, and our whole conduct.

for every man. Dying even *for the ungodly, and rising again for our justification.*

For we cannot suppose that any are called upon to praise God for what they are forever excluded from, without the most dishonourable thoughts of God that can be conceived of.

By these various expressions we see the Choir is composed of the heavens and earth, every part of earth, the ends, the lower parts, the mountains, the inhabitants of the rock, the wilderness, the islands, they that go to sea, and all that is therein: And the Lord at the head of them.

We may next inquire how the Choir is to be employed, or exercised under the direction of him that excelleth.

They are to make a joyful noise *unto the Lord*, sing, *unto the Lord,* a new song, *and his praise* to the end of the earth. *Unto him and his praise;* there it is to centre. They are to shout, to give glory to God, and declare his praise.

The next inquiry, why they are to be thus exercised?

We have the answer in Psalm, xviii. 2, and Isaiah xliv. 22, *The Lord hath made known his salvation, his righteousness hath he openly shewed in the sight of the heathen. I have blotted out as a thick cloud thy transgressions, and as a cloud thy sins. Return unto me, for I have redeemed thee.*

Thus we see for what we are to rejoice, and sing praise, namely, the Lord's salvation, his righteousness, the blotting out of transgression, the work of redemption, which leads to the next inquiry.

What is the new song?

Here it may be said, the Psalmist speaking of Christ in Psalm' xl. 3, brings him in saying, *and he hath put a new song into my mouth, praise unto our God.* His being heard and brought up out of an horrible pit,

pit, and miry clay, and his feet set on a rock, and his goings established, and the new song put in his mouth, is the foundation for the new song to be sung by the united Choir, who are five times called upon to sing a new song to the Lord, brought to view in the new and living way, by the new covenant or Testament inforced by the death of the testator.

In Rev. v. 9, we read of the new song that was sung by the four living Creatures, and four and twenty elders, to the Lamb, which was, *thou art worthy, for thou wast slain, and hast redeemed us to God by thy blood, out of every nation, and kindred, and tongue, and people, and hast made us to our God kings and priests, and we shall reign on earth.* And Rev. xiv. 3, The hundred forty and four thousand *sung, as it were a new song before the throne, and before the four living creatures, and the elders, and no man could learn that song, but the hundred forty four thousand which were redeemed from the earth.*

Perhaps that part of the song, " and hast made us to our GOD kings and priests, and we shall reign on earth," may be peculiar to those described as the fruits to GOD and the Lamb, who were redeemed *out of* every kindred and tongue, and people, and nation, when GOD visited the nations to take *out of them* a people for his name : The great multitude which no man could number, *of all nations,* and kindreds, and tongues, which came out of great tribulation, and have washed their robes, and made them white in the blood of the Lamb, cried with a loud voice, saying, *Salvation to our God which sitteth on the throne, even to the Lamb.*

We have ten thousand times ten thousand, and thousands of thousands of angels, saying with a loud voice, *worthy is the Lamb that was slain, to receive power and riches, and wisdom and strength, and honour and glory, and blessing.* In Rev. v. 13, John saw

the

the whole Choir joined in one. *And every creature which is in heaven, and on the earth, and under the earth, and such as are in the sea, and all that are in them, heard I, say, blessing and honour, and glory, and power, unto him that sitteth on the throne and to the Lamb for ever and ever.*

Upon a review of the extent of the call to join herein, which of us but must wonder with great admiration? Am I included? What I, at the end of the earth, in the lowest part of it? What I, out of sight, on the top of the mountains? I, that am hid in the rock, I, that go to sea, with all that go with me, or were there before? And are we that dwell on the islands to declare his praise? Yes, in welcome, however unworthy in ourselves, by JESUS CHRIST we may offer the sacrifice of praise continually; the fruit of our lips, giving thanks to his name. Only observe the call and the welcome expressed in the repetition of the word Let five times in the passages mentioned. LET the Heavens and the earth; *let* the wilderness, and the cities thereof; *let* the inhabitants of the rock sing; *let* them shout from the top of the mountains; *let* them give glory to GOD, and declare his praise in the islands. This *let* is a most efficacious word, removing every hindrance that is cast in the way, by satan, sin, and law, which unite to object against singing the divine praises, by terrifying our consciencies, and representing GOD, who is love, to be irreconcilable hatred, by which we are shut up in hopeless despair; which causes us to think that these extensive expressions do not really mean what they say. But when the testimony is believed, *I have blotted out as a thick cloud thy transgressions, and as a cloud thy sins. Return unto me, for I have redeemed thee;* and we thus come to understand the ground of this efficacious *let*, all these hindrances are removed; and though we cannot find encouragement in our own character, we find it in his. *By him therefore let us offer the sacrifice of praise continually; the fruit of our lips, giving thanks to his name.* Constrained with all our hearts to sing the song of *Moses* and the Lamb, saying, *great and marvellous are thy works,* LORD GOD *Almighty; just and true are thy ways, thou King of saints; who shall not fear thee and glorify thy name?* Similar to the exhortation in the forementioned passage is *Isaiah, let them give glory to God, and declare his praise in the islands.*

It is undoubtedly incumbent on every member of this Universal Choir, to make it the study of his life, that his thoughts, his speech, and the whole tenor of his life be devoted to the glory of GOD. The inconsistency of a contrary conduct is so obvious, that it is hoped that every one whose mouth is employed in blessing GOD, even the Father, will most determinately watch against profaning his name, or cursing men that are made after the similitude of GOD. Every one's mind and conscience must give in to the truth of what the apostle *James* says, *my brethren, these things ought not so to be.* We praise him as the just GOD, and the Saviour. One sober thought will show the inconsistence of giving way to the temptation that would urge us at every fret, with a fellow-servant, a child, or neighbour, to call on GOD, to damn them; as though the divine character was the destroyer, instead of the Saviour. His call is, look unto me, and be ye saved; his name is Father and Redeemer, from everlasting. How shocking the thought, how great the indignity offered, to call on him to do the work of him, whose name is the destroyer; damn our brother who is his offspring. What greater affront can we give our fellow-men, than to call on them for any thing contrary to their character and station, which would debase them below the character of men. The thought is enough to fill those of us with everlasting

lasting shame and contempt of our own character and conduct, who have indulged such conversation; especially if believing him to be the Saviour, and may now sing his being pacified towards us, for all that we have done.

Remembering the words of the Apostle *Paul*, with them I now close, *Ye are bought with a price; therefore glorify God in your spirits and bodies which are* GOD's.

UNIVERSAL PRAISE.

O HEAVENS, sing your highest praise,
   While we attend to hear;
And let us see what numbers are
   Joined together there.
Ten thousand times ten thousand do
   With voices loud proclaim;
Thousands of thousands join to sing
   The Lamb's most worthy name.
Let earth exceed with higher praise
   Expressing of it thus:
The Lamb is worthy that was slain,
   For he was slain for us.
From earth, from the remotest ends,
   Come join to sing his praise;
And ye that occupy the sea,
   Your voice together raise,
From mountains' tops give ye a shout,
   Shout from earth's lowest parts;
Let those who dwell within the rock,
   Join here with all your hearts.
The wilderness and villages
   Their voice together raise,
While dwellers on the islands too,
   With joy declare his praise.

Hark!

Hark ! and attend to unison,
   When all together join ;
From every part with all their heart,
   The music is divine.
For every one in heav'n and earth,
   And those within the sea ;
And all therein, and under earth,
   Most cordially agree.
In blessing, honor, glory, power,
   With union ; ceasing never ;
To him that sitteth on the throne,
   Even to the Lamb, for ever.

The ends of the earth. Isa. xxiv. 16. *From the utmost ends of the earth have I heard songs, glory to the righteous.*

WHILE thousands, thousands are employed
   Of the angelic host,
In singing worthy is the Lamb,
   Sure men should praise thee most.
For thou for guilty men was slain ;
   Hast bought us with thy blood,
From ev'ry nation, kingdom, tongue,
   Redeem'd us all to GOD.
From ends of earth the most remote,
   Thy praise should ever sound ;
For to the utmost coasts thereof,
   Doth grace and love abound.
While you lament your lonely state,
   Distant from fellow-men ;
Lo, CHRIST is there the source of joy,
   There praise him ever then.
His love be ever on your mind,
   His highest praises sound ;
Your satisfaction will increase,
   Your joy will thus abound.

The Mariner's Song.

O JESUS, ever bleſt,
   Guide thou our heart and tongue,
To magnify thy worthy name,
   In a becoming ſong,
Refreſhed was our mind,
   With condeſcending grace,
To find the ſeaman call'd upon
   To celebrate thy praiſe.   *Iſa.* xlii. 10.
We ſing almighty power,   *Mat.* iii. 24.
   That winds and ſeas obey;   *Mark* iv. 39.
For by thy word the threatning ſtorms
   Are made to calm away.   *Luke* viii. 23, 24.
In ſtorms and dangers great,
   Diſciples hope we'll cheriſh;
With them to thee we'll lift our cry,
   LORD, ſave us, or we periſh.   *Mat.* xiv. 30.
When contrary winds
   Make us cry out for aid,
Our minds are calm'd to hear thee ſay
   'Tis I, be not afraid.   *Mat.* xiv. 24. 37.
If once we knew thy voice,
   'Twould make us all agree;
And we'd receive thee in the ſhip,
   With perfect unity.   *John* iv. 21.

The WILDERNESS.

Pſalm lxxi. 9.   *They that dwell in the wildernefs ſhall bow before him.*

WHEN dwellers in the wildernefs,
   In parched barren land,
The tidings of the goſpel true,
   Are made to underſtand.
The wildernefs doth as a roſe
   With pleaſant bloſſoms blow;

And

And in their straits of ev'ry kind,
  They joy and singing know.
The glory thus of Lebanon,
  Is given unto it;
Carmel and Sharon's excellence
  Doth then upon it sit.
For they now see with great delight
  The glory of the Lord;
The excellence of our God
  Doth songs of joy afford.
For the passengers i'th' wilderness
  Behold he makes a way:
Refreshing streams in deserts flow,
  Their parching thirst to lay.
Both wilderness and cities too
  Are called to rejoice;
And in the new song take their part,
  Uniting heart and voice.

Kedar, with the lower parts of the earth.

KEDAR was the son of Ishmael, who was an outcast from his youth, yet beloved of his father Abraham, who prayed, *O that Ishmael might live before thee;* and was answered, *I have heard thee, I have blessed him.* (If God bless, it cannot be reversed.) *I will make of him a great nation;* consequently that nation is blessed in Christ Jesus, according to the gospel preached to Abraham. Though Kedar signifies blackness or sorrow, though Kedar inhabited villages, and dwelt in tents, and might be reckoned with the lower parts of the earth, yet the villages that Kedar doth inhabit, with the lower parts of the earth, are called upon to take their part in the new song.

YE

SONGS of UNIVERSAL PRAISE.

YE who in lower parts of earth,
 By providence do dwell;
Redeemer's praises you are call'd
 With shouting forth to tell.
Kedar though black and sorrowful,
 Is called to rejoice
In Christ, in whom all nations are
 Bless'd by Jehovah's voice.
Kedar, thy flocks shall gather'd be,
 And with acceptance meet;
With joy then in Immanuel,
 Come worship at his feet.
When earth and seas, and islands too,
 Are called to rejoice,
And sing a new song to the Lord,
 Let Kedar join his voice.

From the top of the mountains, and the inhabitants of the rock. Isa. xlii. 6, 7, 10, 11.

HARK! from the mountains there's a shout,
 And from the rock a song;
Why? what's the cause of music heard,
 As thus we pass along?
Jesus, the people's covenant,
 Light to the Gentile world;
The pris'ners from the prisons freed,
 And darkness from them hurl'd.
When this is known, the new song's sung
 O'er all the earth abroad;
Dwellers in mountains, and in rocks,
 May join with one accord.
Proclaiming praise with joyful sound,
 To his most worthy name;
Ascribing honor, glory, power,
 To the redeeming Lamb.

The isles, and the inhabitants thereof.

Ye who upon the islands dwell,
  Your thankful voices raise,
To him who kindly says of you,
  Let them declare my praise.
This efficacious *Let* removes
  Objections guilt doth raise;
The justifier having said
  Let isles declare my praise.
Doth he say *let*? Then sure 'tis true,
  He hath our guilt remov'd,
And brought us nigh by Jesus' blood,   *Ep.* ii. 13.
  As those in him belov'd.
Then let us study to express
  Our love to him, to those,
Who may be cast away on us,
  And need our food or cloaths.
When thus they entertained Paul,
  They were repaid indeed,   *Acts* xxviii. 1-9.
Diseased in the island were
  Each healed as they'd need.
Thy healing power, Lord impart,
  To each disease of soul,
That breaks our peace and happiness,
  May we be thus made whole.
And rise and walk, leap and praise God,
  In all becoming ways;
By lip and life, and tongue, and song,
  Let isles declare thy praise.

[To

[To fill two or three vacant pages, the reader is presented with, 'A view of the world's misery and happiness in miniature;" alluding to Isa. liii. 6, *All we like sheep have gone astray, we have turned every one to his own way*; and to chap. xlv. 23, 24, *I have sworn by myself, that unto me every knee shall bow*, &c.

LOOK in, look out, look round about,
Where'er I turn mine eye, I soon descry
Profaneness, lewdness, pride and guilt;
In yonder lane, the man profane,
The woman very lewd;
The standers by, most scornful proud.
And though I start, for my own part,
And stop, and look, and stare,
In looking in, I find the sin
In all its parts is there.
My silence broke, and thus I spoke,
Profane he, and lewd she,
With proud we, and guilty me,
Must all agree, to bow the knee
To Jesus, Lord of all.
Both guilty, proud, lewd and profane,
Must kneel, and on him call;
To think to stand in these is vain,
Our loftiness must fall;
For by himself he sware it shall.
But prais'd be grace, that's found a place,
Where he and she, and I and we,
May see his reconciled face.
Though we have destroy'd ourselves,
And sink in guilt and helplessness,
In midst of all our deep distress,
Our help in him is found.
So when we pray, we sure may say,
I in the Lord now find,
Both perfect righteousness and strength,
To ease and heal my troubled mind.

When this we see, let's all agree,
His highest praise to sound ;
Instead of hate, fill'd with debate,
Let Love and Peace abound.

On the Crowing of a Cock.

AS I lay musing on my bed,
  I heard the Cock crow twice ;
My sinful shame of JESUS' name,
  Reproach'd me more than thrice.
That he, for me, should bear the cross,
  And quite despise the shame ;
Who have before my fellow men,
  Refus'd to own his name.

The bereaved Mother.

THY will be done, with me and mine,
  Cease then each murm'ring thought ;
'Tis wise and just, and comes in love,
  As revelation taught.   *Heb.* xii, 6. *Job* v, 17.
My child he gave to my embrace,   *Pro.* iii. 11, 12.
  And blessed be his name ;
He took it to himself again,   *Job* i. 21.
  Repeated be the same.
'Tis fruitless now for me to weep,
  He can't come back I see ;
My lot is now to go to him,   2*Sam.* xii. 33.
  He shall not come to me.
Then let my mind now fix upon,
  (All earthly joys before)
The Living One, who once was dead,
  But lives for ever more.   *Rev.* i. 18.

When

WHEN the Pſalmiſt had ſpoken of the perfect character of the bleſſed man CHRIST JESUS, in the firſt Pſalm, he deſcribes the treatment this bleſſed one met with in the world, from *the heathen, the people,* (viz. *Jews* and *Gentiles*) the Kings of the earth, and the rulers, in the ſecond Pſalm; and the many, the increaſed multitude, in the third Pſalm: He breaks forth in verſe eighth, in an aſcription of Salvation to the LORD: *Thy bleſſing upon thy people.*

SALVATION in thy counſels, LORD,
  Was perfect wiſdom's plan;
Deſign'd in JESUS CHRIST for us,
  Before the world began.
Salvation! O the pleaſant ſound!
  Mine ears attend the voice;
It comes thro' perfect righteouſneſs,
  Then let my heart rejoice.
Salvation wrought in JESUS' life,
  And finiſh'd when he died;
And witneſs'd when he roſe again,
  I know no hope beſide.
Salvation then belongs to him,
  Who wrought it out alone;
'Tis not our act or wiſh, but is
  Thy bleſſing freely ſhown.

Iſaiah xlvi. 3, 4.

EBENEZER the place I'll call,
  Wherein I now do ſtand;
For hitherto I've helped been,
  Jehovah, by thy hand.
Through all my helpleſs infancy,
  And tender feeble youth;
For then thy tender mercies were
  My conſtant ſtay in truth.

In riper age when I grew up,
  Thy love I've not forgot;
For thou in mercy didst maintain
  My undeserved lot.
Through all my wants, and wanderings,
  My guilt, and pressing fears,
I've been reliev'd and helped through,
  For more than threescore years.
'Twas thou in mercy didst me bear,
  And carry to this age;
Then let thy praises high employ
  And fill the present page.
Thy mercies through the path I've been,
  Are ever shining bright;
But when I read the gospel news,
  'Tis as the new day light.
Yea, to old age thou art the same,
  And unto hoary hairs,
My guide thou wilt be unto death,
  As in thy word appears.
Then let me ever rest in thee,
  Although the times seem hard;
And left I murmur or distrust,
  Be ever on my guard.
And keep mine eye upon the hope
  The gospel brings to view,
That I may always joy in what
  Thy wisdom calls me through.

The reflections of an OLD MAN.

THREE score and ten's already past,
  My exit must draw nigh,
When I shall quit the present scene,
  And wholly be laid by.

Myself

Myself a sinner of the chief,
  Conscious I freely own;
Hence hope within or from myself
  I must confess there's none.
But when I read GOD's gracious name,
  Father, Redeemer too,
Who's just, and yet salvation hath,
  My hopes revive, 'tis true.
I feel the force of what was told
  To me in early youth;
Though taught me from my infancy,
  It is a living truth:
That my encouragement to pray,
  Must come from GOD alone;
For from my sinful self I see
  Most surely there is none.
My study be GOD's gracious name,
  In JESUS manifest;
JESUS our head, his life, his death,
  His rising is my rest.

A Practical

A Practical Essay, designed for General Use---In Three Parts.

SECTION VII.

The CONSEQUENT OBLIGATION *of the* BELIEVERS *of the* GOSPEL, *A* PRACTICAL ESSAY, *Designed for* GENERAL USE, *in* Three Parts—*Part I. Addressed to* HUSBANDS *and* WIVES: *Being an answer to two Inquiries; the 1st,* "*What is the most obvious meaning of the word* CHURCH, *in the New Testament? The 2d, How doth* MARRIAGE *convey, as in a mystery, the Union of* CHRIST *and the* CHURCH? *Improved to illustrate the honorable* Relation, *endeared* Affection *and mutual* Duties *of* HUSBANDS *and* WIVES. *With a* SONG *on* MARRIAGE. *To which is added, an* APPENDIX, *with* Some Thoughts *suggested by the provisions of the* Table.——*Part II. Addressed to* PARENTS: *Being* Some Thoughts *on* Education.——*Part III. An* Inquiry *concerning the* CASE *of* CHILDREN, *with an* Exhortation *to them.*

"For the Grace of GOD, that bringeth Salvation, hath appeared to all men." Or, as in the former translation, "The Grace of GOD, that bringeth Salvation to all men, hath appeared, and Teaches us, that we should deny ungodliness and worldly lusts, and that we should live soberly, righteously and godly in this present world." TITUS II. 12.

PART I.
To HUSBANDS AND WIVES.

THE words of the Apostle, in *Ephesians* v. 32, "this is a great mystery, but I speak concerning CHRIST and the church," naturally lead to two inquiries.

1st. What is the most obvious meaning of the word church in the scriptures?

2d How

2d. How doth the marriage union convey, as in a myftery, the union of CHRIST and the church?

For the moft obvious meaning of the word church in the fcriptures, we may look into the various texts where it is mentioned.

I do not recollect that the word is any where ufed in the Old Teftament. The apoftle, in *Acts* vii. 38, ufes it for the Old Teftament church, " this is he that was in the church in the wildernefs with the Angel," &c. The words that are ufed in the Old Teftament are affembly and congregation; *Exodus* xii. 6, " the whole affembly fhall kill it in the evening," that is, the whole church of *Ifrael*, that were bound to keep the paffover; *Pfalm* xxii. 22, " In the midft of the congregation will I praife thee," which the Apoftle, in *Hebrews* ii. 12, calls the church, " in the midft of the church will I fing praife unto thee."

In the New Teftament, the firft mentioned place I recollect, is *Matthew* xvi. 18, " upon this rock will I build my church, and the gates of hell fhall not prevail againft it." Upon this rock, the truth *Peter* had made confeffion of, " thou art the CHRIST, the fon of the living God," is the rock on which the church is built, againft which the gates, the power and policy of hell, fhall not prevail.

Then in the xviiith of *Matthew*, 17, in which fo far as I underftand, JESUS CHRIST is inftructing his difciple's their duty in their particular connection, thofe believers of the apoftles doctrine collected in the profeffion of the name of JESUS, meeting together in one place, was called the church in that place. In *Acts* viii. 1, we read of the church which was at Jerufalem, the firft church gathered by the apoftles after the defcent of the Holy Ghoft; *Acts* xiii. 1, of the church at Antioch; *Acts* xx. 7, and *Revelations* ii. 1, of the church of Ephefus; *Romans* xvi. 3-15, and 1ft o {*Corinthians*, xvi. 19, we

read

read of the church in the house of Priscilla and Aquilla; in *Colossians* iv. 15, of the church in Nymphas's house, and of the church in Philemon's house, in the 2d verse of that epistle.

These particular churches, gathered by the apostle's doctrine, was governed by the will of JESUS CHRIST, as taught by them; and so far as that can be understood from the scriptures, are the rule by which particular churches of CHRIST are to be governed in all ages; but as that would be too lengthy to be here considered, must be passed over.

We read also of the church of the first born, written in heaven, *Hebrews*, xii. 23; of the church for which CHRIST gave himself, " that he might sanctify and cleanse it, by the washing of water through the word, that he might make it to himself a glorious church, not having spot or wrinkle, or any such thing, but that it might be holy and without blemish." *Ephesians* v. 26, 27.

Hence I collect, 1st, That JESUS CHRIST is the foundation on whom the church is built.

2d. That those that were brought by the Apostolic doctrine concerning him, to believe that JESUS is the CHRIST, in the first ages of christianity, were by apostolic authority collected into distinct, particular churches, in such places where there were a sufficient number of believers for that purpose, and were called the church in that place. There is little said about the place of their meeting: I suppose any place that they could obtain, that was convenient for that purpose: The church of Troas met in an upper chamber; *Acts* xx. 7, 8, the church of the Colossians in Philemon's house, as may be seen by comparing those two epistles.

These churches appeared as a representation of the universal church, in their holding the one truth, that JESUS CHRIST is the son of GOD, by which they

were

were all gathered together, this being the sole foundation on which the universal church is built, and in their professed subjection to the authority of JESUS CHRIST, the head of the church, and head over all things for its good.

3dly. That there is a universal church, which will consist of all that are included in that glorious church for whom JESUS CHRIST gave himself; the full meaning of which is the general assembly and church of the first born, written in Heaven; JESUS CHRIST is the first born among the many brethren brought to glory. *Psalm* lxxxix. 27, " I will make him my first born, higher than the kings of the earth ;" *Romans* viii. 29, " the first born among many brethren ;" *Colossians* i. 15, " who is the first born of every creature," verse 18, " the first born from the dead." It is his church, the church of the first born; this church, this general assembly, called *Psalm* cvii. 32, " the assembly of the people, the congregation of the elders," *Psalm* cxi. 1, " the assembly of the upright, and the congregation," *Psalm* clxix. 1, " the congregation of the saints," that are represented to John, *Revelations* v. 8, by the four living creatures and four and twenty elders, and chap. vii. 9, by a great multitude, which no man could number, of all nations and kindred, and people and tongues, in addition to the hundred, forty and four thousand, that were sealed in the former part of the chapter, of all the tribes of *Israel.*— The same sealed number are represented, in chap. xiv. 1, to 5, standing with the lamb on the mount Zion," which did not exclude the preaching of the gospel to every nation and kindred and tongue and people, verse 6; which gospel or word shall not return void, but shall accomplish what he pleases, and shall prosper in the thing whereunto he sends it.

Of this church every believer of the Apostles testimony, or every one that believeth that JESUS is the

C c   CHRIST,

CHRIST, according to *Peter*'s confession, appears, upon the confession of this faith, to be a visible member. And it is the duty of every such person, who can find a particular church built on this foundation, and who in subjection to his authority, make the apostolic churches their rule as to order to join with them in the profession of his name, with them observing all things whatsoever he has commanded, walking together in love, as he hath given commandment; for this they are chosen and called to the faith of the gospel, 1st of *Peter*, ii. 9, Such are made use of for the ingathering of others, 1st of *Thessalonians*, i. 8, " for from you sounded out the word of the LORD;" *Ephesians* i. 9, 10, having made known to us the mystery of his will, according to his good pleasure, which he hath proposed in himself, that in the dispensation of the fullness of times, he might gather together in one, all things in CHRIST, both which are in Heaven and which are on earth, in him." But the Ephesian church being chosen in him before the foundation of the world, to be holy and without blame before him in love, being predestinated to the adoption of children by JESUS CHRIST, according to the good pleasure of his will, to the praise of the glory of his grace, was not to the final exclusion or reprobation of others, but as a means made use of by him, that in the dispensation of the fullness of times, he might gather together all things in CHRIST; chap. ii. 7, " That in the ages to come he might shew the exceeding riches of his grace, in his kindness towards us through CHRIST JESUS." The church then is to hold forth the word of life; the word is to sound out from them. " As oft as ye eat this bread and drink this cup, ye do shew forth the LORD's death till he come :" Thus they boldly bear his name, in opposition to earth and hell; shew that he is precious, and hold forth to the world, that there is no other name under heaven
given

given among men, whereby they muſt be ſaved. Such are the means the great head of the church makes uſe of, as he pleaſes, to the conviction of others: But be the conſequences what they will, it is their duty to teſtify to his name, truth and ways, looking for the time when he will gather all the fruit of his purchaſe into one in himſelf; for every one for whom CHRIST died, ſhall certainly, in his time and way, come to the knowledge of him, and to partake in his ſalvation, as thoſe who have been or are viſible members of his church.—For doth not the ſcriptures ſhew the connexion of the human race with JESUS CHRIST, as their head, in as extenſive a view as their connexion with the firſt Adam, ſee *Romans* v. 14, to the end; *Hebrews* ii. 9, " we ſee Jeſus, who was made a little lower than the angels, for the ſufferings of death, crowned with glory and honour, that he by the grace of GOD, ſhould taſte death for every man." 1ſt of *John*, ii. 2, " he is the propitiation for our ſins; and not for ours only, but for the whole world." And the apoſtle ſays, 2d of *Corinthians*, v. 14, to the end, " we thus judge, if one died for all, then all died; and he died for all, that they which live, ſhould not henceforth live to themſelves, but to him that died for them, and roſe again." This appears to be the deſign of the manifeſtation of this truth, or of perſons being brought to the knowledge of the truth, and to life in CHRIST thereby, that they which live ſhould not henceforth live to themſelves, but to him that died for them, and roſe again;* verſe 16, " wherefore henceforth know we no man after the fleſh;" before they knew the Jews after the fleſh, as thoſe

" to

---

* The thought of this is enough to clothe with ſhame, as a garment, thoſe who have hope of life by Jeſus Chriſt, that this deſign has been no more attended to. For myſelf I can ſay, to me belongs ſhame and confuſion of face. Praiſed be his name, to the Lord our God belongs mercies and forgiveneſs. Though we have rebelled againſt him, may the hope of forgiveneſs ever keep us from deſpair, and be a freſh ſpring of excitement to live to him him that died for us, and roſe again.

"to whom pertained the adoption, and the glory, and the covenants, and the giving of the law, and the service, and the promises, whose were the fathers, and of whom concerning the flesh CHRIST came, who is over all, GOD blessed forever. Amen."

The gospel was first published to them, beginning at Jerusalem; upon their rejecting it, the apostles are sent to the Gentiles, and are taught to call no man common or unclean; what GOD hath sanctified, call not thou common, which the apostle explains, *Acts* x. 28, "GOD hath shewed that I should call no man common or unclean." Why? Because GOD hath cleansed them; I view them cleansed, in that CHRIST died for all, and designs in his time and way to bring them all to the knowledge of himself, and manifest his sanctifying and setting them apart for himself. This destroys all distinction between Jew and Gentile, and not only as the nations of Jews and Gentiles, but of all men in every age, that on some account or other, besides the atonement, would presume to be in, or near, or have a claim upon the divine favour before some of their fellow creatures.— Henceforth know we no man after the flesh, " yea, though we have known CHRIST after the flesh, yet now henceforth know we him no more;" JESUS CHRIST was a minister of the circumcision, was made under the law, fulfilled the righteousness of it, came to his own, sent his gospel first to the Jews; but when his death and resurrection were fully made manifest, and the promises understood, that all the families of the earth were to be blessed in him, that the Gentiles were to glorify GOD for mercy; when these things were made fully manifest, the apostle says, " yea, though we have known CHRIST after the flesh, yet now henceforth know we him no more; therefore if any man be in CHRIST a new creature, these old things are passed away, behold all things are become new."

There

There is not a fragment of the old dispensation, or of the righteousness of our own, can have any admission as recommending us to the divine favour, "all things are become new, and all of God, who hath reconciled us to himself;" us, the apostles and first disciples, with the church of the Corinthians, to whom he wrote, who were together visibly reconciled to himself by Jesus Christ, "and hath committed to us the word of reconcilation;" that is, the word of reconciliation committed to the apostles, "that God was in Christ reconciling the world to himself, not imputing their trespasses unto them." Now then, if God was in Christ reconciling the world unto himself; if he be the propitiation for the whole world; if he tasted death for every man; if Adam was a full figure of him that was to come, and the connection of the human race with Jesus Christ as their head, as extensive as their connection with the first Adam, then we must conceive that the church of the first born, the church for which Christ gave himself, will finally consist of all nations, kindreds, tongues and people; and in this view, the design of mercy forbids calling any man common, and lays a sure foundation of universal love and benevolence to all the human race, and of faith in prayer for them; while those brought to believe that Jesus is the Christ, professing their faith in, and subjection to him, and appearing influenced thereby, are subjects of that gospel charity, which the Apostle enjoins, when he says, "have fervent charity among yourselves," and which I think, appears evidently distinguishable from the universal benevolence due to the whole human race.

Thus from the most obvious meaning of the passages where the word church is used in scripture, these things have been collected. 1st, That Jesus Christ is the foundation on which the church is built. 2dly, A collection of believers professing his name,

name, and in subjection to his authority, observing his laws, in any place, are a visible church there, or a visible representation of the universal church. 3dly, The universal church will finally have gathered into it, or be made up of all for whom CHRIST died.

The second inquiry is, How doth marriage convey, as in a mystery, the union of CHRIST and the church?

Attention to this inquiry will lead us to compare this passage in *Ephesians*, with the beginning of *Genesis*, and various other passages, one with another. In *Genesis* i. 27, we read, "So GOD created man in his own image, in the image of GOD created he him, male and female created he them." There appeared to be male and female created in the one man: The particular formation or building of the woman, was from man, of which we have the account, *Genesis* ii. 21, 22, "And the LORD GOD caused a deep sleep to fall upon Adam, and he slept *; and he took one of his ribs and closed up the flesh instead thereof; and the rib which the LORD GOD had taken from man, builded † he a woman, and brought her unto the man." Thus the woman " is of the man, and for the man," 1st of *Corinthians*, xi. 8, 9, So is the church, in every view, of and for JESUS CHRIST.— *Romans* xi. 36, " for of him, and to him, and through him, are all things." *Colossians* i. 16. " all things were created by him and for him." As the woman was created in him, was of him and for him, so they are called by one name, or she bears his name, *Genesis* v. 2, " male and female created he them, and called their name Adam." When she was brought to him, he says, " she shall be called woman, because she was taken out of man." She shall be called by a name derived from that of man. So the church is called by the same name with JESUS CHRIST; *Jeremiah*

---

* As Adam was a figure of him that was to come, may not this deep sleep prefigure the death of Jesus Christ, from which the church arises.
† See the Hebrew in the bible margin.

miah xxiii. 6, and xxxiii. 16, "he and she are called, the Lord our righteousness." Yet so as to be denominated from him, "he shall be called a Nazarene," they "the sect of the Nazarenes;" he is called CHRIST, "the disciples were first called Christians at Antioch;" names derived from him shewing, that without him they were nothing; that he is their all, and that in him they possess and enjoy all good.

We have the reason of this name, "This is now bone of my bone, and flesh of my flesh; she shall be called woman, because she was taken out of man." "So ought men to love their wives as their own bodies; he that loveth his wife loveth himself, for no man ever yet hated his own flesh, but nourisheth and cherisheth it, even as the Lord the church, for we are members of his body, of his flesh, and of his bones." The circumstances of the church with JESUS CHRIST, are similar to that of Adam with his wife, bone and flesh. "For this cause shall a man leave his father and mother, and be joined to his wife, and they two shall be one flesh: This is a great mystery, but I speak concerning Christ and the church.

"This is a great mystery;" the mystery, that in marriage conveys the union of CHRIST and the church, appears herein: That the woman was created in the man, was united to him before she was distinctly builded a woman: When she was thus builded and brought to him, there appeared the visible marriage union; he said, "This is now bone of my bone, and flesh of my flesh." "Therefore shall a man leave his father and mother and cleave to his wife." Therefore because of the previous union that was the ground of it, "But I speak," says the Apostle, "Concerning CHRIST and the church," this holds forth the union between CHRIST and the church, prior to the visible marriage union which takes place upon any of the children of men, being brought to JESUS CHRIST;

who

who says, "For no man can come to me, except the Father which hath sent me, draw him."

In *Romans* xvi. 7, Andronicus and Junia, are spake of as in CHRIST before the Apostle, though they were together chosen in CHRIST before the foundation of the world. Thus is the whole church in CHRIST, in the most universal sense: He stands answering fully to the figure of him that was to come, the head of every man, as universally as Adam was. In this view there is a union or connection of head and members, even before the members actually appear. "And for this cause shall a man leave father and mother and cleave to his wife." JESUS CHRIST left father and mother in cleaving to his wife; *John* xvi. 28, "I came forth of the father, and am come into the world." In *Matthew* xii. 47, to 50, and *Mark* iii. 32, to 35, His attention to what he had to do for his church, was not diverted by his mother.* JESUS took the churches circumstances as his own; took her debts upon himself; undertook to look after her when lost; and in pursuance of his undertaking, gave his life for her. "Even as CHRIST loved the church and gave himself for it," she wears his name, is complete in him, "who of GOD is made unto her wisdom, righteousness, sanctification, and redemption." It is visibly so with respect to those that are brought by the gospel to the knowledge of, faith in, and subjection to, him: It was really so in the purpose and purchase of JESUS CHRIST, before they came to the knowledge of him, and is really so respecting those who yet know him not, live in unbelief and disobedience; for, says the Apostle, *Hebrews* ii. 8, "Thou hast put all things in subjection under his feet; for in that he put all in subjection, he left nothing not put under him; but now we see not yet all things put under him: But we see JESUS for the sufferings of

---

* Is it not the true antitype of Levi? *Deutreonomy* xxxiii. 8, 9.

of death crowned with glory and honor, that he, by the grace of GOD, should taste death for every man." And the prophet *Isaiah* gives us the divine oath for this, chap. xlv. 22, " Look unto me," (the just GOD and the Savior) " And be ye saved, all the ends of the earth, for I GOD and none else ; I have sworn by myself, the word is gone out of my mouth in righteousness, and shall not return, that to me every knee shall bow, every tongue shall swear, surely shall say, in the Lord have I righteousness and strength, to him shall come;" which must make all that are incensed against him ashamed.

The name of the visible church is, " The LORD our righteousness." All that are brought to him call him so, and are denominated by it, " 'tis the name whereby she shall be called." But we have the divine oath, that " every knee shall bow, and every tongue shall swear, surely shall say, in the LORD have I righteousness and strength." The time and manner is with him, who saith, " I will work, and who shall let it ;" " Who will have all men to be saved and come to the knowledge of the truth ; for there is one GOD, even one mediator, of GOD and man, the man CHRIST JESUS, who gave himself a ransom for all, to be testified in due time."

In CHRIST JESUS, GOD manifest in the flesh, we have the fullness of the divine nature, as is expressed in *Hebrews* i. 3, ", Who being the brightness of glory and the express image of his person." *Colossians* ii. 9, " For in him dwelleth all the fullness of the godhead bodily ;" who could say, " I and Father are one."

Is there not the fullness of the human nature also in him ? The Apostle says, " we are members of his body, of his flesh, and of his bones," Who does he mean ? Doubtless the church, the apostles, the first disciples, the church of the Ephesians, who were visibly so, and those who should believe through their word, in every age; yea, all for whom JESUS CHRIST gave himself. The church, in the most extensive sense, are in this union, and are represented travelling together in pain, till the manifestation of it. *Romans* viii. 22, " For we know that the whole creation," it is the same word we have in *Mark* xvi. 15, " preach the gospel to every creature;" therefore every creature that the gospel is to be preached to, " groaneth and traveleth in pain together; and not only they, but we ourselves that have the first fruits, even we ourselves groan within ourselves, waiting for the adoption, the redemption of our body." By the redemption of our body, I conceive the idea of the body of which Jesus is the head, as captivated, enslaved, sold, and groaning under this bondage; and those whose minds have been led to an understanding of redemption by CHRIST, though their minds are thereby relieved, yet groaning, waiting for the adoption, the redemption of the whole body.

Now that in JESUS CHRIST there is the fullness of the human nature, is it not evident from the consideration of *Genesis* v. 2, where we read of our first parents in their primitive state, " male and female created he them, and blessed them, and called their name Adam, in the day they were created." Whom he blesses are blessed; for his gifts are without repentance. So when we have the account of their being seduced from their allegiance, brought under bondage, and led captive by satan, the curse is denounced upon the serpent, *Genesis* iii. 14; but the way opened through which the original blessedness, pronounced in the day they were created, should be accomplished, verse 15, although they could not sin without smart and sorrow; to the woman, I will greatly multiply thy sorrow; in sorrow shalt thou bring forth children," &c.—to the man, " cursed is the ground for thy sake;

in

in forrow shalt thou eat it all the days of thy life," &c. And as the way in which the original blessing that was forfeited was to be restored and confirmed, was brought to view in the 15th verse; so it is repeated and illustrated in *Gen.* xii. 3, xviii. 18, xx. 18, and xxvi. 4, " In thy seed shall all the nations of the earth be blessed." This the apostles call " preaching the gospel to Abraham," *Galatians* iii, 18, 'Tis agreeable to *Deuteronomy* xxxii. 43, " rejoice, O ye nations, his people ;" *Psalm* lxxii. 11, " all nations shall serve him," verse 17, " all nations shall call him blessed ;" *Psalm* lxxxii. 8, " arise O God, for thou shalt inherit all nations ;" *Psalm* ii. 8, " ask of me, and I will give the heathen thine inheritance, and the utmost parts of the earth thy possession ;" *Psalm* lxxxvi. 9, " all nations shall come and worship before thee, and glorify thy name." *Psalm* c: all the earth are called upon to make a joyful noise to the LORD, on account of his making us his people, and the sheep of his pasture : " Know ye." Who is to know ? Answer, all the earth. Know ye that the LORD, he GOD, * he hath made us, and not we ourselves, his people and the sheep of his pasture. Agreeable to *Psalm* cxvii. " O praise the Lord." Who ? All ye nations ; praise him all ye people." Where are any exempted ? " For his merciful kindness is great towards us." Towards who ? All the earth, as extensive as the call to praise him.— " And the truth of the Lord forever ; praise ye the LORD." His merciful kindness ; how is the greatness of it made manifest, and how doth the truth of the LORD appear to endure forever, but in him, " who is the mercy and the truth," in him " in whom all nations are blessed," in him " in whom thou wilt perform the truth to *Jacob* and the mercy to *Abraham,* which thou hast sworn to our fathers in the days of old. - Now

---

* I read this verse without the words supplied by the translators.

Now this blessedness of the nations, of which these passages speak, was to have its accomplishment in the seed of *Abraham*. " In thy seed ;" which is CHRIST. *Galatians* iii. 6, Now if all the nations of the earth are included in the blessedness in CHRIST JESUS, they are in him as their head ; there is the fullness of the human nature in CHRIST JESUS ; so they were considered in him before the evidences of it appeared in or upon any of them ; and because of this union, he is engaged in all he doth for them, to bring them to himself. " This is now bone of my bone, and flesh of my flesh ; she shall be called woman, because she was taken out of man." " Therefore," because of the previous union, " shall a man leave his father and mother and cleave to his wife, and they shall be one flesh : This is a great mystery, but," says the apostle, " I speak concerning CHRIST and the church." " This is now bone of my bone, and flesh of my flesh ; she shall be called woman ;" she shall wear my name, come into a visible connection and intercourse with me, be interested in what I am and have, &c. So in consequence of this union shall the church, in the most extensive sense, even every member, from all the ends of the earth, be brought to JESUS CHRIST, in his times, who is the blessed and only potentate ; shall bear his name ; be called by the name which the mouth of the Lord doth name : 'Tis by his authority we are assured, she shall be called " the Lord our righteousness." These things shall be made manifest when *Psalm* xlv. 15. 15, and *Psalm* lxxii. from the 9th to the end of the 15th verse, have their accomplishment.

Against what has been brought to view, particularly in the several quotations from the Psalms, arises this objection, that the apostle appears to apply such passages to those gathered by the gospel from among the Gentiles ; not to the Gentiles, in so extensive a manner

manner, as is expressed in the Psalms; and so those passages are to be understood in the limitted sense used by the apostles, who direct their epistles to the believers of their testimony, collected from among the Gentiles.

To this it may be answered, that the epistles of the apostles were wrote to visible churches, and visible believers, for their express direction in their conduct towards God, and one another, and are left on record for the same end, to all believers in all ages, as none but such as are led to the knowledge of Jesus Christ, were capable of understanding the grace there made manifest, and the obligations thence arising to glorify him in their spirits and bodies which are his; but yet it is evident they were designed as a means of communication of the knowledge of Christ to mankind in general. See *Ephesians* i. 9, 10.

Ephesians ii. 4 to 7, " But God who is rich in mercy, for his great love, wherewith he hath loved us, even when we were dead in sins, hath quickened us together with Christ, and hath raised us up together, and made us sit together in heavenly places in Christ Jesus." For what end? " That in the ages to come, he might shew the exceeding riches of his grace in kindness towards us, through Christ Jesus." And in the 3d chapter, from the 2d verse, we have the end of the dispensation of grace, given to the apostle towards the Ephesians, " how that by revelation he made known unto me the mystery, which in other ages was not made known unto the sons of men, as it is now revealed unto his holy apostles and prophets by the spirit, that the Gentiles should be fellow heirs, and of the same body, and partakers of his promise, in Christ by the gospel unto me, who am less than the least of all saints, is this grace given, that I should preach among the Gentiles the unsearchable riches of Christ, and to make all

MEN, see what the fellowship of the mystery, which from the beginning of the world, hath been hid in GOD, who created all things by JESUS CHRIST."

Here we have glad tidings to ALL MEN; to ages to come; to all things in Heaven and earth, in what divine grace did for, and among the apostles and Ephesians. The 5th *Romans*, from the 14th to the end, and 1st of *Corinthians*, v. 15. 19, shew the same thing, but have been already mentioned and need not be repeated.

Thus the second inquiry has been attended to, *viz.* How doth marriage convey as in a mystery, the union of Christ and the church?

From what has been brought to view, we see the obligations those are under, that are brought to the faith of the gospel, to collect together in the profession of his name, and subjection to his authority, after the example of the first disciples in the first churches, to the same end, which will, I conceive, be the duty of the disciples till the second coming of JESUS CHRIST, or till all things are put under his feet; till which time, he will use the same means to the same end.—Much might be said here, " but except the LORD build the house, they labour in vain that build it."

And not only their obligations to stand forth in the profession of his name, observing the order of the gospel, as practised by the first churches, but their obligations to an attention to all the precepts of the new testament, concerning their conduct in every relation they sustain; particularly that of husband and wife, which the apostle has in view in the passage before us, beginning with the wives, verse 22, " Wives submit yourselves unto your own husbands, as unto the LORD." *Col.* iii. 18, " as it is fit in the LORD." *Titus* ii. 4, " That they may teach the young women to be sober, to love their husbands, to love their children, discrete, chaste, keepers at home, good, obedient

dient to their husbands, that the name of God and his doctrine be not blasphemed." 1st of *Peter*, iii. to the end of the 6th verse, " Likewise ye wives in subjection to your own husbands; that if any obey not the word, they also may without the word, be won by the conversation of the wives, while they behold your chaste conversation, coupled with fear."

In these passages, the duty of the wives is made plain; inculcated and enforced from the obligations to JESUS CHRIST, " as unto the LORD, as it is fit in the LORD;" which shews the duty of the wife to flow from the authority of JESUS CHRIST, and to be directed by his will: So that in all her attention and submission to her husband, the authority and directions of JESUS CHRIST are ever to be kept in view, as the first motive the apostle uses, and truly it is no barren one, but full of excitation. The believing wife may thus think with herself, While I am attending my duty to my husband, the ever blessed JESUS, in his adorable condescension, is pleased to accept me as attending to him: Therefore, as to the LORD, will be musical in her mind, and excite to chearfulness therein. The second motive, if it be a distinct one, is, " that the name of God and his doctrine be not blasphemed." *Titus* ii. 4, 5, " That they," the aged women, " may teach the young women to be sober, to love their husbands, to love their children."—Wives are not only taught submission to their husbands from a sense of duty, but " to love their husbands, to love their children;" which will excite them, from inward affection, ever to be studying and pursuing their comfort and happiness, while their own is increased by the comfort of love: And when to the motive, " as unto the LORD," is joined the " love of husbands and children, good, obedient to their own husbands, that the name of God and his doctrine be not blasphemed," will follow; will

follow,

follow, did I say! is it not inseparably interwoven? O my Jesus! is thy name and doctrine concerned in my love and duty to my husband and children; how happy hast thou made me, in making love, which is my happiness, my duty; and bringing thy name and doctrine to my continual view, may it never be blasphemed by my evil conduct towards my husband and children; methought I moved in a low sphere in attending daily to them, but now I find I am exalted to wait on my Lord; he has been pleased to commit his name and doctrine to my daily care: Angels have not higher employment than is appointed me, in the very place where he hath placed me; and when I dwell in love, I dwell in him. The third motive, "that if any obey not the word, they also may, without the word, be won by the conversation of the wives, while they behold your chaste conversation with fear," must also be a powerful one, in the minds of believing wives, to an attention to the hidden man of the heart, in that which is not corruptible, of a meek and quiet spirit, which is in the sight of God of great price. If by the hidden man of the heart, we understand Christ dwelling in the hearts of believers by faith, we are led to that which is not corruptible, and to the pattern, fountain, and foundation of a meek and quiet spirit, which indeed, in the sight of God, is of great price. In *Matthew* xi. 29, Jesus Christ says, "Learn of me, for I am meek and lowly, and ye shall find rest to your souls." The believing wives understand Jesus Christ to be the green olive-tree, from whence this fruit is found. So did their examples in the old times; "The holy women who trusted in God, and thus adorned themselves, being in subjection to their own husbands, even as Sarah obeyed Abraham, calling him Lord, whose daughters ye are as long as ye do well, and are not afraid with any amazement." What doth that import?

import? So long as you are influenced by your duty to Jesus Christ, to attend your duty as wives, you appear to be the children, the followers, or imitators of the holy women who trusted in God; to belong to that family; and need not be afraid with any amazement; for if our hearts condemn us not, then have we confidence towards God. But if instead of attention to the directions of the Apostles of Christ, there is giving heed to temptation, not contented in " modest apparel, with shame-facedness, and sobriety," but giving way to a prevailing solicitude for " the outward adorning of plating the hair," and of " wearing of gold, pearls and costly array," you will appear to be under the influence of your lusts; to be walking according to the course of this world; according to the prince of the power of the air, the spirit that now worketh in the children of disobedience; and the tendency of it will be to darkness and fear with amazement, more especially at times when there is most need of consolation. It certainly doth not become women professing godliness, to be thus adorned; but it becometh them to be adorned with good works. Certainly there appears ability for the good works of the gospel; such as feeding the hungry and cloathing the naked, at least as far as the price of the gold, pearls and costly array beyond modest apparel, that they wear; when the wearing it can be of no use, except evidencing their inattention to the scripture, which prohibits their wearing it; or what is worse, opposition to them. In which case they may be advised to read *James* v. 1, 2, 3, with sober attention, which will shew such a conduct to tend to fear with amazement; which christian women ought to turn from; to walk in love to Jesus Christ, to their husbands and children, according to the directions of the apostles of Jesus Christ, which tends to cast out the fear that has torment.

Verse 24. "Therefore, as the church is subject to Christ, so let the wives to their own husbands, in every thing." Which shews the duty of wives to submit to and seek to please their husbands, in every thing that is not contrary to the mind of Jesus Christ, "as it is fit in the Lord." When the wife makes this the rule of her conduct, she pursues her own happiness in connection with her husband's. When his will is contrary to the mind of Christ, or would wish his wife to do that she is afraid will incur his displeasure, she is then only to point out her reasons from the word, and to persevere in attention to the will of Jesus Christ. But when she sets up her own will in opposition to her husband, and glories in a victory over him, however she may seem to gratify herself, she will find it leads to future shame, and fear with amazement.

We have also, in the passage before us, verse 25, "Husbands love your wives, even as Christ also loved the church, and gave himself for it," &c. Verse 28, 29, and 30, "So ought men to love their wives as their own bodies; he that loveth his wife loveth himself: For no man ever yet hated his own flesh, but nourisheth and cherisheth it, even as the Lord the church. For we are members of his body, of his flesh, and of his bones." From this passage, together with *Colossians* iii. 19, and 1st of *Peter*, iii. 7, we may collect the mind of Jesus Christ, as signified by the apostles, concerning the duty of husbands. 'Tis comprehended in love. "Husbands love your wives." Love is the fulfilling of the law, and the rule or measure of the love of the husband to the wife, is, "as Christ loved the church, and gave himself for it, that he might sanctify and cleanse it, with the washing of water by the word; that he might make* it to himself a glorious church,

not

---

* See the former translation.

not having spot or wrinkle, or any such thing, but that it should be holy and without blemish."

"Jesus Christ loved the church, and gave himself for it." "Husbands love your wives, even as Christ loved the church." Did Jesus Christ give himself; and am I, or have I any thing that is for the comfort and happiness of my wife, that thro' covetousness or self-will I may withhold from her, and yet manifest I love her as Christ loved the church? Jesus Christ paid the church's debt, redeemed her from captivity, directed her in her duty, supplied her wants, knows how to have compassion on the ignorant, and them that are without of the way: He took her circumstances of want, distress and misery upon himself, and communicates of his fulness unto her; is of God made to us wisdom, righteousness, sanctification and redemption;" and is in all an example to direct the love of the husband to his wife; that he attend to all her wants, distresses and miseries; to relieve and supply them according to his measure. And when any thing appears in the conduct of the wife inconsistent with her duty, as the husband is the head of the wife, he is to point out her duty from the word. "Jesus Christ gave himself for the church, that he might sanctify and cleanse it, with the washing of water by the word." If the word be made use of in the exercise of love, the tendency and efficacy would be to heal, as it would always bring Christ's authority to the view of the wife, and keep his example in the view of the husband, and guard against the evil cautioned against in Col. iii. 19, "husbands love your wives, and be not bitter against them." Remember that bitterness always springs from the root of bitterness; "the root that beareth gall and wormwood, from the turning away from the root of the righteous, that beareth fruit." Yet so great is the deceitfulness of our own hearts,

hearts, and so imperceptible the prevalence of the enemy, transformed into an angel of light, that this bitterness may appear to spring from a sort of religious ignorance, or a mistaken religious zeal.

When we read, " That the husband is the head of the wife," and that it is his duty to rule well his own house, a strange notion of headship and rule may take place, that upon every slight occasion there is a bitter resolution ; I will be master of my own house; I will be minded ; it is my duty, &c. That instead of viewing the head as the seat of wisdom, care and tenderness, it is viewed as the seat of domineering ; as if its only care was to see, that my will may be done ; and perhaps for no fault, only that a particular humour is not pleased, there will be a stamp on the floor, enough to make all ring again, and the husband hold himself not guilty, from a religious zeal to be minded to rule his own house. If I find out the man, can he be offended if I should inquire, Dear Sir, where find you this in the example of JESUS CHRIST ?

From this cause often proceeds such discontent with that which the industrious wife has endeavored to prepare, with as much agreeableness to her husband, as the means he had put into her hands was capable of ; that he will despise both it and her ; and instead of coming with gratitude, thankfgiving and satisfaction to his meals, as that which shews his increasing and perpetual obligation to eat, drink and do all to the glory of GOD, there will be bitter uneasiness through the whole of the time calculated for family enjoyment and happiness. If there be such a man, shall I put him in mind, that when JESUS fed the multitude with barley bread and fish, he gave thanks ; and when *Paul*, and those with him on board the ship, were about to eat, " he took the bread and gave thanks to GOD in presence of them all, and

when

when he had broken, he began to eat; then were they all of good chear, and they alſo took meat."— Dear Sir, thankſgiving to God, and all of good chear, becomes a Chriſtian's Table, which the head of the family is to lead in :* Every thing contrary comes from the root of bitterneſs, however diſordered the head may be, ſo as not to ſee whence it is. The caution, " be not bitter againſt them," is to be attended to through the whole of the conduct of the huſband to the wife, with whom he is to " dwell according to knowledge." The above deſcribed conduct muſt flow from ignorance and blindneſs, from the God of this world blinding the mind, though it be with a religious zeal for his own honor as the head of the wife, while the honor that is to be given to the wife as the weaker veſſel, as his own fleſh, as now, " bone of his bone, and fleſh of his fleſh, as heirs together of the grace of life," is not attended to, and their mutual prayers are hereby hindered.

I have been the longer on this, becauſe this evil may proceed from ignorance, and the temptation in it not diſcovered, which, when brought to light, may be the ſooner turned from; for certainly, if a man find a proneneſs to theſe or the like evils, in his temper, it will be natural to ſeek a hiding place, to excuſe and juſtify himſelf, and no where can he find one more eaſy, than under a cloak of falſe religion. But when the true cauſe or ſource is diſcovered to himſelf, he muſt conclude, that it is more agreeable to his duty, when he finds a legal, fretful, froward diſpoſition working in him, only waiting an opportunity of breaking forth, to get alone, and take ſhame to himſelf, before him to whom all things are naked and open, who is " the great High Prieſt that is paſſed into the heavens, Jesus the ſon of God, touched with the feeling of our infirmities, in all points tempted as we

---

* See the appendix.

we are, without sin," and take encouragement from him, " to ask mercy, and find grace to help, in time of need," and take his example with him into his family; who says, " learn of me, for I am meek and lowly." Whence proceeds a gospel disposition, which is meek and quiet.

Now then, if there be any in this honourable relation, " HEAD OF THE WIFE, EVEN AS CHRIST IS HEAD OF THE CHURCH," who with their mouths shew much love to " the grace of GOD that bringeth salvation to all men that hath appeared," who are so far from soberly attending to its teaching " to deny ungodliness and worldly lusts, and to live soberly, righteously and godly, looking for the blessed hope, and the glorious appearing of the great GOD and our Saviour, JESUS CHRIST; who gave himself for us, that he might redeem us from all iniquity, and purify us unto himself a peculiar people zealous of good works," that they give themselves over to ungodliness and worldly lusts, in such a manner, as to neglect their business, their means of providing for the temporal salvation and comfort of their families for idle company, and gaming, till pinched with want, they are fretful and profane in their families, to a degree, that would be a scandal to heathens, whereby the name of GOD and his doctrines are blasphemed. I dare to appeal to their consciences, upon sober reflection (which they must come to, whether they will or no) whether their hearts don't die within them and become as a stone.

I was looking in my own mind, whether there were not a deception some-how attending the temptations, by which these persons are carried away. Perhaps they will say, they thank GOD they are not as other men,—worldly, covetous, afraid of spending a little time or a little money; for their part they don't desire to have their hearts over-charged with cares of this

this life, &c. But do they not see, that this very practice involves them and their families in the utmost perplexity? What, though they may sometimes appear to gain, hath not divine truth said, " wealth gotten by vanity shall be diminished?" Yes, it shall. Divine power is engaged in the cause of divine truth, and it shall be accomplished. Perhaps in this very instance in which you gain, it is fulfilled respecting some other family.

When JESUS CHRIST exhorted his disciples, " Take heed lest your hearts be over charged with surfeiting and drunkenness, and cares of this life, and that day come upon you unawares," did he not give an example of diligence in working the work of him that sent him? Says he, " my meat is to do the will of him that sent me, and to finish his work." Is it not the character of his spouse? " She worketh willingly with her hands, she looketh well to the ways of her houshold, and eateth not the bread of idleness." And doth not his Apostles direct his disciples, 1st of *Thessalonians*, iv. 11, 12, " That ye study to be quiet and do your own business, and work with your own hands, that ye may walk honestly towards them that are without, and ye may have lack of nothing." 2d of *Thessalonians*, iii. 11, 12, " We hear that there are some that walk disorderly, working not at all, but are busy bodies,; now them that are such, we command and exhort, by our LORD JESUS, that with quietness they work, and eat their own bread." *Ephesians*, iv. 28, " Rather let him labour, working with his hands the things that is good, that he might have to give to him that needeth." In this the Apostle was an example, 1st of *Thessalonians*, ii. 9, " For labouring night and day, because we would not be chargeable unto any of you, we preached unto you the gospel of GOD." *Acts* xx. 34, 35, " These hands have ministered to my necessities, and to them that were

were with me : So labouring, ye ought to support the weak, and to remember the words of our LORD JESUS, how he said it is more blessed to give than to receive."

Let these sayings sink down into our ears, and let us remember the exhortation, *Romans* xiii. 13, 14, " Let us walk honestly as in the day, not in rioting and drunkenness, not in chambering and wantonness, not in strife and envy, but put ye on the LORD JESUS CHRIST, and make not provision for the flesh, to fulfil the lusts thereof." 'Tis all day with him; we are naked and open before him; " If I say the darkness shall cover me, even the night shall be light about me; yea, the darkness hideth not from thee, but the night shineth as the day; the darkness and the light are both alike to thee."

As the duty of the husband is now in view, I would take a little more particular notice of the Apostle *Peter's* comprehensive address to them, all contained in one verse, 1st epistle, iii. 7, " Likewise ye husbands dwell with them according to knowledge, giving honour unto the wife as to the weaker vessel, and as being heirs together of the grace of life, that your prayers be not hindered."

" Dwell with them according to knowledge." This may import the knowledge of the mystery contained in the marriage union : as it is a figure of the union of CHRIST and the church, the knowledge of the love, care, compassion, and tenderness, that JESUS CHRIST shews to his church, as an example to the husband, and of what his word and the nature of the marriage union binds upon them."

." Giving honour to the wife as to the weaker vessel." The Apostle says, " If one member suffer, all the members suffer with it; and if one member be honoured, all the members rejoice with it." 'Tis true here, if the head and husband give honor to the
wife,

wife, all the sensible parts of the family rejoice; if she frequently, and without cause, suffer his displeasure, all the family suffer herein. But how may I understand this expression, " honor as to the weaker vessel?" When I look into the house, I see the weaker vessels, the glass, the china, honored with the most attention, the safest and most honorable place assigned to them; they are handled with the greatest care and tenderness; and in *Isaiah* xxii. from the 15th, I read, that when Shebna, who looked upon himself as the nail fastened in the sure place, should be removed, cut down and fall, and the burden on it broken, God would fasten Eliakim, as a type of JESUS CHRIST, as a nail in a sure place; " And they shall hang on him all the glory of his Father's house, all vessels of small quantity, from the vessels of cups, even to all the vessels of flaggons." Here is honour to the weaker vessels. Hence the honour to the wife, denotes the care and tenderness with which she is to be treated; and in all her fears, distresses, and perplexities, to be put in mind of the nail in the sure place, that can never be cut down, and fall.

This is agreeable to what follows: " And as being heirs together of the grace of life." The grace of life, is the grace that reigns through righteousness to eternal life, by JESUS CHRIST our LORD; which comes not by works of righteousness which we have done, but according to his mercy. The idea of heirship, is the idea of inheriting what was not our own, by the will of another. Heirs together of the grace of life, carries the mutual obligation that the grace of the gospel brings us under, to obedience to him in our mutual duties one to another.

" That your prayers be not hindered." The direction, 1st of *Peter*, iv. 7, " Be ye therefore sober, and watch unto prayer," together with the repeated exhortations of JESUS CHRIST, to watch and pray, shews the duty of watchfulness against every thing whereby our prayers may be hindered; and as Jesus Christ, in *Mark* xi. 52, says, " When ye stand praying, forgive, if ye have ought against any," we may easily see that the contrary spirit must hinder mutual prayer; for where envy and strife is, there is confusion and every evil work. That your prayers be not hindered, may have referrence to mutual prayer in the church, which ought to be attended in the exercise of fervent charity, and which may be marred, weakened or broken, by an indulged carriage, unbecoming the gospel of Christ; in which case the direction of Jesus Christ, " If thou bring thy gift to the altar, and there remember that thy brother hath ought against thee, leave there thy gift before the altar, and go thy way, first be reconciled to thy brother, and then come and offer thy gift," ought to be attended to.—It may also have referrence to their mutual prayers in the family, as their circumstances, opportunity, and sense of divine mercy, may call them thereunto: For we have direction to pray with all prayer and supplication in the spirit; and in every thing, by prayer and supplication with thanksgiving, to be making our requests known to God; and it must be the mutual duties of husbands and wives, to guard against that conduct which would hinder the mutual enjoyment of such a privilege.

In what has been brought to view, the scriptures, in their most obvious meaning, have been attended to, as knowing they come with the authority of Jesus Christ, who is Lord of all. The authority of the Apostles is the authority of Christ, as he has connected them with himself; so that he that despises these their exhortations, despiseth not man, but God. And sure I am, that an attention to them, is the surest way to domestic happiness. I have often thought, that if two persons come together in the relation

lation of husband and wife, that wished to live happily in that relation, they could walk by no better rules, even supposing they did not believe the scriptures; but in that case they would have but the body or the letter, without the spirit. The honor, the nearness, the endeared affection, and the obligations mutually arising in that relation, cannot be fully seen but as they center in CHRIST JESUS, in his union with, love to, and care of, his church; in whom the man is not without the woman, nor the woman without the man: " For, OF HIM, and TO HIM, and THROUGH HIM, are all things;" To whom be glory for ever.

AMEN.

To this I would subjoin some thoughts by another hand, collected together some years past.

ON MARRIAGE.

I.

WHEN such as we attempt to sing,
The praises of our heavenly King,
His mercies rise so fast to view,
That still the theme is always new.

II.

In early days his Godlike care
Of all his creatures, did appear;
Each of his kind an help-meet found,
To pass the days successive round.

III.

When man alone no partner knew,
This want was in his Maker's view;
Whose love and pow'r the want suppli'd,
From sleeping Adam's tender side,
Whose rib he form'd a lovely bride,

This

IV.

This good obtain'd, how bless'd had been
Man's happy state, unstain'd by sin ?
But too, too soon th' unthinking pair,
By Satan's arts beguiled were.

V.

From this foil'd source did soon arise,
Lusts of the flesh, the world and eyes ;
Whose all predominating power,
The happiest days of man devour ;

VI.

Disturb the joys of social life,
And discord spread t'wixt man and wife ;
But praise and thanks to thee shall rise,
The joyful sound shall reach the skies ;

VII.

That peace and good on earth proclaim'd,
And man, th' ungrateful subject, nam'd,
Whom boundless mercy doth arrest,
And thus compelleth to be bless'd.

VIII.

Which brings to view eternal joy,
Which can't admit of an alloy :
To purchase which the SON of GOD
Did shed his own most precious blood.

IX.

This glorious news proclaim'd abroad,
Makes wandering man return to GOD ;
And thus the mind from earth is rear'd,
And with eternal joy is chear'd.

X.

Thus o'er this short, contracted span,
Which is assign'd to mortal man,
The gospel casts a smile of peace,
And bids our anxious cares to cease.

XI.

By this the husband and the wife,
Are taught to pass the days of life :

Their

Their duty and their happiness,
Most closely here connected is:
XII.
Each tender passion doth revive,
And mutual duties keep alive.
Th' unbounded love which CHRIST hath shown,
Who for his church his life laid down,
XIII.
Is to the husband brought to view,
A pattern of affection true.
The church, his spotless bride, likewise,
Doth as the wife's example rise.
XIV.
'Tis thus the gospel doth revive,
And keep each gen'rous thought alive;
Arrests those lusts which bitter life,
And teach to live like man and wife.

APPENDIX.

APPENDIX.

Containing thoughts occasioned by the provisions of the table.

Upon looking over the time calculated for family enjoyment, happiness, &c. mentioned in the 221st page; some thoughts occurred on the provision of the table, which swelled beyond the compass of a marginal note, and are brought in by way of appendix, as follows.

WHEN the head of a family retiring from his business to his meals, has the happiness to make them all set down around him, and the example of JESUS CHRIST and the apostle, to direct, excite, embolden, and encourage him to give thanks before them all, if his mind is led to understand the glory of the gospel, what can hinder his breaking forth into praise, for all spiritual blessings in heavenly things, in CHRIST JESUS, as they are brought to his view in the bounties of providence on his table; yea, though it be at a time of poverty, and there be only bread and water, to preserve life, till some further provisions can be procured, yet even that would point us to the bread and water of life, for even they were made by him, and for him, and do silently, eminently and constantly hold forth his glory; if with them I have a piece of a broiled fish, shall I be discontent because I have no more, and seem as if the meal was not large enough to call me to thanksgiving; or shall I not rather remember it is the same with which JESUS fed the multitudes, after he had given thanks; the same that was laid on the coals, *John* xxi. 9, to which he called his disciples to " come and dine," verse 12; or would my discontented mind find fault with my bread,

bread, because I cannot obtain every day the finest of the wheat, let it rather remind me, that it was barley bread with which JESUS fed the multitude, *John* vi. 9. If the adversary, whose name is legion, for they are many, attempt like the Midianites that typified them, *Judges* vi, to destroy the increase of the earth, by introducing murmuring, discontent and uneasiness, instead of thanksgiving at my table, may this barley bread with which the multitudes were fed, remind me of what the barley cake did, in the host of the Midianites, and be as efficacious to take away my murmuring; for will it not pierce my heart with grief and shame that I should murmur at that for which my Lord gives thanks! Can I have the least appearance of a servant or disciple, to be thus above my master and Lord, while a " perfect disciple shall be as his master." *Luke* vi. 40. Herein is the love perfect in us, that we should have boldness in the day of judgment, for as he is, so are we in this world." 1st of *John* iv. 17, Methinks here is also a further lesson for me; when a lad had only five barley loaves, and two small fishes, they were all at the service of JESUS CHRIST, of whom and for whom he had them. If I am favoured with meat, it is calculated to lead me to the meat that endureth to eternal life, which the Son of man shall give, who says, " my flesh is meat indeed." If I have a dinner of herbs, and the sense of divine love exciting me and my family to love one another, it is better than a stalled ox, and hatred to my GOD, and family therewith: Shocking the thought! that my ungreatful heart is capable of this! If I cast my eye on the salt, while I reach after it, it would silently remind me of the favour of the knowledge of CHRIST, made manifest by his apostles in every place, " which is the salt of the covenant of GOD, that never should be lacking," typified by that which was to accompany all the offerings of the children of Israel, and which

was

was given them in Ezra's time, by Darius, chap. vi. 9, and by Artaxerxes, chap. vii. 22, at the commandment of the prieſt, without preſcribing, pointing forward to the favour of the knowledge of CHRIST, which my ſalt would remind me of: This turns my mind to an inſtruction we have in *Ezra* iv. 14, " Now becauſe we are ſalted with the ſalt of the palace, it was not meet for us to ſee the kings diſhonour:" This is the inſtruction my ſalt, which was created by him, is of him, and for him, would communicate to me. Is my table furniſhed, and am I favoured with roots, and will they not turn my mind to the " root of Jeſſe," *Iſaiah* xi. 10, " the root out of a dry ground." chap. liii. 2, " the root of the righteous that yieldeth or giveth," *Proverbs* xii. 12. For my roots were by him, they are from him and for him, to hold forth his glory. Do I find my table enriched with fruits, the fruit of the vine; have I a cup of wine there, ſurely it ſo fully points to JESUS CHRIST, that as oft as I drink it I ought to remember him, whether it be at the LORD's ſupper, or at my own table. Do I ſee the beans, peas and ſquaſhes on my table, either of theſe are the fruit of the buſh, and would lead my mind to the angel of the LORD, or the agent Jehovah, that appeared to Moſes in the buſh, which burned with fire and was not conſumed, which cauſed Moſes to turn aſide, to behold with attention, when he was told to put off his ſhoes from off his feet, in token of reverence and reſignation to his LORD, which he did, and was then inſtructed in the meaning, which led Moſes to underſtand, that though the poſterity of Abrahram, Iſaac and Jacob, were in bondage in Egypt, ſighing and groaning, and was expelled a ſtranger in Midian, a ſtrange land, yet GOD ſaw their trouble and heard their cry, and ſaid unto him, " I am the GOD of thy father, the GOD of Abraham, of Iſaac and of Jacob, this is my name forever, and my memorial unto all ages;"

ages;" I that delivered Abraham, Isaac and Jacob in all their distresses, particularly that saved Jacob, and his family when in danger of being burnt up with famine, by bringing them into Egypt, and giving them there the blessing of Joseph, with which he blessed his land in the seven plenteous years, even the sweetness of heaven, the dew, and the deep, and the sweet increase of the sun and the moon, the precious things of the mountains and hills, and the precious things of the earth, and the abundance thereof; whereby the good will of him that dwelt in the bush, rested on Joseph, and upon the top of the head of him that was separated from his brethren, as a type of him in whom all fulness dwells.

" I AM that I AM, I am the God of Abraham, of Isaac, and of Jacob; this is my name forever, and my memorial throughout all generations; I know the sorrows of their posterity, therefore I am come down to deliver them."—And is there not in this name and memorial joy to the whole earth? Is he the God of the Jews only, and not of the Gentiles also? Yes, " even of the Gentiles also; the God of the whole earth shall he be called." The promise to Abraham is, " In thy seed shall all the nations of the earth be blessed." So that there is not held forth to Moses in the burning bush, the distressed state of the children of Israel and their deliverance only, but of the whole human race, who by the curse of the fiery law, appeared in danger of being burnt up without remedy; but JESUS " was made under the law, to redeem them that were under the law;" he sustained the fire, and freed us from being consumed. His sustaining of, and deliverance from it was the beginning of revenges on the enemy; on which the call is, " Rejoice O ye nations, his people." In view of which, in the xlviith *Psalm,* " All people" are called to " clap their hands, and shout with the voice of triumph; for the Lord, most High, terrible, a Great King over all the earth, he hath subdued the people under us, and the nations under our feet." The nation and people of the Jews, apprehended themselves above the Gentiles, and despised them; but since " God is gone up with a shout, the Lord with the sound of the trumpet," it is evident he hath chosen our inheritance for us, " the excellency of Jacob, whom he loved."

Our inheritance: All people, the Gentiles, who are fellow heirs, and of the same body, and partakers of his promises in Christ by the gospel, and all people are called on, Sing praises to God; sing praises; sing praises unto our King, sing praises; for God is King of all the earth; sing ye praises that have understanding: God reigneth over the heathen; God sitteth upon his holy throne."—Agreeable to *Psalm* ii. where it is said, " Yet have I set my King upon my holy hill of Zion: Thou art my Son, this day have I begotten thee," (referring to the resurrection) " ask of me, and I will give the heathen thine inheritance, and the utmost parts of the earth thy possession." Upon his resurrection, it is manifest they are his purchased possession. This King now manifestly appears to reign in righteousness: " I have set my King upon my holy hill of Zion." So in the above xlviith *Psalm*, on his ascension, he is " King of all the earth," he " reigneth over the heathen," he " sitteth on his holy throne," he is come whose right it is; thus " the princes of the people are gathered together, the people of the God of Abraham;" he not only shielded Abraham's family in their affliction, but " the shields of the earth belong unto the Lord; he is greatly exalted."

Is there not a lesson for me, under my distressing trials, of what sort soever, to realize the reverence and subjection that is due to my Lord, as in the case of Moses, *Exodus* iii. 5, and *Joshua* v. 15, resigning myself

self up to him as not my own, but redeemed by him? Now this was the manner in Ifrael, concerning redeeming and changing—to eftablifh all things, a man plucked off his fhoe, and gave it to his neighbour, and this was a fure witnefs in Ifrael, that he had refigned his right, and it was the property of him that redeemed it; which I am of my LORD Redeemer, and ought to realize it with reverend fubmiffion, under every affliction, knowing that in his everlafting name, his memorial through all generations, there is a fountain of all-fufficient confolation.

Am I prefented with the fruit of the apple-tree, to bring to my mind the tree of life, which bear twelve fruits, and yielded her fruit every month; which fruit was for meat, and the leaf for medicine; "the leaves of the tree for the healing of the nations?" If my apple fhould remind me of the fruit of the forbidden tree, by which fin and death entered, it will alfo lead me to CHRIST, by and for whom the apple-tree was created; for as the apple-tree among the trees of the wood, fo is my beloved among the fons." I have all in this tree; for the fruit is for food and the leaf for medicine. What may I underftand by the leaves of the tree? In a natural fenfe, it fhows that which evidences of what fort the tree is: Thus the fig tree was known it had leaves; and as the leaves of a fig-tree, were fewed together for aprons, after the fall, to hide nakednefs and fhame, as has been the manner ever fince, " to cover with a covering, but not of GOD's fpirit," to go about to eftablifh our own righteoufnefs, which covering is too narrow, a man cannot wrap himfelf in it; fo when JESUS came, the LORD our righteoufnefs, he faith to the fig-tree, the emblem of feeking life by our own righteoufnefs, " never man eat fruit of thee henceforth for ever, and immediately the fig-tree withered away;" but his leaf fhall not wither—his profeffion.

The

The truth he heard of GOD at this baptifm, " this is my beloved Son, in whom I am well pleafed," the truth he taught through his life and miniftry, that he witneffed a good confeffion to, before Pontius Pilate, that was witneffed in his refurrection, whereby he is " declared the Son of GOD, with power according to the fpirit of holinefs," this truth, which Peter made confeffion of, on which he will build his church, is, I apprehend, what we are led to for the meaning of the " leaves of the tree, that are for the healing of the nations," whofe virtues fhall prevail, 'till " there be no more curfe."

PART

PART II.

THOUGHTS ON EDUCATION.

ADDRESSED TO PARENTS.

Ye honored, respectful sires,
   A motive now appears,
Of cautious circumspection to'ards
   Your children young in years.

Provoke them not to wrath, lest they
   Discourag'd should appear;
But by the nurture of the Lord,
   Their tender spirits cheer.

He in his word doth nurture give,
   And admonition too;
Let it imparted be to them,
   With faithfulness by you.

And may you ever sit with joy,
   At our Emanuel's feet,
To learn with wisdom and with love,
   The little ones to treat.

PARENT and child comprehends more endearing, engaging, and respectful ideas, than I can conceive, much less express the fulness of: But when I think of them, they appear as harmonious notes in agreeable musick, which may delight the ear of him who cannot give them their proper sound. Notwithstanding, I shall attempt something that may be useful in conducting in that endeared relation.

It is the place and duty of a child to be in his parents presence with reverence and delight; and it is the duty of the parent to guard against a childless familiarity, that would tend to make the child humoursome, and bring the parent into contempt; and against such an austerity as would make their presence a dread which the child would seek to avoid. It is their duty also to guard against ill names, and such phrases and expressions as would intimate to the minds

minds of the children, that their parents have not the fear of God before their eyes. If inſtead of the paternal, endearing expreſſions of—my dear child, my ſon, my daughter—it is—you little cur, you dog, you plague—or the like ; it is, what ſhall I call it! a violent rape on the morals of the child. Such children are early capable of reaſoning after this manner—if I am ſuch a creature, what is my father that begat me, or my mother that brought me forth? And they ſoon get emboldened to uſe the ſame expreſſions, at leaſt to thoſe that offend them; which is productive of wrath and ſtrife, and promotes an undeſirable hardneſs and harſhneſs of temper and manners.

Parents muſt likewiſe guard againſt a cuſtomary threatening which alienates the mind, and ſowers the temper of the children, and produces contempt of the parents, when they ſee their threatenings are only verbal, never to be feared except when they get into a paſſion. Threatenings ought to be given out with great caution and care; to be what will be the parents indiſpenſible duty in the threatened caſe: They ought to be confined to moral evils; ſuch as apparent wilful diſobedience, lying, cheating, or profaneneſs; any thing that is an apparent ſin againſt God or our neighbour: And when judicioufly given out, they ought to be punctually executed, not in paſſion and anger, but in love and faithfulneſs. And when any accidental miſcarriage takes place, ſuch as the breaking an earthen veſſel, or a ſquare of glaſs, it ſhould meet with a gentle admonition, never carried ſo high as to tempt the children to lie to hide it, for fear of the wrath of their parents.

Here I would take notice of the apoſtolick direction, *Epheſians* vi. 4, " And ye fathers provoke not your children to wrath, leaſt they be diſcouraged, but bring them up in the nurture and admonition of the Lord."

" Left

"Left they be discouraged." Doth it not include in it every thing in the education of children, that would give them a dreadful discouraging idea of God, or of their natural parents, so as to cause them secretly to wish they could hide themselves from him or them, or to make them unhappy, at the thought of being always in the divine presence (a source of security and happiness where his name is known) or at the thought of coming into the presence of their parents.

The scripture account that God is love, and the way in which it is made manifest, is calculated to shew our highest happiness in his presence and favour; and what is to be most feared, is that which will displease him, and procure his frown. In like manner, if parents conduct by the divine rule, their children will be happiest in their presence and favour, and it must be a great punishment to be turned away from them, as a token of displeasure, but for an hour. But when, on the contrary, they cannot come where they are, without some hard names or dreadful threatenings, they are provoked and discouraged.

"But bring them up in the nurture and admonition of the LORD." Nurture conveys the idea of nursing or nourishment, agreeable to 1st of *Thessalonians*, ii. 7, "We were gentle among you, as a nurse cherisheth her children;" 1st of *Peter*, ii. 2, "As new born babes desire the sincere milk of the word, that ye may grow thereby;" 1st of *Timothy*, iv. 6, "Nourished up in the words of faith and good doctrine." Admonition conveys the idea, to counsel, advise, instruct, warn and reprove.

The admonition of the LORD, leads my mind to 1st of *Corinthians*, x. 11, Where the Apostle, speaking of the things written in the Old Testament, says, "they are written for our admonition." The scriptures of the new began to be spoken by the LORD, and

and was confirmed to us by them that heard him. They are the admonition of the Lord; not only the sayings of CHRIST himself, but of his Apostles, that he connects with himself, " He that heareth you, heareth me;" are the admonition of the LORD, as is expressed 1st of *Thessalonians*, ii. 11, " As ye know how we exhorted, and comforted, and charged, every one of you, as a father his children, that ye would walk worthy of God, who hath called you to his kingdom and glory."

1st. For nurture. Let the children have the sincere milk of the word, that they may grow thereby; let them suck and be satisfied with these breasts of consolation. Only let us look into the various passages, in which JESUS CHRIST spake of, to, or about little children: See *Matthew* xviii. 1, to 14, chap. xix. 14, 15. *Matthew* xxi. 16. *Mark* xi. 13, to 16. *Luke* xviii. 14—16. And see if there is any thing besides glad tidings of great joy to them: If it be so, let the dear children know it as soon as they are capable of understanding; let them be " nourished up in the works of faith," in those truths that are to be believed, " and good doctrine;" the good news, the glad tidings that the GOSPEL contains. Or is there any threatenings of eternal damnation to children, by the Apostles of CHRIST? If not, who dare ring them in their ears!

There is indeed, temporal destruction, with the greatest infamy, threatened disobedient children, *Proverbs* xxx. 17, which is a part of the second branch: The admonition of the LORD so is, *Luke* xv. 15, where the prodigal, from a father's house, where is bread enough, and to spare, is brought to be a poor hungry swine-feeder.

So is every caution and warning through the scriptures, especially the New Testament, which the parents ought to be acquainted with, and bring to the children's children's view, for warning, reproving, counselling, advising, and instructing on all occasions, particularly upon any thing that is sinful: The divine admonition ought to be brought immediately from the lively oracles, and they convinced it is disagreeable to the will of their Creator, Preserver, and redeemer, on whom their all depends.

For an example of admonition, we have one drawn to our hands by the Apostle, 1st of *Corinthians*, 1 to 11, which being well considered, may help parents to make use of other scriptures in a similar way, as there may be occasion.

Thus have I given some thoughts on the education of children, to whom I wish the blessedness of an early acquaintance with what God has done for them, and their obligations of gratitude to him. 'Tis the duty of parents, from childhood, to acquaint them with the holy scriptures, wherein these things are contained (as Timothy was) " which are able to make wise unto salvation, through faith in CHRIST JESUS:" 'Tis with him to communicate the knowledge of himself, according to his good pleasure: To whom be glory and dominion, for ever.

AMEN.

PART III.

An INQUIRY *into the* CASE *of* CHILDREN, *with an* EXHORTATION TO THEM.

MATTHEW xviii. 4.—*Even so it is not the will of my Father which is in Heaven, that one of these little ones should perish.*

Third epistle of JOHN, 4:—*I have no greater joy than to hear that my children walk in the truth.*

WHEN I meditate on the case of children, and propose an exhortation to them, instead of being governed by the various opinions there are about them, I would turn to the scriptures, and form my apprehensions from them, that I may know what ground there is for a word of exhortation to them. In *Matthew* xviii. 5, and *Mark* ix. 37, JESUS CHRIST says, "Whosoever shall receive one such little child in my name, receiveth me." One such;—it was a child he took in his arms, in *Mark*; a little child in *Matthew*: And in *Luke* xviii. 15, they brought infants, and JESUS said, "Suffer the little children to come unto me, and forbid them not, for of such is the kingdom of Heaven." How comes infants constituted of the kingdom of Heaven? *Matthew* xviii. 11, shews JESUS CHRIST came to save them; therefore, "take heed that ye despise not one of these little ones; for I say unto you, that in Heaven, their angels do always behold the face of my father, which is in Heaven; for the son of man is come to save that which is lost." Their angels; What is the office of the holy angels? "Are they not all ministring spirits, sent forth to minister for them that shall be heirs of salvation?" If their angels always behold the face of the GOD and Father of our Lord JESUS CHRIST, who is in Heaven, doth it not convey the idea, that nothing can be done againſt them, in a way of deſpiſing them, but what muſt be immediately known there? And if angels miniſter to infants, are they not heirs of ſalvation? How came they heirs; are they not by nature children of wrath; are they not loſt in Adam, their head; how came they heirs of ſalvation? Verſe 11 informs us, " For the ſon of man came to ſave that which was loſt." Though they are really loſt in union with the firſt Adam, and however they may appear loſt in their own utter helpleſſneſs, and the various diſtreſſes and miſeries, even death itſelf, that they are expoſed to; yet if the ſon of man is come to ſave that which is loſt; has taken hold of them, taken their nature into union with himſelf, and conſtituted them of the kingdom of GOD, by virtue of his own righteouſneſs, who ſays, *Luke* xviii. 16, " for of ſuch is the kingdom of GOD," then " take heed that ye deſpiſe not one of theſe little ones." Are they not deſpiſed by thoſe that freely and frequently ſpeak of the everlaſting damnation of infants? Do they get it from any word of JESUS CHRIST concerning them? Why is it ſo? That they are loſt is readily acknowledged; but the ſon of man came to ſave that which was loſt: Will he not accompliſh his deſign; is he not mighty to ſave? He is the ſhepherd that looks after that which is loſt," that " takes the lambs into his arms, and carries them in his boſom:" " How think ye, if a man have an hundred ſheep, if one of them be gone aſtray, doth he not leave the ninety-nine, and goeth into the mountains and ſeeketh that which is gone aſtray; and if ſo be that he find it, verily I ſay unto you, that he rejoiceth more of that than of the ninety-nine that went not aſtray: EVEN ſo it is not the will of your Father who is in Heaven, that one of thoſe little ones ſhould periſh." If JESUS Chriſt came to ſave them, and it is not the will of

your

your Father in Heaven that one of them should perish, must not the despisers of them, that so freely treat of their damnation, suspect themselves as advocates for the destroyer? Do they not prevail to draw a veil over the power and compassion of the Saviour, and destroy the peace of thousands?

It may not be amiss to illustrate this, by bringing in the testimony of the prophets and apostles. When God, by his prophet *Jeremiah,* was comforting ancient Israel in what he would do for them, chap. xxxi. 1, to 14, the ground and reason of which, we have in the 11th verse, " For the Lord hath redeemed Jacob, and ransomed him from the hand of stronger than he." Having redeemed and ransomed him— " He that scattered Israel, will gather him, and keep him as a shepherd his flock: Therefore they shall come and sing in the height of Zion ; and they shall not sorrow any more at all ; then shall the virgin rejoice in the dance, both young men and old men together ; for I will turn their mourning into joy, and make them rejoice from their sorrow, and I will satiate the soul of the priest with fatness, and my people shall be satisfied with my goodness, saith the Lord." That this good news may reach the bottom of their affliction and sorrow, expressed in verse 15, in a prophetic view, of the destruction of the children of Bethlehem, by Herod, it is said, verse 16, " refrain thy voice from weeping, and thine eyes from tears, for thy work shall be rewarded, saith the Lord; and they shall come again from the land of the enemy, and there is hope in thine end, saith the Lord, that thy children shall come again to their own border."— Death was the enemy where they went ; from which they shall come again, and inherit their own border, in him, or by virtue of union with him, " who through death, destroys him that had the power of death ; that is the devil." " Thus saith the Lord, even the

captives

captives of the mighty shall be taken away, and the prey of the terrible shall be delivered; for I will contend with him that contendeth with thee, and I will save thy children, *Isaiah* xlix. 25," " They shall come again from the land of the enemy."

" And there is hope in thine end that thy children shall come again to their own border." What is their own border? 'Tis the fruit of the purchase of JESUS CHRIST, called their own in virtue of their union to him. To this I would add the apostle Peter, in *Acts* ii. 39, " For the promise is to you and to your children, and to all that are afar, of even as many as the Lord our GOD shall call." The promise to you and your children, as extensive as the call of the gospel, which is directed to every creature, and expressed in this language by the prophet, " Look unto me, and be ye saved, all the ends of the earth."

It may not be unsuitable to take notice here of the error of many parents, and others, who comfort themselves concerning their infant children, when they die, from their innocency, saying, they are undoubtedly gone to happiness; and rob the Saviour of his glory, and themselves of any true comfort. If they would think a few minutes, if the salvation by JESUS CHRIST is excluded, and they gone to happiness by virtue of their own innocency, it is a happiness that they themselves can never be admitted to; " for there is no other name under Heaven among men, whereby they can be saved, but the name of JESUS." They seem not to attend to the apostle; he hath concluded all under sin, that he might have mercy upon all."

The apostle John, when writing to the disciples, under the character of little children, says, " I write unto you, little children, because your sins are forgiven, for his name sake: I write unto you, little children, because you have known the Father." The

Father

Father is not known to any, but to whomsoever the son will reveal him. When they understood the forgivness of sins for his name's sake, they know the father: Thus is he, who is love, made manifest. And this is what little children in CHRIST's school are taught by an aged apostle, "I write unto you, little children, because your sins are forgiven you, for his name's sake" which he lays in the foundation of his exhortations to them, "Love not the world," &c.

I am aware of an objection against what I have brought to view. How can these things be so, when we see children, as soon as they grow up, turn after their own lusts, after "the course of this world, according to the prince of the power of the air, the spirit that now worketh in the children of disobedience?" Do we not see children and youth soon arrive at a shocking pitch of profaneness and immorality? Yes, verily, multitudes of them appear to be in the snare of the devil, and led captive by him, at his will: But whose are they? Do they belong to him who hath insnared them, and leads them captive; yea, tho' he so blind their minds as to lead them to profane the name of their rightful owner, and to say he shall not reign over us, doth it alienate the property of them? May they not be told with truth and propriety, that they are not their own, they belong to JESUS CHRIST, to whom they must give an account of their conduct, who will bring every knee of them to bow to him; that they are working out their own shame and confusion of face before him? May they not be called to repent; to return to their rightful proprietor, owner and LORD?

But how repent, unless they are wrong in their alienation to JESUS CHRIST, and in their walking according to the spirit that now worketh in the children of disobedience? How return, if they have not gone astray; if they belong not to their LORD Redeemer, er, if he be not the shepherd and bishop of their souls? Is not this idea held up in every call to repentance? *Isaiah* xliv. 22, " Return, for I have redeemed thee." *Jeremiah* iii. 12, " Return, thou back-sliding Israel, saith the LORD;" 14, " Turn, O back-sliding children, saith the LORD, for I am married unto you;" 22, " Return, ye back-sliding children, I will heal your backslidings." The idea of his right as Redeemer, Husband and Father, is implied in the call to return, and every call to repentance supposes mercy: " There is forgiveness with thee, that thou mayest be feared," and we cannot conceive of mercy but in a consistency with justice: If justice is satisfied, mercy flows without obstruction, " Return, for I have redeemed thee."

Besides, as they are in the snare of the Devil, led captive by him at his will, " for this purpose was the son of God manifest, that he might destroy the works of the Devil."—When the prophet *Isaiah* introduces the inquiry, chap. xlix. 24, " Shall the prey be taken from the mighty, or * the lawful captive delivered?" † The answer is, verse 25, " But thus saith the Lord, the captives of the mighty shall be taken away, and the prey of the terrible shall be delivered, for I will contend with him, that contendeth with thee, and I will save thy children." He will not leave them in his hands; no, not one of the hundred; the shepherd will not lose one of the hundred sheep; he came to save that which is lost; he came to do his Father's will, and it is not his will " that one of these little ones should perish."

Thus much OF CHILDREN; what follows is addressed TO CHILDREN.

Children—

---

* Hebrew, in the bible margin, " The captivity of the just."

† By " the lawful captive," or " the captivity of the just," I understand, that those who were taken captive by the mighty adversary, were taken from where they lawfully belonged, led captive from the just one, their rightful owner.

Children—Let me ask your attention to what is laid before you, simply from the scriptures,—Are these things so? If so, methinks it is "glad tidings of great joy," and shews the ground of obligation that lies upon you to look upon yourselves as not your own, as not at liberty to walk after your own lusts, as not belonging to Satan, however he may seek to devour or insnare you,—you belong to JESUS CHRIST, OUR CREATOR, PRESERVER, AND REDEEMER, he has bought you with his blood, and therefore you are under the highest obligations to "glorify him in your spirits and bodies which are his;" and is it not in this view, most ungrateful, base and wicked, to walk contrary thereunto? I have thought whether it were not the ignorance of children about what our LORD and SAVIOUR is to them, has done, and is doing for them, that was the cause of their sinking so low into the mire and filth of profaneness and immorality; while a sense of love always carries with it, a sense of obligation to grateful obedience: Where this is the case, it would be natural to turn our minds to the exhortation of the apostle to children, "children obey your parents in the Lord for this is right." When we consider the wretched, helpless circumstances we come into the world in, and view the GOD and Father of our Lord JESUS CHRIST, the Father of mercies, giving paternal love, tenderness and compassion to our parents, and by this means, daily loading us with his benefits; as soon as we are capable of reflecting, it must give us a view of obligation to gratitude and thankfulness, which cannot be expressed, without a sense of obligation to obedience; therefore, children "obey your parents in the Lord, for this is right, it must commend itself to your own consciences as right.

I wish to unfold something of the meaning of this expression; if I could, it would discover such obligations

gations as could not be broken through, without doing violence to our own consciences, our peace and comfort, for it must lead to a united view of what our JESUS CHRIST has done, and is doing for us, and what he makes our parents to us, and does for us by their means, which would lead our minds to all the thought, care, toil and labour of the father, and to the compassionate tenderness of the mother, who often, with much pain and pleasure, nourishes her offspring from her own body, both night and day; well might the apostle say, " children obey your parents in the Lord, for this is right." Here also is a direction to children, when they come to years capable of understanding the will of GOD in CHRIST JESUS concerning them; if ever the parents, through the prevalency of temptation, command any thing contrary to his revealed will, to remember the words of the apostle to the rulers who commanded them contrary to the will of the Lord, " we ought to obey GOD rather than man," and dutifully to remind their parents of the reasons of their conduct; to obey in any thing contrary to his revealed will, would not be to obey them " in the LORD."

" Honor thy father and mother," which is the first commandment, with promise, " that it may be well with thee, and that thou mayest live long on the earth;" a contrary conduct, slights the divine authority that commands, and the divine promise annexed thereto; it slights our own welfare, and forfeits life upon earth. What base folly, guilt and shame, doth disobedience to parents carry along with it!

When the apostle to the Romans, speaks of GOD's giving over the Gentiles to a reprobate mind, and rehearses what they were filled with which led thereunto, we find in the catalogue, " disobedience to parents," *Romans* i. 30, So when he speaks of the perilous times that should come in the last days, one part of the description is, " disobedience to parents," 2d. of *Timothy* iii. 2.

This is that which, besides the ingratitude, baseness and wickedness that appears in it, has a leading tendency to various others, if not all kinds of vice and wickedness; Therefore, " children obey your parents in the Lord;" Honor thy father and mother, that it may be well with thee, that thou mayest live long upon the earth," even till it please GOD in his providence, to call you by a natural death, in his own time and way, and not hurry yourselves, by your disobedience, into the hands of civil justice, to an untimely death, to which it has a tendency.

When JESUS CHRIST addressed his disciples under the character of little children, *John* xiii. 33, the exhortation he had to give them, to which he thus called their attention, was, verse 34, " a new commandment I give unto you, that ye love one another; as I have loved you, that ye also love one another."— This is the duty of every one, more especially of all who hope for salvation from the love of the Saviour, which ought to excite children to treat one another with kindness and love, not to wish evil to any that offend us, not to " render evil for evil," not to despise those that are poor, but endeavour to think of the forgiveness and condescension of JESUS CHRIST, agreeable to the exhortation of the apostle, *Ephesians* iv. 31, let all bitterness, and wrath, and anger, and clamour, and evil speaking, be put away from you, with all malice, and be ye kind one to another, tender hearted, forgiving one another, even as GOD in CHRIST hath forgiven you."

Here I would take notice of what I have seen in some instances, with sorrow. When young persons have been intrusted with the care of little children, either at home, or to lead them abroad, they have seemed to lose all sense of that kindness and tenderheartedness,

heartedness, of which the apostle speaks; and as it were, cruelly divert themselves with telling the dear little ones frightful stories, and giving out many threatenings to them, until fear and distress has banished every agreeable feeling from their tender breasts, and they burst forth into sobbing and crying; for which they have been called cross—twitched, scolded at, threatened and beaten: Which conduct, in many cases, has been of very hurtful consequences. How contrary is this to the obligations we are under to walk in love one to another!

There is one consideration I would suggest to all that have the care of little children; i. e. what JESUS CHRIST said, " of such is the kingdom of Heaven," and in that remarkable passage, *Mark* ix. 36, 37, " he took a child and set him in the midst of them, and when he had taken him in his arms," (observe the bigness of the child, a child in the arms) " he said unto them, whosoever shall receive one of such children, in my name, receiveth me, and whosoever shall receive me, receiveth him that sent me." Would we treat JESUS CHRIST in the above manner were he upon earth! And will not the above passages warrant us to say that he is now on earth, in the least of these his brethren; so that as ye did unto them, ye did unto him; and on reflection on the above conduct, any of us that have been guilty, on recollecting what we have done when we thought no one saw us, may well be afraid, and say—surely GOD was in the place, and I knew it not.

May the thought ever excite to an attention to the forementioned exhortation, " Let all bitterness and wrath, and anger, and clamour, and evil speaking, be put away." Evil speaking comes from a little member, but " 'Tis a fire, a world of iniquity; it sets on fire the course of nature, and is set on fire of hell," saith the Apostle, *James* iii. 6, It would perhaps

haps be impossible to describe the variety into which this fire blazes and unfolds itself. Without attempting this, I shall just take notice of it, as it discovers itself in profaneness, uncleanness, covetousness, stealing, and lying.

To begin with profaneness.—Can there be any thing more base, ungrateful, and wicked, than to profane that worthy name, which is above every name, in which there is salvation, the just GOD and the Saviour, EMANUEL, GOD with us. We know not God but as he is thus manifest: So there can be no species of profaning that name, but it includes in it the base ingratitude of profaning the Saviour. If the consideration of his being their GOD, was used as an argument against profaneness with ancient Israel, as *Leviticus* xix. 12, " Neither shalt thou profane the name of *thy* God," certainly the grace manifested in the gospel hath the same obligations in it; and opens up a ground of perpetual praise and thanksgiving: And who of us are not at some times constrained to acknowledge it; and with our tongues to bless GOD, even the Father ? Shall we therewith curse our fellow-creatures, " that are made after the similitude of GOD ?" *James* iii. 9, Certainly these things ought not so to be; the grace of the gospel teaches, by precept and example, " to bless them that curse you, bless and curse not, love your enemies; do good to them that hate you, and pray for them that despitefully use and persecute you." Here we are warranted to make use of the Saviour's name, in praying for our enemies; he bids us, and sets the example. How contrary the profane practice of calling on his name to damn those we think injure or displease us! It comes as evidently from the destroyer, our adversary, the devil, as the above-mentioned precepts and examples come from the Saviour. Stop dear child! stop young man, over-heated with passion and resentment,

and

and hurried by temptation! stop one minute and consider which you ought to follow: Hear the apostle, " Let all evil speaking be put away from you, with all malice."

The next branch of evil speaking I would take notice of, is uncleanness. If we consider the warnings and cautions given against it by the apostles of CHRIST,* we must see the the propriety of our children's being warned to shun the appearance of this evil; to shun the speeches, behavior and company, that tends hereunto. What shameful ingratitude doth it discover, when we see our children, who are privileged in their education so as to be able to write their thoughts legibly, defiling the fences, as they pass the streets, with shameful uncleanness! writing what they would at first be afraid to speak, until their minds are hardened by writing, then reading and repeating, until they contract a habit of evil speaking; which has a tendency, as they grow up, to lead after all uncleanness with greediness. I think I may tell them with truth, if they should live two or three times twenty years after, it would not obliterate, but increase the shame that such conduct must produce, upon the remembrance of such follies; for old age has a lively remembrance of what is done in youth, though it forgets later transactions; and the sense of forgiveness doth not take away the ground of shame,

but

---

* See *Galatians* v. 19, *Ephesians* v. 3, to 6; *Colossians* iii. 5, to 8, 1st of *Thessalonians*, iv. 3, to 8, 1st of *Peter*, iv. 2, 3. And in the epistle to the *Corinthians*, the apostle says, " What know ye not that your bodies are the members of CHRIST; shall I then take the members of CHRIST, and make them the members of an harlot? GOD forbid.— What! know ye not that he that is joined to an harlot is one body, for two shall be one flesh; but he that is joined to the Lord is one spirit. Flee fornication: Every sin that a man doth is without the body; but he that committeth fornication, sinneth against his own body. What! know ye not that your body is the temple of the holy ghost in you, which ye have of GOD, and ye are not your own, for ye are bought with a price? Therefore glorify GOD in your body and in your spirit, which are GOD's." 1st of *Corinthians*, vi. 15, to the end.

but increases it, agreeable to *Ezekiel* xvi. 63, "That thou mayst remember and be ashamed and confounded, and never open thy mouth any more because of thy shame, when I am pacified towards thee for all that thou hast done, saith the Lord God." This I would close with the advice of Divine wisdom, *Proverbs* vii. 24 to 27, "Hearken unto me now therefore, O ye children, and attend to the words of my mouth; let not thine heart decline to her ways; go not astray in her paths; for she hath cast down many wounded, yea, many strong have been slain by her: Her house the way to hell, going down to the chambers of death."

I might mention the scripture warnings and cautions against covetousness, stealing and lying. Covetousness in children discovers itself in a fretful uneasiness for what belongs to other children, prompting them to attain it by any means, if it cannot be had, as they say, by fair means, and tempts them to steal, and then to lie to hide the crime. The story of Achan is left on record for warning and admonition, which we have in *Joshua* vii. particularly verses 20 and 21, where Achan says, "Indeed I have sinned against the Lord God of Israel, when I saw among the spoils a goodly Babylonish garment, and two hundred shekels of silver, and a wedge of gold, of fifty shekles weight, then I coveted them and took them, and behold them hid in the earth, in the midst of my tent," &c.

Covetousness is idolatry, it makes an idol of what it fixes on: Can there be any thing more base and disingenuous, when we consider what God is to us, and hath done for us, than to prefer any thing our peevish minds covet after, and in pursuit of it to disobey him. The apostle speaking to the Ephesians, who were in some measure acquainted with what God in Christ was to them, and had done for them, says,

chap.

chap. iv. 28, " Let them that stole, steal no more, but rather let him labour, working with his hands the thing that is good, as shewing a more excellent way of attaining what we need, and helping those that may need help from us. And in the same chapter, he exhorts to put away lying, and speak truth " every man to his neighbour," from this motive, " for we are members one of another;" therefore, in this view, we act as if we would deceive ourselves, as if the eye should purposely betray the feet into the mire.

By what has been brought to view of the ingratitude and baseness of some of the many works of the flesh, something is discoverable of the source from whence they proceed, and of the darkness, distress and misery to which they tend: It may lead to the same reflections on all the works of the flesh, which are brought to view by JESUS CHRIST, *Matthew* xv. 19, 20, *Mark* vii. 21, 22, and by the apostle, *Galations* v. 19, 20, 21, It might be very seasonable and profitable by way of contrast, to consider the source and leading tendency of the fruits of the spirit, against which there is no law, the very mention of which, as they are enumerated by the apostle, *Galatians* v, 22, 23, wears the aspect of delight and satisfaction, both as they flow from the love of JESUS, and lead to an imitation of him, and satisfaction in him: But as I mean not to burden young minds with what is over lengthy, I only hint at these things, to open a field for themselves to walk in with pleasure, delight and thanksgiving,* as they come to be capable; knowing that the path of the just one, which he trod and laid out for his followers to walk in, who has given us an example

---

* Thanksgiving is a grateful, delightful expression of our obligation to GOD, for the manifestation of himself, " in CHRIST JESUS who is love; " and for all the mercies that flow to us from that fountain, both temporal, spiritual, and eternal, which is to be expressed in thinking, speaking, singing and living his praise, to which children are encouraged, by the gracious acceptance the children met with from JESUS CHRIST, in their hosanna's to the son of David, *Matthew* xxii. 15, 16.

example, " that we should follow his steps, is as " the shining light that shineth more and more unto the perfect day," while the way of the wicked one, into, which he seeks to insnare his followers, is as darkness. *Proverbs* iv. 18, 19.

Thus, dear children, I have endeavoured to lead your minds to the grace revealed in the gospel, and to the view of the obligations this grace lays upon us ;—if you accept my attempt, and are hereby excited to turn over the pages of revelation, and to attend to Jesus Christ and his apostles, speaking in them, I have all I wish for from you : I know I am not my own, and that every opportunity and talent I have, belongs to my Redeemer ; therefore, so far as duty to him, and love to you hath excited me hereto, I have reason to be satisfied, whatever reception it hath. To his honor and glory, and your comfort and benefit it is devoted. To the only wise God our Saviour, glory and majesty, dominion and power, both now and ever,

A M E N.

SECTION VIII.

A Dialogue between Teacher and Scholar, for the benefit of young men: Or, an attempt to imitate Timothy's Catechism; who from a child knew the Holy Scriptures, that were able to make him wise to Salvation, through the faith which is in Christ Jesus, 2d. Tim. iii. 15. Being an attention to two questions arising from what the Scriptures principally teach, viz. 1st. What is Man to believe concerning God? 2d. What doth God require of Man?

SCHOLAR.

Sir, I have been attending to the Assemblies Catechism, and the three first answers appear intelligible; but when I come to the question, What is God? I would say, As the chief end of man is to glorify God and enjoy him forever, and the scriptures are the only rule to direct us how we may thus glorify and enjoy him, and they principally teach what man is to believe concerning God, and what he requires of man, in order to this chief end, I would wish to be taught from this only rule, supposing it more plain and easy to be understood than any other. I therefore ask, that I may be taught from the scriptures what I am to believe concerning God.

Teacher. Though your request is singular, I can't but suppose it is reasonable, although it makes me at a loss how to answer you; if I should attempt it by bringing to your view some of the many passages of scripture in which it hath pleased God to reveal himself unto us; I would first take notice that the scriptures are often spoken of as the Old and New-Testament, or the old and new, first and second Covenant;

venant; the letter and the spirit, the law and the gospel; and in order to understand them, we are to distinguish between the language of the law and the language of the gospel, or else we shall be in danger of viewing one passage of scripture contradictory to another. For instance:

The law saith,

Gal. iii. 10, *Cursed is every one that continueth not in all things written in the book of the law to do them.* The gospel saith, Gal. iii. 13, *Christ hath redeemed us from the curse of the law, being made a curse for us.*

Isaiah speaking in the language of the law, saith, chap. v. 25, and ix. 12, and xvii. 21, and x. 4, After repeating various judgments that befel the people of Judea, and Jerusalem, in consequence of their transgressions, repeateth, *For all this his anger is not turned away, but his hand is stretched out still.*

The same prophet speaking the language of the gospel, saith, chap. xii. 1, *In that day thou shalt say, O Lord I will praise thee; though thou wast angry with me; thine anger is turned away, and thou dost comfort me.* Chap. xxv. 10, *For in this mountain shall the hand of the Lord rest.*

Whatever they suffered consequent on their rebellion, there was no atonement; justice was not satisfied, but his hand is stretched out still. But speaking gospel language, he points to Jesus under the name of this mountain, where the hand of the Lord rests.

Joshua speaking in the language of the law, saith, chap. xxiv. 19, *Ye cannot serve the Lord your God, for he is an holy God, he is a jealous God, he will not forgive your transgressions nor your sins.*

Isaiah speaking in the language of the gospel, in the name of the LORD, saith, *I am he that blotteth out thy transgressions for my own name sake.* And Ezekiel

xx.

xx. 40, faith, *For in mine holy mountain, in the mountain of the height of Zion, there shall all the house of Israel, all of them in the land serve me, and there will I accept them.*

SCHOLAR. You remember, sir, the question was, What is GOD? which I wished to be answered from the scriptures?

TEACHER. I supposed the observations I have made, needful for the understanding of it, under the law, we read *that God would dwell in the thick darkness: And Moses drew near to the thick darkness where God was; and he spake to all the people out of the midst of the fire, and out of the thick darkness; he made darkness his pavillion round about, darkness was under his feet, &c.* Under the gospel we read *God is light, and in him is no darkness at all;* that God who dwelt in thick darkness is made manifest to us in Christ Jesus, the great mystery that was hid in the thick darkness of the former law dispensation, is laid open under the gospel, *God was manifest in the flesh.*

John faith *no man hath seen God at any time. The only begotten Son which was in the bosom of the Father he hath declared him, no man knoweth the Father, save the Son, and he to whomsoever the Son will reveal him: if ye had known me, ye should have known my Father also, and from henceforth ye know him and have seen him.* Philip upon this, faith, *Lord shew us the Father, and it sufficeth us.* Jesus faith unto him, *have I been so long time with you, and yet hast thou not known me, Philip; he that hath seen me hath seen the Father, and how sayest thou, shew us the Father, believest thou not that I am in my Father, and the Father in me.* A view of these things shew that the knowledge of God was to be more fully manifested under the gospel dispensation.

The light of the knowledge of the glory of GOD is given to us under the gospel dispensation in the face of JESUS CHRIST, *who is the image of the invisible God,*

God, the brightness of his glory, and the express image of his person.

SCHOLAR. Doth not the scriptures speak of GOD as unchangeable, how then am I to understand the distinction you speak of?

TEACHER. To illustrate my meaning I would say, if I were convicted as a criminal or desperate debtor; I could see nothing but what the law manifested as my portion, which would make all distress and darkness to me, look which way I would; and coming to the judgment seat, could expect nothing but that it was a sure step to the infliction of the penalty of the law upon me; but to my surprise it was manifested beyond all contradiction, that my father, my friend, my husband, my brother, whom I look on as my enemy, and had no expectation from, by reason of my crimes, has, unasked, suffered the penalty and paid the debt, that in the nature of law and justice I was discharged, and to my surprise found this united character was my advocate and judge. Then that essential love which was the moving cause of all that was done for me which before was hid in thick darkness was now made manifest, which took place before the manifestation of it to me, and was as true before I knew it as afterward;—The way is now open for your question, which you wished to be answered from the scriptures.

SCHOLAR. The question is, What is GOD?

TEACHER. GOD is love.

God is light and in him is no darkness at all.—Saith John.

The God of peace.—Saith the Apostle to the Hebrews.

The God of patience and consolation.
The God of hope.—Saith Paul.
The God of all grace.—Saith Peter.

SCHOLAR.

SCHOLAR. Your anſwer is taken from the New-Teſtament; doth the Old-Teſtament afford evidence of the ſame truth?

TEACHER. Yes; when the law of Moſes, the Prophets and the Pſalms ſpeaks in goſpel language.

SCHOLAR. This is an intereſting ſubject, and I wiſh to have a ſpecimen from each of them.

TEACHER. It muſt be but a ſpecimen, for neither the time nor my capacity will admit of conſidering it fully.

SCHOLAR. Perhaps your mentioning a few inſtances may help me in my further ſearching the ſcriptures.

TEACHER. Moſes hath this name manifeſted to him, * *The Lord deſcended in a cloud, and ſtood with him there, and proclaimed the Lord, the Lord God merciful and gracious, forgiving iniquity, and tranſgreſſion, and ſin; and that will by no means clear,—* (the two words following) viz. *the guilty* are of a different character, to ſhew they were ſupplied by the tranſlators, and they appear to darken the ſenſe of the paſſage; for we can't conceive of the forgiveneſs of iniquities, tranſgreſſions, and ſin; while he will by no means clear the guilty: And therefore I conceive the words refer to the ſurety on whom the Lord laid the iniquities of us all, and ſpared not his own Son, but delivered him up for us all. This name being thus manifeſted to Moſes, or as it is expreſſed in Pſalm cii. *He made known his way unto Moſes,* His way of ſhewing mercy; and his name the Lord God merciful and gracious, &c. being the ſame when this is manifeſted to Moſes, in a time of great diſtreſs, when the people of Iſrael had rebelled and were threatened with being diſinherited, he pleads the divine name on their behalf, " *And now I beſeech thee let the power of my Lord be great, according as thou haſt*

* Exodus, xxiv. 5, 6, 7.

haſt ſpoken, ſaying, The Lord is long-ſuffering and of great mercy, forgiving iniquity, tranſgreſſion, and ſin, and by no means clearing; (having direct respect to the ſurety who his own ſelf bear our ſins in his own body to the tree.) *Pardon, I beſeech thee, the iniquity of this people, as thou haſt done from Egypt until now,* the anſwer follows, *I have pardoned according to thy word.*"*

SCHOLAR. I take notice you have not mentioned a part of the above paſſages where it is ſaid, Viſiting the iniquities of the fathers upon the children, to the third and fourth generation. I wiſh to hear your thoughts upon it.

TEACHER. When I have thought on the paſſage, I ſuppoſed it had reference to what was to take place under the law diſpenſation, till the coming of Chriſt; we read *of the generations from Abraham to David, and from David to the carrying away into Babylon, and from the carrying away into Babylon, unto Chriſt;* now Jeſus Chriſt came under this third diviſion, diſpenſation, or generation, for he was made under the law, came under that diſpenſation, and introduced the goſpel diſpenſation; and in this view may be called the third and fourth generation, till which time the law diſpenſation laſted, and iniquities were thus viſited; this is the cleareſt account I am at preſent able to give, and ready to attend to any one who hath a clearer view of the paſſage.

SCHOLAR. You will pleaſe to proceed to the anſwer to the queſtion from the prophets.

TEACHER. It is to be obſerved with joy that the prophet Iſaiah unites in the Divine character thoſe perfections which ſecure our ſalvation; † *I the Lord and no God beſides me; the juſt God and the Saviour, none beſides me,* which agree with ‡ Zechariah, *Behold thy King cometh unto thee, he is juſt, and having ſalvation,*

---

* Numbers xiv. 17 to 20.   † Iſaiah xlv. 21.   ‡ Zechariah ix. 9.

ion, so he connects the character of Creator, King, Lord, Father, Husband, &c. with Redeemer.

* *Thy Maker, thy Husband, the Lord of Hosts his name, the God of the whole earth shall he be called.* Passing the various passages where this consoling connection is repeated, in the abovementioned prophet; I will just mention the last that I remember in the prophesy where it is called his name from everlasting: † *Doubtless thou art our Father, though Abraham be ignorant of us, and Israel acknowledge us not, thou art our Father, our Redeemer, thy name from everlasting.* Jeremiah speaks of him, as calling rebellious Israel children, ‡ *turn O backsliding children*: § *Will thou not from this time cry unto me, my Father thou be guide of my youth,* and the compassionate tenderness of a Father is expressed: ‖ *Return, I will not cause my anger to fall upon you, return ye backsliding children, I will heal your backslidings*: Not, and I will as a condition, the and, in both verses, is supplied by the translator; but 'tis return, I will heal your backslidings. Return, I will not cause mine anger to fall upon you, for I am merciful, saith the Lord. When our minds are led to the understanding view of the riches of Divine grace appearing herein, we may well, with astonished admiration, call to mind that majestic expression, ** *Behold I the Lord,* THE GOD OF ALL FLESH. *Is there any thing too hard for me ?* blessed be his name, he condescends to say, †† *I am married unto you,* ‡‡ and this is his name whereby he shall be called, THE LORD OUR RIGHTEOUSNESS.

Perhaps I should tire you to turn to the rest of the prophets, to collect a specimen of their answer to the question; therefore, shall leave it to your delightful contemplation when you have opportunity.

SCHOLAR.

* Isaiah liv. 5. † Isaiah lxiii 16. ‡ Jeremiah iii. 14. § Verse 4. ‖ Verse 12. ** Jeremiah xxxii. 27. †† Jeremiah iii. 14. ‡‡ Jeremiah xxvi. 3.

SCHOLAR. You may remember, you mentioned the psalms, from which I should be glad to hear something.

TEACHER. I need only remind you, that GOD is frequently called in the psalms, the GOD of our Salvation; and that agreeable to the description in the prophet Isaiah, the just GOD and the Saviour: So righteousness and salvation is connected in the psalms: For example, see psalm. xcviii. 2, *" The Lord hath made known his salvation, his righteousness hath he openly shewed, in the sight of the heathen, he hath remembered his mercy, and his truth towards the house of Israel. All the ends of the earth have seen the salvation of our* GOD;" which if we compare with the direction to all the earth, in the xcvi psalm, 1, 2, *To shew forth his salvation from day to day*, we may with pleasure, see the connection in the call to praise and thanksgiving in both psalms, for all the earth, the heavens, the sea and the fulness thereof; the fields, the trees, the floods and the little hills, which are all called to be joyful together. The matter of the joy is, the LORD hath made known his salvation, his RIGHTEOUSNESS hath he openly shewed in the sight of the heathen, &c.

SCHOLAR. What you have made mention of appears scriptural and comfortable; in every view it seems suitable to adopt the language of lxii psalm, " *My soul wait thou only upon* GOD, *for my expectation is from him, he only is my rock and my salvation, my defence, I shall not be greatly moved; in God is my salvation and my glory, the rock of my strength; and my refuge is in God; trust in him at all times ye people, pour out your hearts before him. God is a refuge for us.*"

But I recollect you said, under the gospel, God is manifest in the flesh, and what we know of God, is manifest in Christ Jesus, *who is the image of the invisible*

visible God, the brightness of his glory, and the express image of his person. I wish you to express yourself a little upon it, to help my understanding.

TEACHER. It is worthy of remark, that when Moses was sent to the children of Israel, to say to them, The God of your fathers hath sent me unto you, and they should say, What is his name? The answer was, *I AM that I AM, and thus shall thou say to the children of Israel, I AM hath sent me unto you.* When JESUS asked the band and officers that came to apprehend him, Whom seek ye? they said JESUS of Nazareth,* JESUS saith unto them, *I am;* as soon then as he said unto them, *I am, they went backward and fell to the ground.* And again he says to them, † *Before Abraham was, I am.*

SCHOLAR. If you please, I should be glad of some farther particulars.

TEACHER. I will proceed to instance 1st. in creation. Moses saith, Genesis i. 1, *In the beginning GOD created the heavens and the earth.* Nehe. ix. 6, *Thou, thou art Lord alone: Thou hast made the heaven, the heaven of heavens, with all their host; the earth, the seas, and all that is in them.* John speaking of JESUS, saith, chap. i, 3, *All things were created by him, and without him was not any thing made that was made:* Verse 10, *the world was made by him.* Colossians i. 16, 17, *For by him were all things created that are in heaven and that are in earth, all things were created by him and for him.*

2dly. Preservation. Nehemiah adds, *And thou preservest them all.* Psalm xxxvi. 6, *O Lord, thou preservest man and beast.* So Paul, speaking of JESUS saith, *By him all things consist.* Hebrews i. 3, *Upholding all things by the word of his power.*

3dly. Redemption is ascribed to GOD. Psalm cxxx. 8, *He shall redeem Israel from all his iniqui-*

L l *ties.*

* John xviii. 4, 5. † John viii. 58.

ties. And he is called our Redeemer nine times in the prophecy of Isaiah. The name JESUS was given, *for he shall save his people from their sins;* and Paul speaking of him, in his epistle to Titus, saith, chap. ii. 14, *Who gave himself for us that he might redeem us from all iniquity.*

4thly. Forgiveness of sins belongs to GOD, Psalm ciii. 3, *Who forgiveth all thine iniquities.* It belongs to *Christ in whom we have redemption through his blood ;* * *the forgiveness of sins,* who said, † *Man thy sins be forgiven thee,* and to her, ‡ *Thy sins are forgiven.*

5thly. The knowledge of the hearts of men is ascribed to GOD only. 1st of Kings, viii. 39, *For thou, thou only knowest the hearts of all the children of men.*

In Matthew xii. 25, we read, JESUS *knew their thoughts.* And John ii. 24, JESUS *knew all men; he knew what was in man.*

6thly. Healing the sick. Exodus xv. 26, *I am the Lord that healeth thee.* Psalm ciii. 3, *Who healeth all thy diseases.*

We read in Matthew iv. 23, JESUS *went about all Gallilee, healing all manner of sickness, and all manner of disease among the people.*

7thly. GOD is the only object of Divine worship, Deu. x. 20, *Thou shalt fear the Lord thy* GOD *; him shalt thou serve, and to him shalt thou cleave ; and swear by his name. It is written, thou shalt worship the Lord thy* GOD, *and him only shalt thou serve.* In Matthew viii. 2, we read concerning JESUS, *There came a leper and worshiped him, saying, Lord if thou wilt, thou canst make me clean.* Of the woman of Canaan, we read, Mat. xv. 25, *Then came she and worshipped him, saying, Lord help me. And they stoned Stephen, calling upon and saying, Lord Jesus receive my spirit.* And it is the description of the disciples, them that call

---

* Ephesians i. 7.   Colossians i. 14.   † Luke v. 20.   ‡ Luke vii. 48.

call on the name of Jesus Christ our Lord.—Well may we with convinced Thomas, say, *My Lord and my God*. Thus have I given you some instances, which may assist your further searching the scriptures, as you have opportunity.

SCHOLAR. When I think of the various passages that have been produced, which manifests, that what was ascribed to GOD in the Old Testament, is ascribed to Jesus Christ in the New; so that divine worship is paid to him, as one with the father; according to the divine will, *that all men should honor the Son, even as they honor the Father*, I inquire, how are we to understand these passages that speak of Jesus Christ, as GOD's servant, as sent of GOD; and wherein he says, My Father is greater than I.

TEACHER. We may conceive among men of an equal, voluntarily putting himself into the place of a servant, and being sent to accomplish some particular business in which he that sends is greater than he that was sent, though in other respects they were equal. We read of JESUS *who being in the form of* GOD, *thought it no robbery to be equal with* GOD; *but made himself of no reputation, and took upon him the form of a servant, and was made in the likeness of men, and being found in fashion as a man, he humbled himself, and became obedient unto death, even the death of the cross; wherefore,* GOD *hath highly exalted him, and given him a name, above every name, that in the name of* JESUS, *every knee should bow, in heaven and in earth, and under the earth; and that every tongue should confess, that Jesus Christ is Lord, to the glory of God the Father.*

In his taking our nature, and coming to do the will of GOD, took the form of a servant, and was capable of humiliation and exaltation.

SCHOLAR. Did not you mention in the name of JESUS, is it not said, *at* the name of JESUS every knee should bow? TEACHER.

TEACHER. I know we read it thus; but from the mouth of two or three witnesses, I have been informed it is not so in the first reading, but is the same word; we have in Colossians iii. 17, Which is there rendered, *whatsoever ye do in word or deed, do all in the name of the Lord Jesus.* God is manifested *in* Christ Jesus; therefore, he is thus to be worshipped, thus he blesses his people with all spiritual blessings *IN* Christ Jesus, and hath made us set together *in* heavenly places *IN* Christ Jesus. All the promises are *IN* him: Not because of him, or for his sake. The promise to Abraham, *IN* thy seed shall all the kindreds, nations and families of the earth be blessed. The Psalm saith, *Men shall be blessed IN him*: The prophet saith, *The nations shall bless themselves IN him, and IN him shall they glory.* By the apostle we are said, 'to be chosen *IN him*, to be gathered together *IN him*, to be rooted and built up *IN him*, to be justified *IN him*, to be made the righteousness of God *IN him*, to be sanctified *IN* Christ Jesus, to be compleat *IN him;* therefore *IN* the name of Jesus every knee shall bow.

SCHOLAR. I took notice when you said all the promises of GOD are *IN* him: You added not because of him, or for his sake. Is it not said by the apostle, when exhorting to forbearing and forgiving one another, even as God for Christ sake, hath forgiven you? What difference is there between being blessed in him, and because of him; or for his sake?

TEACHER. As to the first part of your question, we read in Ephesians iv. 22, *Be ye kind one to another, tender hearted, forgiving one another, even as* GOD *for Christ sake hath forgiven you*; but it is likewise said to be the same word as the other, even as GOD *IN* Christ hath forgiven you.

SCHOLAR. What difference is there between being blessed *IN* him, and because of him; or for his sake?

TEACHER.

Teacher. It may be said, one person, a mere stranger, may come to another to obtain something for the sake of a third person, who sent him, and obtain it, and be a stranger still, but if a wife, or a son, go *in* the name of the husband or father, there is union. So if we are blessed IN him, there is union. If we seek to be blessed because of him, it denotes a stranger. I think the distinction is obvious, though I believe it is not generally perceived, yet I think it deserves to be soberly considered.

Let us attend to the similitude a little.—A husband or father has his wife or son in view in all he does, and their welfare flows to them through him; according to the nature of it, the love and care is unceasing in every circumstance of sickness and health, as long as the relation lasts. So is their confidence in him perpetual, according to his ability and their wants, they bear his name, and rise and fall with him: But let a stranger come to the same man with an order from another; if the order is accepted, the sum is paid, or the thing delivered, and the matter is over, and they remain the same strangers, the man hath no further care, and the other hath no further expectations. The above mentioned union is spoken of, Ephesians v. 30, *For we are members of his body, of his flesh, and of his bones;* and blessed be his name. Jesus told his disciples, John xiv. 20, *At that day ye shall know that I am in my father, and you in me, and I in you.*

Scholar. In attending to the answers to the question, What is God? I wished to hear you express your thoughts on the subject of the various passages in the New-Testament, in which mention is made of Father, Son, and Holy Ghost, as in the commission Jesus Christ gave to his disciples, and in the form of blessing, the Apostle makes use of in his second epistle to the Corinthians, which John mentions, 1st epistle,

tle, v. 7, *For there are three that bear record in heaven, the Father, the Word, and the Holy Ghost, and these three are one.*

TEACHER. I would take notice that three persons is no where mentioned; that is a tradition (perhaps from the assemblies catechism,) which I wish to avoid, but the scripture expression is, These three are one.

SCHOLAR. That is the thing I wish to have my mind assisted in the understanding of.

TEACHER. James iii. 9, Speaks of men as made after the similitude of God. Now if man consists of body, soul and spirit, are not these three, one. Again, the same person may at the same time be in the relation of father and son, and that filial respect, that influences a reverential, suitable deportment towards his father, may be fitly called the spirit of the son, that same spirit manifesting itself in the paternal love and care of his offspring, may fitly be called the spirit of the father, or if spoken of to his children, the spirit of your father. The same spirit influencing his general conduct, is called the spirit of the man; as 'tis often said among men, I am satisfied that this speech, this work, or this gift, come from such an one, 'tis the spirit of the man. Now in this view, is not the Father, the Son, and the Spirit one man? Are not these three, one? What hath been brought to view, brings to mind several passages, as John x. 30, *I and father are one.* John xv. 26, *The comforter, the spirit of truth; which proceedeth from the father.* Gal. iv. 6, *God hath sent forth the spirit of his son into our hearts.* And in Rom, viii. 9, *the spirit of God and the spirit of Christ* are both mentioned in one verse.

SCHOLAR. If I understand you, when I read these various expressions, they speak of the same spirit.

TEACHER.

TEACHER. Yes, I understand them to speak of the same spirit, according to the various manifestations of it. So when our minds are contemplating the character of the one only living and true God, it must be in the way he manifests himself to us; therefore if we attend to the manifestation of him, as Father, Son, or Holy Ghost, we attend to the manifestation of the same one God.

SCHOLAR. I would wish to have this matter illustrated further from the Old Testament scriptures?

TEACHER. Have we not the three in one expressly mentioned, Genesis i. 2, *And the spirit of the Lord moved on the face of the waters.* And verse 26, *Let us make man in* our *image, after* our *likeness.* Verse 27, *So God created man in his own image, in the image of God created he him, male and female created he them.*

This seems likewise to be expressed in the form of blessing, in Numbers vi. 24, 25, 26, *The Lord bless thee, and keep thee. The Lord make his face to shine upon thee, and be gracious unto thee. The Lord lift his countenance upon thee, and give thee peace.* Surely the repetition is not a vain repetition. Compare it with 2d of Corinthians, xiii. chapter and 14 verse.

The Lord bless thee and keep thee.	The love of God the Father.
The Lord make his face to shine upon thee, and be gracious to thee.	The grace of our LORD JESUS CHRIST.
The Lord lift up his countenance upon thee, and give thee peace.	The communion of the Holy Ghost, be with you all.

In the first expression, the Lord bless thee, and keep thee; we are led to the love of God, the fountain of life; in the next, the Lord make his face to shine upon thee, and be gracious unto thee; we are led to the manifestation of this love in Christ Jesus, the light in which we see light. The

The last expreſſion in the bleſſing, the Lord lift his countenance upon thee, and give thee peace; leads to the communion of the Holy Ghoſt.

This might be further illuſtrated by attending to Proverbs viii. 22, to the 31ſt, Which may be left to your peruſal at your leiſure.

Scholar. Tho' I would make the inquiries with reverence, remembering Job's queſtion, *Canſt thou by ſearching find out God? Canſt thou find out the Almighty to perfection?* And his aſſertion, *the Almighty, we cannot find him out;* yet bleſſed be his name, he hath manifeſted himſelf to us in Chriſt Jeſus under the goſpel: and it is thoſe manifeſtations I am endeavouring to underſtand. As you have given a ſimilitude from the New-Teſtament, if you recollect one from the Old, I wiſh you to mention it.

Teacher. I wiſh to ſpeak of theſe things with the higheſt reverence, and to ſpeak of nothing but what the ſcriptures fully warrant; but in anſwer to your inquiry, I would ſay, I have ſomtimes thought of the paſſage in the xxxvi. Pſalm, 7, 8, 9, 10, *How excellent is thy loving kindneſs, O God; therefore the children of men put their truſt under the ſhadow of thy wings. They ſhall be abundantly ſatisfied with the fatneſs of thy houſe; and thou ſhalt make them drink of the river of thy pleaſure; for with thee is the FOUNTAIN of life, in thy light we ſee light.*

If we ſtand at the head of a fountain where we can find no bottom, it appears unſearchable; but it is manifeſted to be a fountain, by the conſtant rivers and ſtreams flowing from it; and by theſe rivers and ſtreams there is a conſtant communication of fertility to the adjacent lands; and of drink for the inhabitants, their children and their cattle, whereſoever the rivers come; beſides the other advantage from the mills, whereby the corn is prepared for bread, and innumerable other benefits, by the communication of the rivers flowing from the fountain, and as the fountain is unsearchable and manifested by the rivers: So if we follow the rivers all running into the sea, and returning to the place whence they came, we are lost in the contemplation: So also, if we trace the benefits received, or the communion and communications we enjoy by the waters, it will presently carry us beyond our comprehension, and if we are lost in the contemplation of ourselves, and the things which we see, no wonder the things of God knoweth no man but the spirit of God; therefore in our inquiries after the knowledge of him, we are to keep close to the scriptures, wherein we have the mind of the spirit.

SCHOLAR. I would wish to detain you to hear of the other branch of the original question, that as you have indulged my inquiries respecting what we are to believe concerning GOD, you would also consider what GOD requires of man?

TEACHER. In general it may be said, that whatever we are to believe concerning God, shews our obligation to him in that relation or manifestation of himself to us.

If we contemplate him as our Creator, we are his, and consequently to pursue the chief end of our creation—to glorify and enjoy him.

If we consider him as our Lord and King, it binds us to every thing whereby a loyal subjection to him may be manifested; a contrary conduct must weaken our confidence in his protection, and tend to our unhappiness.

If we attend to the manifestation of himself to us as our Redeemer, it will shew us we are not our own, but belong to our Lord, Redeemer; being bought with a price, we are to glorify him in our spirit and body, which are his. Our obligations hereto will rise as we are acquainted with the price of our redemption. *Forasmuch as we were not redeemed with*

M m *corruptible*

corruptible things as silver and gold, but with the precious blood of Christ, as of a lamb without blemish and without spot.

His condescending to call himself our * husband, binds singleness towards him, which increases our happiness in him.

His relation to us as a father claims our honour, filial affection, and obedient behaviour, particularly it brings to mind the exhortation, *Love your enemies, bless them that curse you, do good to them that hate you, and pray for them that despitefully use and persecute you, That you may be the children of your Father, which is in heaven; for he maketh his sun to rise on the evil, and on the good; and sendeth rain on the just and on the unjust,* that you may be *children of your Father;* they were so, but this is to act in character as such.

If we consider God is love, we love him; because he first loved us, and 'tis his direction that we love one another, as he hath loved us.

If we attend to his character as the God of peace, it will lead us to follow peace with all men.

Or as the God of all grace; *his grace which hath appeared, bringing salvation to all men; teaches to deny ungodliness, and worldly lusts; and to live soberly, righteously, and godly in the world.*

SCHOLAR. The remarks you have made, seem to arise very naturally from the characters mentioned; but I was ready to expect something particularly from the scriptures.

TEACHER. This would lead to another general view of the substance of the epistles, of the apostles; in the former part of them they treat of the grace of God made manifest in Christ Jesus: Then of the duty of the disciples consequent thereon. Therefore for that which is particularly enjoined upon us, I refer

---

* See 2d Corinthians, xi. 2, 3.

fer you to the application of the epistles of the apostles, of the Lord and Saviour. I having already mentioned the direction of Jesus Christ, to love our enemies, bless them that curse us, and pray for them that despitefully use us, to which I would add that comprehensive direction: Therefore, *all things whatsoever ye would that men should do to you, do ye even the same to them; for this is the law and the prophets.*

SCHOLAR. It may be of service to me to have those parts of the epistles of the apostles, that you mentioned, pointed to, that I may turn to them with greater readiness, when my mind is inquiring, what doth God require of man?

TEACHER. You will easily see in reading them over; but for your present assistance you may take for one lesson, or for your entertainment at one time, the xii and xiii chapters of the epistle to the Romans, and attend to what we are called too, as members of the one body, of which Christ is the head; according to the place in which we are set by the various gifts bestowed upon us without slothfulness; being fervent in spirit, serving the Lord: And to see that we be not overcome of evil, but overcome evil with good—whatever abuse we may meet with in the world. And that we live in a quiet subjection to the government, that God in his providence has placed over us, and render to all their dues, attending to that love which comprehends every commandment, worketh no ill to his neighbour, and is the fulfilling of the law.

SCHOLAR. As you mentioned subjection to government in this passage, I wish to have you a little more particular on this head, if I should not take up too much of your time.

TEACHER. Civil government derives its honourable origin both from Divine and human authority; as we see by comparing Romans xiii. 1, with 1st of Peter, ii. 13, it is said in one to be ordained of God, and in the other it is called the ordinance of man. The

The blessing of good government is the greatest of all temporal blessings, without it no outward privilege, nor even life itself can be enjoyed with any security; and as it is so extensive and universal a blessing, it carries, in its own nature, universal obligation to honour civil rulers, and to pay a ready and chearful obedience to the wholesome laws that are established for the welfare of the whole political body. As this sentiment must approve itself to every one's conscience, he that resisteth must receive to himself condemnation in the very nature of it, as well as by the law of God; but as professing christians, we are bound to be subject for conscience sake. In the above mentioned Rom. xiii. 1st of Peter, ii. from the 13th to the 18th, and Titus iii. 1, we have the exhortations of the apostles of Jesus Christ, upon this subject, to which every one that calls Jesus, Lord, would do well to take heed: And a little attention to the connection that these exhortations stand in to the grace of the gospel: The grace that brings salvation to all men, will shew the indisputable, indispensible obligations of Christ's disciples hereunto; so that civil government cannot be knowingly resisted by them, without resisting an ordinance of God; without slighting the authority of Jesus Christ, and acting counter to the obligations his grace lays on them, and consequently receiving to themselves self-condemnation.

SCHOLAR. Please to proceed to the other passages you would turn me to.

TEACHER. For another opportunity you may turn to the epistle to the Ephesians, from the 22d verse of the fourth chapter, to the eighteenth verse of the sixth chapter. And at another time take Colossians iii, from the beginning, to the end of the 6th verse of chapter iv; with 1st of Peter, iii, from the beginning to the end of 13th verse. Your attention at another time may be profitably drawn to 1st Thessalonians, iv, from the beginning, to the end of the 12th verse,

verse, and then to the 5th chap. from the 15th verse, to the end of the 22d, and 2d epistle, 3d chap. from the 7th to the end of the 12th verse.

SCHOLAR. I am obliged by your thus turning me to those passages, and purpose as I have opportunity to attend to them.

TEACHER. In the above mentioned passages we have cautions against every hurtful vice and exhortations, to a conduct and conversation becoming the gospel, in following every thing virtuous, praise worthy, and of good report, in the several relations we sustain, as husbands or wives, parents or children, masters or servants, in a diligent attention to the business to which we are called, that we may walk honestly, eat our own bread, and have to give to him that needeth, all built upon, connected with, or flowing from the grace of the gospel, the grace that reigns through righteousness to eternal life by Jesus Christ; in attending to them, you take your direction plainly from the authority of the scriptures, not from the traditions of men; and I would add that I would not have my silence about the epistles that have not been mentioned, esteemed as neglect; they have been passed over only for brevity's sake, therefore, as the scriptures principally teach what man is to believe concerning God, and what God requires of man; let them dwell in you richly, be your study and your guide, and may the Divine Teacher lead your mind to the understanding of them, that you may grow in acquaintance with the grace therein revealed, even in the knowledge of our Lord and Saviour Jesus Christ, to him be glory, both now and forever,

A M E N.

APPENDIX.

APPENDIX.

THE study of the Scriptures having been recommended, it may not be amiss to mention one motive in particular to search them; that deserves our most serious attention, contained in the exhortation we have in Job xxii. 21, *Acquaint now thyself with him, and be at peace, thereby good shall come unto thee.* If we take notice of the character to whom this exhortation is given in the foregoing part of the chapter, verses 5, 6, 7, 9, 10, 11 and 13, to whom he brings to view as a warning, the old way which wicked men have trodden, which were cut down out of time, whose foundation was overflown with a flood, we shall find it a sinful, distressed character; yet even to such a character acquaintance with God is able to give peace, because *God was in Christ, reconciling the world unto himself, not imputing their trespasses unto them.*

Among men, if any person is proposed or introduced to us for an acquaintance, we are desirous first to know his name, then his character; and on knowing his character, if it strike our minds agreeable, we wish to know his thoughts.

Well then, if we wish to comply with the above direction as an external means of our acquaintance with God, let us search the scriptures, where we may find his name, his character, and his thoughts.

If it should please him who caused the light to shine out of darkness in the first creation, to shine into our hearts, to give us the light of the knowledge of the glory of God in the face of Jesus Christ, we shall be at peace.

When

When Moses speaks of him, he calls *him the rock, his work is perfect, for all his ways are judgment, a God of truth, and without iniquity. Just and righteous is he;* but we need not look for his character distinct from his name, as we do among men, where the name only serves to distinguish the person, and doth not communicate the character, but the name of which we speak in the various expressions of it, which we find in scripture, always conveys his character; for instance, if we should attend to the name father, so often made use of in the scripture, we should find every thing signified by that name in its perfection in him.

It is a name that conveys an indissolvable relation: Even among men, there is no prodigality or enormity that a son can commit, that can dissolve the relation; and I suppose it scarce possible to find among earthly parents that are evil, an instance of one that would not wish with all his heart for the reformation of his most profligate son; in most cases parental affections work most strongly towards such a one, and are often expressed in ardent prayer to the father of mercies, and in application to such friends as might be supposed to have influence over such a one, for his reformation; and finally, it must be for want of wisdom, or power in the parent, if it is not accomplished; yet after all the parent is obliged to own and notice this son, or it will break his will in other instances.

But all this parental affection is but a stream from the fountain; *if ye then that are evil know how to give good gifts to your children, how much* MORE SHALL YOUR HEAVENLY FATHER.

But hath it pleased GOD thus to reveal himself in the scriptures? Yes; verily *have we not all one father, hath not one God created us,* Malachi ii. 10. *Thus saith Lord, Israel is my son,* Exodus iv. 22, *For I am a fa-*

ther to Israel, and Ephraim is my first born, Jeremiah xxxi. 9, Is he the God of the Jews only, and not of the Gentiles? Yes, of the Gentiles also; the Apostle of the Gentiles thus speaks of and to them, *For this cause I bow my knees to the father of our Lord Jesus Christ, of whom the whole family in heaven and earth is named, one God and Father of all, who is above all, and through all, and in you all,* Ephesians iii. 14, 15, and iv. 6, If so, then both Jew and Gentile are in an indissolvable relation to him, for we are all his off-spring.

But have not both Jew and Gentile been so captivated by satan, and alienated from God, as to be denominated the children of the devil, who led them captive at his will, and usurped dominion over them? Undoubtedly; but this, notwithstanding they belong to their Father, who is their Redeemer, in Isaiah lxiii. 16, Father and Redeemer are united, our Father, our Redeemer, thy name from everlasting. O the grace that appears in this name to the captivated children of men! how agreeable to hear the repetition of it eleven times in the prophecy of Isaiah, as well as in other parts of scripture! how cheering to captives to hear of a Redeemer; is there one that is able to accomplish it? Yes; as for our Redeemer, the Lord of hosts is his name; but who knows it? Read Isaiah lx. 16, *thou shalt know that I the Lord am thy Saviour and thy Redeemer, the mighty one of Jacob,* and not only thou, but as it is expressed, Chap. xlix. 29, *All flesh shall know that I the Lord am thy Saviour and thy Redeemer.* Surely acquaintance with his name tends to peace.

Among men the redemption price may be paid for a captive, and something may take place to prevent salvation from captivity; but here Saviour and Redeemer are united in the Lord; the Lord of hosts, the mighty one of Jacob, the Lord thy Redeemer, the

the holy one of Israel; so that salvation and redemption comes in a sure connexion in consistence with perfect holiness, agreeable to Zechariah ix. 9, *He is just, and having salvation,* and to Isaiah xlv. 21, *I the Lord and no God else beside me, a just God, and a Saviour, there is none beside me.* If there is no God beside the just God and the Saviour, there is salvation in his name; and to know the only living and true God in Jesus Christ, is life eternal; the knowledge of God is the knowledge of the Redeemer and Saviour; the just God and Saviour, therefore the sure hope of eternal life, or the beginning of life eternal, is thereby conveyed to the mind, therefore acquaintance with God is the way of peace, and this would be evidence from every manifestation of himself in the scriptures of truth: If we turn our mind to what Moses was directed to say to the children of Israel in Egypt, *I am the God of Abraham, of Isaac and of Jacob; this is my name forever, and my memorial through all generations.* It brings to view the gospel preached to them, that in thy seed, which is Christ, *Shall all the nations, kindreds and families of the earth be blessed.* It will correspond with Isaiah liv. 5, *The God of the whole earth shall he be called.* Thus acquaintance with his name is acquaintance with his character and his thoughts. The prophet Jeremiah, chap. ix. 11, was directed to tell the captives in Babylon, *I know the thoughts that I think towards you, thoughts of peace and not of evil.* Surely his character and his name of Saviour and Redeemer, gives ground of hope, that these are his thoughts respecting every of the captived children of men, whom satan hath led captive at his will: For; *thus saith the Lord, the captives of the mighty shall be taken away, and the prey of the terrible shall be delivered.*

The foregoing hints may serve to open a subject to contemplation, that will never close: but these hints may lead our minds to the further study of his name, in the various manifestations of it, expressed in the scripture; forever blessed be his name, he hath manifested himself to us therein.

If the study of his name is accompanied with the illumination the disciples were favoured with, when he opened their understandings, that they might understand the scriptures, it will open up the plain meaning of such passages, as shew the name of the Lord, a strong tower, to which the righteous run and are safe, *They that know thy name, will trust in thee; in his name shall the Gentiles trust.* The Gentiles, those who were accounted far off, sinners of the Gentiles, the most destitute in themselves, in all parts of the earth, the north and the south, which he has created, Tabor and Hermon, (east and west) *shall rejoice in thy name.* Thus will the ground of those exhortations be understood, which direct, *To rejoice ever more, to rejoice in the Lord always, and again to rejoice, and the poor among men, shall rejoice in the Holy One of Israel, who remembered us in our low estate, for his mercy forever.*

ADVERTISEMENT.

AS the foregoing Dialogue with the Appendix, is designed for the benefit of young men, it may not be amiss to mention a little piece, called the HISTORY of the MOTHER and CHILD, calculated for the entertainment and instruction of young Children, which may be had at the places where this book is sold—Price 5 Cents.

. SECTION

SECTION IX.

Introduction.

THE Pfalms, or book of Praifes, are like a treafure locked up, which cannot be feen without the key, to open that wherein the riches is contained: However, we may admire the external ornaments of the covering.

While we view them as teftifying of good men, we are blundering after creature righteoufnefs, wifhing we could come to their attainments, that we could fay as good David did in many of the expreffions of uprightnefs, fincerity and love to the divine precepts, which are found in the Pfalms; then we were ready to imagine we fhould have hope, &c.

Whereas, if we view David's character as a man, we fhall find it juftly fummed up by himfelf in three words, *I have finned*, and his hope could only be found in the gofpel preached to him by the prophet Nathan, *The Lord hath put away thy fin—thou fhall not die.* With an eye to the fame all-fufficient and exclufive ground of hope, contained in the appearing of Jefus Chrift to put away fin by the facrifice of himfelf.

But when it is given us to underftand the expreffions of our Lord and Saviour to his difciples, when he difcourfed with them of the Pfalms, concerning me, and of the Apoftle, Acts ii. 25, "for David fpeaketh concerning him," verfe 31, "he feeing this before, fpake of the refurrection of Chrift, that his foul was not left in hell, neither did his flefh fee corruption." We are helped to the key according to the Apoftle, when it fhall turn to the Lord, the vale fhall be fha-

ken

ken away; then the expressions of sincerity, uprightness and love to the divine precepts, appear to be the truth as it is in Jesus: Who being our head, is made to us of God's wisdom, righteousness, sanctification, and redemption: And our compleatness is in him, then shall we *abundantly utter the memory of thy great goodness, and sing of thy righteousness*, which will cause us to cease from man, from any pretence to, or hope in creature righteousness.

The first Psalm speaks of Jesus as the blessed man, and points out his perfect character, which cannot be assumed by, or applied to, any other. When this blessed one appeared in the world, bringing grace and salvation to men, we have the heathen, and the people, Jews and Gentiles raging, imagining a vain thing, the kings of the earth, and their rulers taking counsel against the Lord, as recorded in the 2d Psalm, and in the 3d Psalm, the many, the increasing multitude rising up against him, with how great propriety is the 8th verse ushered in, salvation to the Lord, thy blessing upon thy people; surely Jew and Gentiles, Kings and Rulers, with the increasing multitude must join in not unto us; not unto us, but to thy name, give glory, for thy mercy and truth's sake.

To this mercy and truth manifested in Christ Jesus as the center of all our hopes, the subject of all our songs, the Hymns, and Spiritual Songs, are attempted to be directed in plain scriptural languages, which is esteemed to excel poetical elegance, as tending more to edification, by bringing to view the holy scriptures, which are able to make wise to salvation, through faith which is in Christ Jesus.

A small

A small Collection of PSALMS, HYMNS, and Spiritual SONGS.

The connexion of the first and second PSALMS.

I.

THE blessedness of the man,
  Of which the psalms relate,
Employ with joy, my mind and pen,
  They are exceeding great.

II.

Behold this ever blessed man,
  Who never walketh in
Ungodly counsel, nor will stand
  With those who live in sin.

III.

Nor can we see him while we sit
  With pride, in scorner's chair;
This spotless character cannot
  Appear as sitting there.

IV.

For in the perfect law of GOD,
  He plac'd his whole delight,
Attending to it constantly,
  Both in the day and night.

V.

'Tis he the precious tender plant,
  Of which *Isaiah* shew,
The righteous branch, plant of renown,
  The Prophets had in view.

VI.

He's like a tree that planted is
  By rivers fertile sides,
That in his season yields his fruit,
  And ever green abides.

VII.

Profperity on him attends,
 Whatever he commands,
The pleafure of JEHOVAH fhall
 Still profper in his hands.*

VIII.

Not fo the ungodly, no, his hope
 Shall never with him ftay;
But like the chaff before the wind,
 Be driven clean away.

IX.

He therefore in the judgment fhall
 Unable be to ftand,
Nor in the affembly of the juft,
 The finners of the land.

X.

Becaufe the LORD, the righteous way
 With approbation knows,
While the ungodly in his way,
 He wholly overthrows.

The fecond PSALM.

I.

WHY? When this bleffed man appears,
 In perfect purity,
Who has profperity infur'd,
 Why rage the heathen? Why?

II.

The people too, a vain thing think,
 Tho' prince and rulers join,
And fet themfelves againft the LORD,
 Againft his CHRIST combine.

III.

* Ifaiah liii. 10.

III.

Their bands, in union caſt on us,
    Forbiding us to teach,
And ſtraitway charging in that name,
    We never more ſhould preach.

IV.

Lets' break by ſaying unto them,
    Judge ye if that we may,
Adhere to you, more than to GOD,
    Thus caſt their cords away.*

V.

He that in Heaven ſits ſhall laugh,
    At all the ſons of pride,
That thus combine againſt his CHRIST,
    The LORD ſhall them deride.

VI.

In his diſpleaſure and his wrath,
    He then to them will ſpeak,
What muſt them vex, while they oppoſe;
    His will they cannot break.

VII.

Yet tho' you plot and rage 'tis vain,
    I've ſet my King upon,
Zion my hill of holineſs,
    He 'ſtabliſh'd is thereon.

VIII.

JESUS the firm decree declares,
    The LORD hath ſaid to me,

Thou

---

* In the ſecond Pſalm, the word *ſaying* at the end of the ſecond verſe, that appears ſupplied by the Tranſlators, ſeems to make the third verſe the language of thoſe that take counſel againſt the LORD; but is there not ground to conſider the third verſe as the language of the LORD's people, when the very perſons ſpoken of in the Pſalm charged them, *not to ſpeak at all, nor teach in the name of Jeſus*? They break their bands by ſaying, *Whether it be right in the ſight of God to hearken unto you more than unto God, judge ye, for we cannot but ſpeak the things which we have heard and ſeen; we ought to obey God rather than man*; Acts iv. 17, 18, 19, 20—25, 26, 27, and chap. v. 29.

Thou art my Son, this very day
  I have begotten thee.*

IX.

Ask of me thine inheritance,
  The heathen I will give,
Possession thine's the utmost parts,
  Of earth where men do live.

X.

Their opposition shall be broke,
  As with an iron rod,
And dash'd as Potter's vessel is,
  That under foot is trod.

XI.

Now therefore, O ye kings be wise,
  Princes instruction gain,
Serve him with fear, and trembling joy,
  For's mercies yet remain.

XII.

You perish by his anger sure,
  In keeping your own way,
Then kiss the Son, for blessed are
  All who upon him stay.

Psalm

---

* JESUS CHRIST through his whole life, particularly in his publick ministry, claimed the character that is declared in this seventh verse of the second Psalm, agreeable to the truth he heard of GOD at his baptism, and supported his claim by the works he did in his Father's name, which bear witness of him. He was charged with blasphemy, because he said, *I am the son of God*, making himself equal with GOD ; the decision of the controversy was put on his resurrection from the dead, by which, as faith the Apostle, Rom. i. 4. *He is determined the Son of God, with power according to the spirit of holiness.* So the Apostle, when treating of the resurrection of JESUS CHRIST, Acts xiii. 30 to the 33d, says, *but God raised him from the dead, and he was seen many days of them which came up with him from Gallilee to Jerusalem, who are his witnesses unto the people, and we declare unto you glad tidings, how that the promise that was made unto the fathers, God hath fulfilled in that he hath raised Jesus again,* as it is also written in the 2d Psalm, *Thou art my Son, this day have I begotten thee*; shewing it referred to the day of his resurrection, when the controversy is determined, and the decree declared.

PSALM LXXXVII.*

I.

HIS foundation for his church
 Immovably is laid,
In holy mountains, where it stands,
 Securely ever staid.

II.

The LORD the gates of *Zion* loves,
 Tho' barr'd to human pride,
To JESUS, and through him to his
 Are ever open wide.

III.

Not Jacob's dwellings ever can
 Be so divinely fair,
As to produce a character,
 That claims admittance there.

---

* This 87th Psalm appears to be a prophetic description of the gathering all things into one in Christ Jesus, under the metaphor of a city, which is God's building, taking notice first of the security of the foundation, as fixed in the holy mountains. Jesus, the foundation of the church, is the holy one: Then of the gates, which the Lord loves more than all the dwellings of Jacob; by the gate, the way, the door, we understand the entrance. Thus Jesus is the way, Jesus is the door, and saith, by me, if any man enter in, he shall be saved. The entrance into this city, being Jesus, in whom the father is well pleased; Jesus, his beloved Son, in whom we are accepted, he having made us accepted in the beloved, the dwellings of Jacob cannot procure a character that can be accepted out of him.

Then the prophetic description goes on, taking notice of the glorious things spoken of the city of God. These are so great, that the mention of them is ready to stagger the faith even of those that know him, to whom he condescends to make mention of Rahab and Babylon. Rahab, or Egypt, where the children of Israel were in bondage 400 years, had their deliverance, the same day that had been before appointed; and thus was likewise accomplished their return from Babylon after a captivity of 70 years, according to the promise of God by Jeremiah, Chap. xxix. 10.

Behold Phylistia and Tyre, with Ethiopia. This was born there. When we object to the salvation of the heathen, because they know not God, we lose sight of the Gospel preached to Abraham, and even forget that God knows them.

But those things that appear as hindrances, or those places that appeared as enemies, are shewn to be the places where this is born to view, which was to be more particularly understood in Zion, where this and that man, reputed enemies and friends, Jew and Gentile were united as one. Born to view as one new man in Christ, which union into one building, one city, should be established by the Most High, who when he took account of the particular inhabitants, though a great multitude, which no man could number, yet are all included in one in Christ Jesus, which being understood, set every form of praise in motion; the grand chorus of the Song is, all my springs are in thee.

IV.

Exceeding great, and glorious things,
  Are spoken in the word,
To be accomplished in thee,
  O city of the LORD.

V.

Should any doubt, they'll be fulfill'd,
  Of those my name that know,
Egypt nor *Babel* could not let,
  What I purpos'd to do.

VI.

The *Gentiles*, *Palestine*, and *Tyre*,
  With *Ethiopia* too;
Instead of hindering is the place,
  Where this is born to view.

VII.

Of *Zion* too it shall be told,
  Both this and that man were,
Both *Jew*, and *Gentile*, one in CHRIST,
  Each born together there.

VIII.

'Tis not the wisdom, or the power,
  Of any mortal men;
It is the work of the Most High,
  She shall be stablish'd then.

IX.

The LORD when he the people writes,
  Tho' more than men can count, *Rev.* vii. 9.
This one new man in JESUS CHRIST,
  Makes up the whole amount.

X.

Those who can sing, and cheerful say,
  For ever praise the LORD,
With those on Instruments that play,
  Shall join with one accord.

XI.

To shout the praises of thy love,
  For all their song shall be,
My springs of hope, of life, and joy,
  Are ever all in thee.

PLALM

PSALM CXVII.

I.
LET nations all, of every tongue,
 Unite to praise the Lord;
And people all, of every land,
 To praise his name accord.

II.
Because his kindness merciful,
 And truth forever sure,
Is most exceeding great to us,*
 And ever shall endure.

III.
Let old and young, let low and high,
 Together here accord;
And every soul, from all the earth,
 Unite to praise the Lord.

PSALM CXXXIII.

The spirit of Prophecy in this Psalm appears to point to the love among the first Disciples on the day of Pentecost, the fruit of the Spirit sent down consequent on the Great High-Priest's going into the heavenly holy place, in virtue of his own blood, now to appear in the presence of GOD for us.

I.
BEHOLD! a good and pleasant sight,
 In brethren that agree,
In CHRIST their head, and thence are led
 To love and unity.

II.
Like precious ointment that ran down,
 The head of *Israel's* Priest,
To's garments, where their names he wear,
 That thus they might be blest.

III.

---

* To us, the mercy and truth is doubtless as extensive as the call to praise him; for Psalm lxxii. 17, " all nations shall call him blessed." Jeremiah iv. 2, " the nations shall bless themselves in him, and in him shall they glory."

III.

Like fruitful *Hermon*'s useful dew,
  That blessings there produce,
Which *Zion*'s mountains plenty shew,
  For *Israel*'s daily use.

IV.

These shew the blessing GOD commands,
  Laid up in plenteous store,
In JESUS sure it shall endure,
  'Tis life forevermore.

PSALM CXLVIII.

I.

A UNIVERSAL shout of joy,
  Now to Jehovah bring,
Ye heav'ns high, ye angels all,
  Unite his praise to sing.

II.

Praise him ye sun, and moon, and stars,
  Ye heaven of heavens too,
And waters that above them are,
  For he created you.

III.

His glorious power, his arm of might,
  Upholds you where you are;
By his established decree,
  You ever stand fast there.

IV.

Let dragons, deeps, and cattle all,
  Praise him from earth below;
Fire, hail and vapor, join herein,
  With stormy wind and snow.

V.

Let mountains praise, and all the hills,
  And fowls of every wing,
The fruitful trees, and cedars all,
  And ev'ry creeping thing.

VI.

VI.

Come and agree his name to praise,
   Ye Kings of noble birth,
Together with each one that makes
   All people of the earth.

VII.

Princes to him by whom you rule,
   Your grateful homage bring;
And all the judges of the earth,
   Praise our Almighty King.

VIII.

Both young men and the maidens too,
   Old men and children small,
In consort here most gladly join,
   His praise becomes you all.

IX.

Come one and all unite to praise,
   The Lord's exalted name;
In which his glory is above
   Both earth and heaven's frame.

X.

This is the name that JESUS hath,
   Above each name always,
That in his name each knee should bow,
   And tongue confess his praise.

XI.

Thus he exalts his people's horn,
   That's raised up for us,
E'en our salvation's mighty horn,
   In's servant David's house.

XII.

He is the subject of the praise,
   Of all with one accord,
His saints, his Israel, near to him,
   O then praise ye the Lord.

Deut.

Deut. x. 21. *He is thy praise.*

I.

THE glory of the church's head,
 Be ever on our mind,
The subject of our songs in him,
 May we forever find.

II.

From antichristian pride in songs,
 May we be safe preserv'd,
Nor ever dare of our own worth,
 To sing before the LORD.

III.

To him whose life fulfill'd the law,
 Whose death doth sin attone,
Whose resurrection from the dead,
 Proves him the HOLY ONE.

IV.

To him who lives for evermore,
 A priest to intercede,
And all who come to GOD by him,
 Can save in utmost need.

V.

E'en him who to the holiest
 Is gone, with his own blood,
And ever pleads his worthiness,
 Before the throne of GOD.

VI.

To him who came to seek and save,
 The altogether lost,
Be our high praises in our songs,
 For evermore address'd.

VII.

To him who sav'd the dying thief;
 Call'd persecuting *Saul*;
Look't *Peter* to repentance too,
 After his fearful fall.

VIII.

To him who set th' Adulterous free,
  And wash'd *Corinthians* stain,
Who found *Ephesians* dead in sin,
  And quicken'd them again.

IX.

To him who the redeemed church,
  Ascribe all worth alone,
And constant pay their solemn praise,
  Agreeing all in one.

X.

To him then be all praise ascrib'd,
  With universal reign,
And glory, honour, power, and might,
  For evermore, AMEN.

CHRIST RIDING TO JERUSALEM.

I.

REJOICE, O *Zion's* daughter here,
  With joy, exceeding great, rejoice:
And let *Jerus'lem's* daughter too,
  Join in with joyful shouting voice.

II.

Behold thy King cometh to thee,
  With splendid ornaments divine;
He's just, and yet salvation hath,
  In lowly meekness he doth shine.

III.

BEHOLD him riding in upon
  A colt his own, for him prepar'd,*
On which no man before had sat,
  Attend and hear the King declar'd.

---

* The owners held their title under their Lord: So Jesus saith to his disciples, "say the Lord hath need of him, and straitway he will send him." *Mark* xi. 3, 5, 6. *Luke* xix. 33. Is not this for our instruction, and a rebuke to our covetousness, that would withhold what he in his members hath need of.

IV.

A multitude, lo! very great,
  With chearfulness their garments lay;*
Others cut goodly branches down,†
  And joyful spread them by the way.

V.

Hark! hear the shout of highest joy,
  Of which we heard the prophet treat,
By those that go along before,
  Which they who follow loud repeat.

VI.

Hosanna, blessed *Israel's* King,
  That cometh in the name, the Lord,‡
Hosanna to King David's Son,
  Hosanna high with one accord.

VII.

Look! see among the crowded throng,
  Children aloud hosanna cry;§
But it offends chief priests and scribes,
  Who were spectators standing by.

VIII.

Were I among the multitude,
  Methinks I'd listen then to hear,
Doth he reject, or now accept,
  The praises of the children dear.

IX.

From babes and sucklings he approves,
  The praises of his worthy name,
And asks chief priests and scribes, if they‖
  Remember'd not to read the same.

X.

But 'ere I leave this wond'rous sight,
  Methinks I long to hear the King,
His speech, the laws, his will, the news,
  He doth his vast dominions bring.

XI.

---

* Matthew xxi. 8. † Mark xi. 8. ‡ Matthew xxi. 9. Hosanna seems to be the acclamation of salvation and praise, or salvation and praise to the son of David. § Matthew xxi. 15. ‖ Matthew xxi. 16.

XI.

He to the heathen shall speak PEACE,*
  The ancient prophet testifies;
Peace in the Heav'ns; and glory in†
  The highest; multitudes replies.

XII.

PEACE comprehends the blessed news;‡
  And tho' I cannot longer stay,
To hear his speech, his laws, his will,
  I'd bear this olive-branch away.

FRIENDSHIP.

PROVERBS xvii. 17.

A Friend loveth at all Times.

I.

FRIENDSHIP, thou easy pleasing word,
  How soon art thou profess'd;
Friendship, thou active, helpful thing,
  By whom art thou possess'd;

II.

But could I find the happy souls,
  Who friendship fast did tie,
I could not here with safety trust,
  Because the friends must die.

---

* *Zechariah* ix. 10.   † *Luke* xix. 37, 38.
‡ *Isaiah* liii. 5, "The chastisement of our peace was upon him, lvii. 19. I create the fruit of the lips; peace, peace to far off and to near, saith the Lord." *John* xvi. 23. "These things I have spoken unto you, that in me ye might have PEACE. *John* xix. 19. Jesus stood in the midst, and said unto them, PEACE unto you; verse 21, then said Jesus unto them again, PEACE unto you; verse 26, PEACE unto you." *Acts* x. 36. "Preaching peace by Jesus Christ." *Ephesians* xi. 14, "for he is our PEACE; verse 17, and came and preached PEACE to you that were a far off, and to them that were nigh."

III.
Then look away for friendship sure,
  Beyond the dying race,
To him who lives forevermore,
  Time cannot his deface.

IV.
My earthly friend forgets my pain,
  My sorrow and my woe;
Yea, mothers! strange! of children too
  May thus forgetful grow.*

V.
But he, the never failing FRIEND,
  Before the world had frame,
Had his delights with sons of men,
  And ever is the same. †

VI.
He had them graven on his heart,‡
  With all their guilt and woe,
To save them he their natures took,
  And answers what they owe.

VII.
They ow'd obedience to the law
  Which they could never pay,
But lo! I come to do thy will,§
  The FRIEND is heard to say.

VIII.
What law and justice both demand,
  The soul that sins shall die,
He as their Head and in their stead,
  Doth dying satisfy.

IX.
In proof the debt is fully paid,
  Death could not him detain, ¶
Hark! hear the glad important news,
  Lo! JESUS rose again.

X.

---

* Isaiah xlix. 15.   † Proverbs viii. 31.   ‡ Isaiah xlix. 16.
§ Psalm xl. 7, 8.   Heb. x. 7, 9, 10.   ¶ Acts ii. 24.

X.

He's gone, the great High-Priest is gone,
  To Heaven itself indeed,
In virtue of his precious blood,*
  For us to intercede.

XI.

Then nothing sure can separate
  Us from his friendly love,
Nor tribulation, nor distress,†
  Nor depth, nor height above.

XII.

For these he loves, tho' in the world,
  He loves unto the end :‡
This, this is our beloved Sire,
  And our eternal FRIEND.

JOHN xv. 15.

I have called ye Friends.

I.

JESUS my ever present FRIEND,
  Thy Friendship ever sure,
Thro' time, thro' all eternity
  Unchanging doth endure.

II.

What tho' my earthly friends grow cold,
  Nor ask me in their door,
Where I was welcome in and out
  With freedom heretofore.

III.

JESUS reminds me, I'm the door,
  Come enter, I will save,
Come in and out and welcome you,¶
  By me shall pasture have.

IV.

---

* Heb. ix. 24. † Rom. viii. 35, 39. ‡ John xiii. 1. ¶ John x. 9.

IV.

In thy sure Friendship may I joy,
  Forever night and day,
With fullest satisfaction, when
  My earthly friends decay.

V.

And may the pure unmixed love,
  That did thy friendship place
Upon our nature in our sin,
  Which reacheth all our race.

VI.

May love self mov'd, and thus extent,
  Be constant on my mind,
That I may treat the purchas'd race
  With tender Friendship kind.

The Love of JESUS CHRIST, *made manifest to little* CHILDREN.

I.

HOW shall a child aright conceive,
  Of JESUS and his Love;
That shines in all he doth so bright,
  'Tis angels thoughts above.

II.

He took a child into his arms, *
  There union with him see;
Who doth receive such in my name,
  He saith, receiveth me.

III.

JESUS, both yesterday, to day,†
  And ever is the same:
He on young children laid his hands,‡
  And blessed be his name.

IV.

---

* Mark iv. 36, 37.   † Hebrews xiii. 8.   ‡ Matthew xix. 10, 15.

IV.

Of such my heav'nly kingdom is,*
  Then let them come to me ; †
Thus safety for a helpless child,
  And joy and comfort see.

V.

Whoever through his haughty pride,
  Disdains to take it so,
While that prevails they never shall,
  Into his kingdom go.‡

VI.

O may I from my early youth,
  Have constantly in mind,
The condescending love and grace,
  Of child and infants friend.

VII.

O may I early know thy name,
  And always trust thy care ;
Help me Lord JESUS by thy word,
  My conduct all to square.

Consolation in CHRIST *for little* CHILDREN.

I.

WHERE shall a feeble, helpless child,
  Find courage to its mind ;
But in the power and grace of him,
  Who came the lost to find.§

II.

As he that hath an hundred sheep,
  If one of them doth stray,
Leaves ninety-nine to go and seek,‖
  And bring it on his way.

---

* Matthew xix. 14. † Mark x. 14. ‡ Mark x. 15. § Matthew xviii. 11. ‖ Matthew xviii. 12.

III.

Your heav'nly father, JESUS faith,
    As in his word we're told;
Will not have one such little one,
    To perish from his fold.*

IV.

O may I know his worthy name,
    And trust his faithful care;
In every gloomy fearful thought,
    Find help and safety there.

V.

Since GOD is love, and hath it shewn,†
    In JESUS unto me;‡
May I from slavish dread of him,
    Be evermore set free.

VI.

And ever have upon my mind,
    A sense I'm not my own;
But am most gratefully oblig'd,
    To live to him alone.

HOSEA xiv. 8.

From me is thy fruit found.

I.

O MY ungrateful barrenness,
    Is ever cause of shame,
When for a theme of fruitfulness
    I have the Saviour's name.

II.

When e'er I sit at home alone,
    Can I be at a loss
For entertainment to my mind,
    Since CHRIST dy'd on the cross.

---

* Matthew xviii. 14.   † 1st of John, iv. 8, 16.   ‡ 1st of John, iv. 9.

III.

Can I be lonely, low or dull,
  When Scriptures afcertain
This glad, this all-important news,
  That Jesus rofe again?

IV.

Can I my fellow-finners meet,
  Silent about the news,
That brings complete falvation to
  Our loft perplexed views?

V.

And doth afford a lafting fund
  Of gladnefs, love and joy,
To ranfom'd captives long enflav'd,
  Their praifes to employ.

VI.

This is the ground we finners have
  To worfhip, when we meet,
'Caufe Jesus dy'd and rofe again,
  Our hope is now complete.

VII.

And tho' in view of what we are,
  Our mouths are wholly ftopp'd,
Yet viewing him, we may draw near
  With an affured hope.

VIII.

The healing of my barrennefs,
  No other where I fee,
But in the union with the Vine,
  And fruitful Olive-Tree.

1 Corinthians,

1 CORINTHIANS, xi. 24.
This do in remembrance of me.

I.

O THOU, the Churches strength and song,
Be pleas'd to teach our minds and tongue
   To sing aright of the display.
Of wisdom, justice, grace divine,
That meet, that harmonize and shine
   In JESUS taking sin away.

II.

And in that firm foundation laid,
The night in which he was betray'd,
   To bring himself and love to view;
Which in his life and death he shew,
And rose again to prove it true,
   A theme the Church holds ever new.

III.

The slain LAMB's worthiness they sing,
Their sacrifice, their Priest and King,
   With lovely harmony they sound;
On whom alone their hopes do rest,
To whom their loyalties express,
   While they appear his table round.

IV.

But who of all the guilty race
May at his table find a place?
   A wretch replete with guilt as I;
Because the LAMB that once was slain,
Arose, and ever lives again,
   May be encourag'd to draw nigh.

V.

The obligations this doth bind,
Conception here is lost to find,
   May we as one while here combine
Our highest gratitude to show,
By following him where'er he'll go,
   In hopes eternal praise to join.   LUKE.

LUKE xxii. 19.

This do in Remembrance of Me.

I.

WHEN in ourselves we view our state,
  Both shame and guilt and fear,
Arises to our anxious minds,
  We're lost and in despair.

II.

But when we read the Gospel news,
  A ray of hope creeps in,
Jesus was born, liv'd, dy'd and rose,
  And put away our sin.

III.

Tho' Satan accuse, the law condemns,
  And conscience guilty cries,
There's life and hope in Gospel news,
  'Tis God that justifies.*

IV.

He's just herein for Jesus dy'd,
  Yea, rather rose again,
Thus law and justice hath its due,
  The case is very plain.

V.

Here's now the baptism that saves,
  Not washing hands or head,
But conscience furnish'd with reply,†
  By's rising from the dead.

VI.

Therefore we meet and break the bread,
  And take and eat and drink,
In mem'ry of his dying love,
  Of which we speak and think.

VII.

* Romans viii. 33.   † Peter iii. 21.

VII.

In happiness and liberty
   We glory since we've found
That we are not our own, but are
   Thy servants bought and bound.

Psalm cxi. 4.

He hath made his wonderful works to be remembered.

I.

O FOR a song of grateful praise,
   For love surpassing thought,
Which gladsome tidings unto us,
   Are by the Gospel brought.

II.

For him who knew no sin at all,
   To be made sin for us;
For us under the curse of law
   Himself was made a curse.

III.

That we in him might now be made
   The righteousness of GOD,
And have full freedom from the curse,
   The purchase of his blood.

IV.

And have a token of his love
   'Till he again shall come,
And see the travel of his soul,
   And take his purchase home.

V.

May hearts and lips, and lives and tongues
   Conceive and speak his praise,
As it becomes the Gospel news,
   Through our remaining days.

PSALM lxviii. 19.

Blessed be the Lord who daily loadeth us with benefits, the God of our salvation; Selah.

I.

COME let us join as one and sing,
The praises due to *Zion's* King,
   For joy of life, and health, and friends,
And let our raiment and our food,
Be always by us understood,
   As what he undeserved sends.

II.

Protection too from dangers great,
Which multiply while we relate,
   From childhood both by night and day,
From water, fire, wounds and falls,
From sickness rais'd aloud it calls,
   That we a grateful tribute pay.

III.

Our dwelling places found intire,
When oft' indanger'd by the fire,
   A mercy think how very great;
His favour undeserv'd admire,
He doth it certainly require,
   While we the circumstance relate.

IV.

These mercies which we now relate,
Altho' they are exceeding great,
   And claim our constant praising breath,
Yet even in their highest prime,
Are chiefly bounded here by time,
   And ending in our day of death.

V.

But when we're taught of God to look,
Into the volume of his book,
   For his designs of grace therein;
Eternal mercies there unfold,
Which eye ha'nt seen, nor ear heard told,
   And thought is lost where to begin.

VI.

VI.

But may our song arise and swell,
While by it we attempt to tell,
   What's far beyond the reach of tho't;
Eternal Wisdom's perfect plan,
Beyond—Beyond device of man!
   To us by Revelation brought.

VII.

Which opens up designs of grace,
For sinners of the human race,
   Long back from all eternity!
To come to view to them in time,
When not for his but for their crime,
   The spotless Son of God did die.

VIII.

'Tis finished, he then could say,
The debt discharg'd, he had to pay,
   Justice is fully satisfy'd,
His resurrection fully shews,
This glad, this all important news,
   Death could not hold him when he dy'd.

IX.

He rose, he lives for evermore,
The great High-Priest is gone before,
   To Heaven itself, the holy place,
For us, (with joy be't understood,)
To plead the virtue of his blood,
   Before the Holy Father's face.

X.

This is the hope within the vail,
We may lay hold and cannot fail,
   'Tis there that our forerunner's gone,
The anchor holds, the head's secure,
The members then must all endure,
   They're only safe in him alone.

XI.

The knowledge of this truth should cause,
That we with gratitude should pause,
   And know our lips, and lives, and tongues,
Belong to him to shew his praise,
In dutiful becoming ways,
   With sweetest, softest, highest songs.

A MORNING THOUGHT.

On Psalm lxviii. 19.

I.

MERCIES with mornings multiply,
   The Lord be ever blest,
Who with them daily loadeth us,
   And nightly gives us rest.

II.

To think how high our praise should rise,
   To view the joyful clause,
The God of our Salvation sure,
   Let Selah make the pause.

An ADDRESS to the READER.

PERHAPS you may be ready to say, on looking over the foregoing, I find, as far as I have read, every song centers in the resurrection of Christ: Why, or whence is it that *that* event is so much insisted on? I answer, for the same reason,* that the Apostles of Christ in all their preaching and writing had this truth in view, as the only foundation of their hope:

If

---

* Acts ii. 32,—Ib. ch. iii. 15—iv. 10—33—v. 30—vii. 52, 55, 56.—x. 40—xiii. 30, 33, 34, 37.—xvii. 3, 31. Thus for the Apostle's preaching, to turn to their writings on this hand would be too lengthy.

If CHRIST be not raised our preaching is vain, ye are yet in your sins, and those who have fallen asleep in CHRIST are perished; but now is CHRIST risen from the dead, and by his accomplishing a perfect obedience to the divine Law, and suffering the penalty annexed to our transgression, was fulfilled the prophecy of the Old Testament, of his finishing transgression, making an end of sin, bringing in everlasting righteousness; so that the universal Church shall call him the LORD our righteousness, and every member shall say, *Surely in the Lord have I righteousness.* Now when he was on earth, claiming the character of him who was to accomplish this, and proving it by his works, he is called a blasphemer, the issue of the controversy is put on his resurrection, and this event taking place, he is *declared the Son of God with power according to the Spirit of Holiness,* and made it evident that he has accomplished our deliverance from the curse of the law, by *being made a curse for us;* in that law and justice could hold him no longer, *for it was not possible he should be holden of death.* Hence, saith the Apostle, *He died for our offences, and rose again for our justification,* and hence we read of the *answer of a good conscience by the resurrection of* Jesus Christ; and that *it is God that justifieth, who is he that condemneth? It is Christ that died, yea rather that is risen again:* Consequently, the Apostle took great care to keep this in the memory of the Disciples, *Remember that Jesus Christ, of the seed of David, was raised from the dead, according to my gospel,* 2 Timothy, ii. 8. Salvation by the death and resurrection of Christ, is the gospel, the Apostles preached among them, by which, saith *Paul, Ye are saved if ye keep in memory what I preached unto you.* To keep this truth in my own and your memory is the design in view, as the understanding, remembrance of this truth will save us from the distressing anxiety

anxiety of the curse of the law, and the innumerable perplexities consequent thereon through life, and at the hour of death, to which we are all without exception hastening; *For it is appointed unto man once to die.* Surely then, that by which we are saved from the sting of death, ought to be ever had in remembrance.

Hebrews ix. 27.
It is appointed unto Man once to die.

I.
Hark! from the word a solemn truth
   Doth thence salute our ears,
Which equally concerns us all,
   Alarming all our fears.

II.
Sin came by one man in the world,
   Thereby death enter'd in,
So death hath pass'd upon all men,
   For all partake therein.

III.
Ah! death, sin arm'd thee with thy sting,
   And caus'd thee forth to go
Against mankind, as if thou wert
   Their universal foe.

IV.
Not youth, nor health, nor usefulness,
   Can ward thy fatal blow;
The rich, and those in honour high,
   Must at thy summons go.

V.
The learn'd, the pious, and the wise
   Must to thy stroke submit,
Nor can the mighty of the earth
   Resist the force of it.

VI.

The peasant low, and most obscure
  Cannot escape thine eye,
O thou dread monarch who regards
  The low as well as high.

VII.

The tender bands that wedlock ties
  By thee, alas, must break!
Most kind and loving partners thou
  Dost from each other take.

VIII.

Where then shall we console ourselves,
  In thought that we must die,
But in the righteousness of one
  Complete to justify.

IX.

O death and grave, where's now thy sting?
  Since JESUS CHRIST did die,
Thanks to his name, who doth thro' him
  Give us the victory.

LUKE xv—1 to 7.

I.

WHEN publicans and sinners wish'd
  That they might JESUS hear;
And both were led with hasty feet
  Together to draw near;

II.

The scribes and pharisees agree
  To murmur at the sight;
This man receives the sinners, and
  Eats with them with delight.

III.

He kindly asks them, which of you
   An hundred sheep that own'd,
If one be lost would cease to seek,
   Till he the wanderer found.

IV.

If he had earn'd them, or if they
   Were what his father gave,
There was not one that he would lose,
   Were it his power to save.

V.

For tho' its lost, and stray'd away,
   'Tis still his property,
Nor can it be detain'd from him,
   Paying the damage fee.

VI.

It might, alas, beyond the sight,
   Of feeble mortals stray,
Or want of power, or want of love,
   Prevent being brought away.

VII.

But praises high be ever sung,
   The Shepherd great and good,
Hath eyes like to a flaming fire,
   That pierces through the wood.

VIII.

He wants not riches, love, or power,
   The sheep he knows his own,
To ransom all his property,
   He hath his life laid down.

IX.

He rose, he lives eternally,
   In proof he's paid the cost,
His sheep shall have eternal life,
   Nor one of them be lost.

X.

His love be ever on our mind,
 With gratitude and joy,
Attending daily to his voice,
 As our most sweet employ.

Isaiah xli. 4.—xlviii. 12. and xliv. 6.

Thus saith the Lord the King of Israel, and his redeemer the Lord of hosts, I am the First, and I am the Last; and besides me there is no God.—Rev. i. 8, 11, 17, and xxii. 13. *I am the First, and the Last.*—That these two passages in the Revelations speak of Jesus Christ, is evident from the connexion of the 17th and 18th verses of the first chapter, *I am the First and the Last; I, he that liveth and was dead, and behold I am alive for evermore:* And from chap. ii. 8. *These things saith the First and the Last, which was dead and is alive.* Consequently, Jesus Christ, is the Lord, the King of Israel, and his Redeemer, the Lord of Hosts, the First and the Last; besides whom is no God, or the one only living and true God, is manifest in Christ Jesus, the just God, and the Saviour: There is none besides, as saith John, 1st Epistle, v. 20. *We are in him that is true, in his Son Jesus Christ; this (viz.* God in Christ*) is the true God and eternal life.*

I.

JESUS our subject in the First,
 Our grateful song is in the Last,
He doth begin our confidence,
 Then let us hold him ever fast.

II.

Our confidence in him's secure,
 And never can or will us fail,
His Priesthood ever shall endure,
 He's gone fo us within the vail.

III.

III.

The great and sure foundation laid,
  Is Jesus Christ and him alone;
Other than this can no man lay,
  He is the chief and Corner-Stone.

IV.

In him we've consolation strong,
  Our refuge that will never fail,
The only hope before us set,
  Our Anchor sure within the vail.

V.

Jesus thy love shall close our song,
  That flow'd unsought through ages past,
And flows to all eternity,
  Thou art our ALL—our First and Last.

A M E N.

"*O Israel,* thou shall not be forgotten of me, *I have* blotted out as a thick cloud thy transgressions, and as a cloud thy sins: Return, for *I have redeemed thee*: Sing, O ye Heavens, for the Lord hath done it! Shout, ye lower parts of the earth, break forth into singing ye mountains, O forest, and every tree therein: For *the Lord hath redeemed* Jacob, and glorified himself in Israel. O praise the Lord all ye nations: Praise him, all ye people; both young men and maidens, old men and children; let them praise the name of the Lord. *Ye that fear the Lord,* praise him: Speaking to yourselves and one another, in Psalms, Hymns, and Spiritual Songs, singing and making melody in your heart to the Lord: Let every thing that hath breath praise the Lord."   Isaiah, David, Paul.

SECTION

SECTION X.

Introduction.

THE method of teaching children and youth by catechifing, is undoubtedly very inftructing, if the matter taught is acceptable words, even written upright words of truth, which flow from divine wifdom, and are as goads and nails faftened, for the direction of mafters of affemblies, which are given from one fhepherd. The Affemblies catechifm being thought exceptionable in many places, when compared with this rule, hath induced fome among us to lay it afide; and having been requefted by fome worthy friends, to endeavour to put into their hands fomething in this way as an affiftant in inftructing their children, I have thought that as the Affemblies fhorter catechifm had been made familiar by ufe, and contained many excellent things, it might comport with the requeft of my friends. To endeavour a more plain fcriptural anfwer to fome parts of it, and to prefent it in every anfwer agreeable to the fcriptures of truth; an acquaintance with which, is a principal end we ought to have in view in the inftruction of children and youth; for this end, I have fet the proofs in the margin, as well as to appeal to them for the truth and confiftency of the anfwers. All that can be faid to recommend it, is, it is an affemblage of divine fcriptures, calculated to inftruct the mind in a more plain, eafy and fatisfactory manner, than can be done in words which man's wifdom teacheth, by the moft refpectable affembly of mortal men. As it is, it is commended to the only wife GOD our Saviour, praying he would pleafe to accompany it with the enlightening influences of his holy fpirit to thofe who read or ufe it. AMEN.

A SHORT CATECHISM, &c.

Scripture Truths and Precepts.—A Short Catechism, with Proofs; designed for the assistance of such persons as wish to search the Scriptures for a consistent view of the Doctrines and Duties contained in them. With an Appendix, concerning Baptism; and a concluding Remark on the Lord's Supper.

But their minds were blinded: For until this day remaineth the same Vail untaken away, in the reading of the Old Testament; which Vail is done away in CHRIST, 2 Corinth. iii. 14. When it shall turn unto the LORD, the Vail shall be taken away, verse 16.

Question. WHAT is the chief end of man?

Answer. Man's chief end is to glorify God and enjoy him forever. — Coll. i. 16. John xvii. 24.

Q. What rule hath God given to direct us how we may glorify and enjoy him?

A. He hath given us in the Scriptures of the Old and New-Testament, the only rule to direct us how we may glorify and enjoy him. — Psalm cxix. 9, 105.

Q. What doth the Scriptures principally teach?

A. They principally teach, what man is to believe concerning God, and what God requires of man. — Isai. xlv. 21. Matt. vii. 12.

Q. What is God?

A. God is a Spirit, infinite, eternal and unchangeable, in his being, wisdom, power, holiness, justice, goodness, and truth. — John iv. 24. Mal. iii. 6.

Q. Are there more Gods than one?

A. There

A. There is but one only living and true God.

Q. *How doth the only living and true God make himself known?*

A. He maketh himself known as a Father in Christ Jesus, who is by nature his only begotten Son, and at all times, and in all places, by his operations as the Holy Spirit.

Q. *How may I understand your expression, "Who is by nature his only begotten Son?"*

A. Referring to the expression of the apostle, "When ye knew not God, ye did service to them that by nature are no gods;" which shews, that the apostles and first disciples worshipped Christ as God by nature.

Q. *If Christ be the only begotten Son of God, how are believers called the sons of God?*

A. As having the adoption of children by Jesus Christ.

Q. *What further evidence is there that Jesus Christ is God by nature?*

A. When he took on him our nature, thereby taking the human nature into union with himself, God was manifest in the flesh; creation, providence and redemption, being attributed to him; in which the eternal purpose of God, according to the counsel of his own will, for his own glory, is executed.

Q. *What is the work of creation?*

A. The work of Creation is God's speaking all things into being, by the

---

Marginal references:

Deuteronomy vi. 4.

Isai. lxiii. 16.
Eph. i. 3.
2 John, 3.
Gen. i. 2.

Gal. iv. 8.
Acts vii. 59.
1 Cor. i. 2.

John i. 12.
Eph. i. 5.

John i. 1. and 12.
1 Tim. iii. 16.
John i. 3.
Heb. i. 3.
Coll. i. 14.
Eph. i. 7.

Gen. i. throughout.
Psalm xxxiii. 9.

the word of his power, in the space of six days, and all very good.

Q. How did God create man?

A. In the image of God created he him, male and female created he them, and he blessed them, and called their name Adam. *Gen. i. 27, and v. 2.*

Q. What are God's works of Providence?

A. His works of providence are, his most holy, wise, and powerful preserving and governing all his creatures, and all their actions. *Psalm cxix. 91. Matt. x. 29, 30, 31.*

Q. What special act of providence did God exercise towards man in the state wherein he was created?

A. When God created man, he gave him a test of his obedience, forbidding him to eat of the tree of knowledge of good and evil, upon pain of death. *Gen. ii. 17, and iii. 3.*

Q. Did our first parents continue in the state wherein they were created?

A. Our first parents fell from the state wherein they were created by sinning against God. *Gen. iii. 6, 11, 12, Rom. v. 12.*

Q. What is sin?

A. Sin is the transgression of the law of God. *1 John iii. 4.*

Q. Did all mankind fall in Adam's first transgression?

A. By one man, sin entered into the world, and death by sin, so death passed upon all, for that all have sinned, being included in the one as their head. *Rom. iii. 23. Rom. v. 12.*

Q. Into

Q. Into what estate did the fall bring mankind?

A. Into a state of sin and misery. [Rom. viii. 22, & iii. 16.]

Q. Did God leave all mankind to perish in the state of sin and misery?

A. God having, out of his mere good pleasure, made known the mystery of his will, which he hath purposed in himself, that, in the dispensation of the fulness of time, he might gather together in one, all things in Christ, hath manifested that he hath not left them to perish in a state of sin and misery, but hath brought them into a state of salvation in a redeemer. [Eph. i. 9, 10. Eph. ii. 13.]

Q. Did Jesus Christ, thus taking our nature, as our head, accomplish our redemption?

A. He was made of a woman, made under the law, to redeem them that were under the law: taking our nature into union with himself, the law took hold of him as our surety, and was fully satisfied, by his perfect obedience to the will of God, and his one sacrifice (which was witnessed in his resurrection.) Thus he hath appeared to put away sin by the sacrifice of himself; and by his own blood; he entered into the holy place, having obtained eternal redemption. [Gal. iv. 4, 5. Chap. ix. 12, 26.]

Q. How are we made partakers of the redemption which is in Christ Jesus?

A. By the effectual application if to to us, by his Holy Spirit. [1 Cor. ii. 10, 11, 12.]

Q. How

Q. How doth the Spirit apply this redemption to us?

A. By taking of the things of Christ, and shewing them to us, enabling us to perceive the certain evidences of the truth testified of him, as our Lord and Saviour.

John xvi. 14, 15.
Titus i. 4.

Q. How doth the Spirit shew to us that Jesus is the Lord?

A. By satisfying our minds of the truth of the Scriptures, wherein this is made manifest, and subjecting them to his authority; for no man can say that Jesus is the Lord but by the Holy Ghost.

1 Cor. xii. 3.

Q. How doth the Spirit shew to us that Jesus is the Saviour?

A. By enlightening our minds, to understand the types, prophesies, priesthood, and sacrifices of the Old Testament, to center and have their complete fulfilment in the priesthood and sacrifice of Christ, the Lamb of God, who taketh away the sin of the world; so as to cause us, with satisfaction of mind, to look to, and rest in him, as our complete and only Saviour.

Acts x. 43.
Acts xiii. 23.
Heb. ix. 7—12.

Q. What benefits do they that are taught of God to know Jesus Christ, as their Lord and Saviour, partake of in this life?

A. They that believe that Jesus Christ is their Lord and Saviour, do in this life partake of justification, adoption, and sanctification, and the several benefits which in this life do accompany or flow from them.

Rom. iii. 26, 28.
Gal. iii. 26.
Acts xv. 9.

Q. *What is justification?*

A. Justification is a freedom from condemnation, by the satisfaction of law and justice, even by Jesus Christ, who hath delivered us from the curse of the law, being made a curse for us. Or thus; justification is an act of God's free grace, wherein he pardoneth all our sins, and accepteth us as righteous in his sight, only for the righteousness of Christ, imputed to us, and received in believing.

<small>2 Cor. v. 21. Gal. iii. 13.</small>

Q. *What is adoption?*

A. Adoption is of God's free grace in Christ Jesus, in whom we are received as children, heirs of God, and joint heirs with Christ.

<small>Gal. iv. 4, 5.</small>

Q. *What is the spirit of adoption, as received by us?*

A. The spirit of adoption is the right understanding and firm belief of our union with Christ, and sonship in him, whereby we are enabled to call God in Christ our Father.

<small>Rom. viii. 15. Gal. iv. 6.</small>

Q. *What is sanctification?*

A. Our sanctification, as well as adoption and justification, is in Christ, who is made to us of God, sanctification, who, that he might sanctify the people with his own blood, suffered without the gate.

<small>1 Cor. i. 30.</small>

<small>Heb. xiii. 12.</small>

Q. *What is the difference between sanctification and justification?*

A. Justification conveys the idea of our being furnished with a righteousness teoufnefs which the law demands, which we have in Chrift Jefus, who of God is made unto us righteoufnefs. Sanctification leads to the idea of that purification we ftand in need of in our ftate of pollution and defilement, by our difobedience, which we have in Chrift Jefus, who faid, " Lo I come to do thy will ;" by the which will we are fanctified, through the offering of the body of Jefus Chrift once. Heb. x. 9, 10.

Q. *What are the benefits which in this life do accompany, or flow from juftification, adoption and fanctification?*

A. The benefits that accompany or flow from them, are affurance of God's love, peace of confcience, joy in the Holy Ghoft, increafing in the knowledge of the grace which is in Chrift Jefus, as their only hope to the end. 1 John, iv. 16. Rom. v. 1, 11.

Q. *What benefits do believers hope for from Chrift at their death, and in the refurrection?*

A. That he may be with them through the dark valley of the fhadow of death, and that they may be with him to behold his glory. Pfalm xxiii. 4, 6. John xvii. 24. 1 Theff. iv. 17.

Q. *What is the duty which God requires of man?*

A. The duty which God requires of man, is obedience to his revealed will. 1 Sam. xv. 22.

Q. *What did God reveal to man, as the rule of his obedience?*

A. God

A. God gave to the children of Israel, from mount Sinai, wrote on two tables, the ten commandments, commonly called the moral law.

Exodus xx.

Q. *In the fourth commandment, thus delivered to Israel, the seventh-day sabbath is enjoined; how doth it appear, that believing Gentiles are freed from it?*

A. They were never under it: Neither did Jesus Christ, who is the Lord of the sabbath, in any of his expositions of the law, or his exhortations to the people, enjoin it upon them, nor any of his Apostles after him; but sufficiently shew, that it was not the design of the gospel to bring Gentile believers under the law.

Mark ii. 28.
Luke vi. 5.
Acts xv. 24 to 29, and the Epistle to the Gal.

Q. *The law of the seventh-day sabbath is a portion of Scripture, and is it not for our learning, on whom the ends of the world is come?*

A. Yes, verily! it was given for a sign to the children of Israel, that they may know that I am the Lord that doth sanctify them; therefore it leads us to the thing signified by that sign.

Exod. xxxi. 13, 16, 17.

Q. *What is signified to us thereby?*

A. It leads to the Lord, that doth sanctify both them and us, even Jesus Christ, who is made to us of God sanctification.

1 Cor. i. 30.

Q. *How doth the sabbath point to Christ?*

A. It

A. It was a perfect rest, in commemoration of the creation, when God rested from all his works of creation, because they were very good, pointing to and centering in, the finished work of redemption, producing the new creation, in which we are created anew in Christ Jesus. *Heb. iv. 10.*

Q. *What authority have we, from the New Testament, to conclude the sabbath thus applies to Christ?*

A. The sabbath is mentioned as the shadow of things to come, but the body is Christ; in the shadow, they were to do no manner of work, because in six days God finished the work of creation, and rested the seventh: In the substance, Christ Jesus having finished the work of redemption, we are, through the whole of this gospel day, to rest in it, because in it the Father is well pleased; as complete, that nothing can be added by us, any more than to work of creation, to which our attention is particularly called, on the first day of the week. *Col. ii. 16, 17. Isai. xi. 10. Matt. xi. 28, 29. Isai. xlii. 21. Matt. iii. 17.*

Q. *What warrant have Christ's disciples for observing the first day of the week?*

A. It was the day on which Jesus Christ rose from the dead, which evidenced the completion of the work of redemption; on that day he appeared to his disciples the first and second time; the first publick meeting *Mark xvi. beginning. John xx. 19, 26.*

meeting of the Apostles and first disciples was on that day, viz. the day of Penticost, which was the morrow after the Jewish sabbath; and from that day, ever after, they met on the first day of the week; and the observation of the first day of the week has ever since been in practise, down to our day.

Acts ii. beginning.

Q. *Was there any type of this change under the Old-Testament dispensation.*

A. The first fruits were offered on the morrow after the sabbath; the eighth day was the great day of the feast of tabernacles; the Nazarite was accepted on the eighth day; the cleansed leper was to bring his offering for cleansing on the eighth day. After Aaron, the Jewish high priest, and his sons had been consecrated seven days, the offering for them and the people, was on the eighth day; when, in token of acceptance, fire came out from before the Lord, and consumed the offering; all pointing to, and entering in the antitype of these offerings and purifications. Their being offered on the eighth day, appears to point to the resurrection of Jesus Christ, the manifestation of his acceptance as our high priest and purifier; and in his, we have the witness of our acceptance, justification, sanctification and redemption: And by believing, we enter into the rest he

Lev. xxiii. 11.
Lev. xxiii. 36.
John vii. 37.
Numb. vi. 10.
Lev. xiv. 10, 23.
Lev. ix. 1, 30.

hath

hath entered into, as our head; and are partakers of an holy sabbath kept through time and eternity.

Q. What doth the observation of the first day of the week imply?

A. Though multitudes observe it from tradition, without under- standing, yet it is plain to those who understand, that, in the nature of it, it implies a belief that Jesus is the Christ, the Saviour of the world. John iv. 42.

Q. How ought the disciples of Christ to conduct in the observation of this day?

A. By endeavouring to acquaint themselves with the Scriptures, that testify of the character and finished work of Christ, and shew the import of his resurrection, that they may with understanding, celebrate it with joy and thanksgiving, and by meeting together, to worship God in Christ; to hear of his glory, and sing of his grace and mercy, and to break bread, in remembrance of him, in imitation of the first disciples in the primitive churches. Acts xx. 7.

Q. What rule is given to believing Gentiles, under the New-Testament dispensation?

A. Jesus Christ hath summed up the moral law in these words, "Thou shalt love the Lord thy God, with all thy heart, and with all thy soul, and with all thy mind. This is the first and great commandment, and the second is like unto it, "Thou shalt Matt. xxii. 37, 38, 39, 40.

Luke x. 27.

shalt love thy neighbour as thyself. On these two hang all the law and the prophets."

Q. *How is this understood?*

A. To love God with all the heart, will exclude any other God, and excite to worship him in Christ Jesus, which is to worship him in spirit and truth, to reverence his name, and observe his institutions. To love our neighbour as ourselves will excite honour, duty and respect to magistrates, parents and superiors, and prevent hatred, malice, murder, fornication, adultery, theft, false witness, and covetousness. Love worketh no ill to his neighbour, therefore love is the fulfilling of the law.

margin: 1 John v. 3.
margin: Rom. xiii. 1.

Q. *What doth the preface to the ten commandments, delivered to Israel at mount Sinai, teach us?*

A. The preface, which is, "I am the Lord thy God, which brought thee out of the land of Egypt, and out of the house of bondage, teacheth us, that because God is the Lord and our God, and Redeemer, therefore we are under the highest obligations to obedience to him."

margin: Exod. xx. 2.
margin: Isai. xliv. 22.

Q. *Is any man able to keep the commandments of God?*

A. No mere man, since the fall is able, in this life, perfectly to keep the commandments of God, but doth daily break them, in thought, word and deed.

margin: Gen. vi. 5, and viii. 21. Matt. xv. 11.

Q. *Where*

Q. *Where is then our hope?*

A. If any man sin, we have an advocate with the Father, Jesus Christ the righteous; and he is the propitiation for the sins of the apostles and believers; and not only for them, but for the whole world. He was manifested to take away our sins; and in him is no sin. 1 John ii. 1. 1 John, ii. 2, 1 John, iii. 5.

Q. *How are the believers of this Gospel to conduct themselves?*

A. They are to manifest their gratitude by a thankful, cheerful obedience to his will, attending to his word and institutions, with prayer for his grace, that they may adorn the doctrine of God their Saviour, by a conversation becoming the Gospel. Psalm. l. 23. Phill. i. 27.

Q. *How is the word to be attended to for this end?*

A. The reading and preaching of the word is to be attended with diligence, that we may, by a growing acquaintance with the grace therein exhibited, be more and more acquainted with our obligations to the duties therein enjoined upon us, in every relation and circumstance of life. Col. iii. 16, 17.

Q. *What are the institutions of the New-Testament?*

A. The institutions of the New-Testament have been commonly called baptism and the Lord's supper. Matt. xxviii. 19. 1 Cor. xi. 23, 24, 25, 26.

T t Q. *What*

Q. What is baptism?

A. The New-Testament speaks of John's baptism, and the baptism of Christ.

Acts i. 5.

Q. What is John's baptism?

A. John, as the forerunner of Christ, baptized with water, calling the people to repentance of every expectation of salvation from the observation of the law, or from any supposed superiority one over another, by strict attention to it; full salvation being in the Messiah, for all, without distinction; for John verily baptized with water, saying, "To the people, that they should believe on him that should come after, that is Christ Jesus."

Matt. iii. 11.
Acts xix. 4.

Q. What is the baptism of Christ?

Q. There is the baptism that Christ was baptized with, and the baptism wherewith he baptized.

Q. What is the baptism that Christ was baptized with?

A. That of which he spake, when he said, "I have a baptism to be baptized with; and how am I straitened until it be accomplished;" in which he spake of his agony and death, that he tells the sons of Zebedee they should partake in.

Luke xii. 50.

Mark x. 39.

Q. How is that to be understood?

A. By that union which was manifested in his drawing all men unto him, when he was lifted up, and tasting death for every man; so that when one died for all, all died.

John xii. 32.
Heb. ii. 9.
2. Cor. v. 14.

Q. What

Q. *What evidence have we of this, seeing it was spoken only to the sons of Zebedee?*

A. The Apostle appears to have it in view, when he speaks of being buried with him in baptism, and says, "Know ye not, that so many of us as were baptized in Jesus Christ, were baptized into his death," as being considered in him in his sufferings and death, and partakers of the benefit of it. Col. ii. 12. Rom. vi. 3.

Q. *Why was Jesus Christ baptized with water in John's baptism?*

A. He gave the answer to John, "Thus it becometh us to fulfil all righteousness," speaking as the head, and intimating his relation to the people. This took place under the law dispensation; and Jesus Christ being made under it, that not one jot or tittle of the ceremonial, as well as the moral law, should fail; thus fulfilled the righteousness of it, and had this testimony by a voice from Heaven, "This is my beloved Son, in whom I am well pleased;" and was thus evidenced to John to be he that should baptize with the Holy Ghost. Matt. iii. 15. Matt. v. 18. Matt. iii. 17. John i. 33.

Q. *What was the baptism wherewith he baptized?*

A. John says, "I indeed baptize with water, but he shall baptize you with the Holy Ghost;" and Jesus told his disciples, before his ascension, "Ye shall be baptized with the Holy Ghost." Acts i. 4, 5.

Q. *What*

Q. What is intended by being baptized with the Holy Ghost?

A. Baptizing with the Holy Ghost immerses the mind in the doctrine of Christ, so as to perceive the evidence of the truth and the fulness of the salvation exhibited in the Gospel, freeing from condemnation, and furnishing the answer of a good conscience towards God, by the resurrection of Christ.

Q. What may be understood by the passages where mention is made of Christ baptizing with the Holy Ghost and with fire?

A. Fire communicates light and heat, refines gold and silver, and consumes every thing that is fuel for it; so the baptism of the Holy Ghost both enlightens the mind to understand the doctrine of Christ, and warms the heart with gratitude and joy, under a sense of the exceeding riches of the grace therein made manifest, and gives a lively hope of deliverance, in due time, from all the defilement that cleaves to us; and that every thing, wherewith we are encompassed through the temptations of Satan and the weakness of the flesh, as wood, hay, stubble, tares or chaff, shall be entirely separated from us, by him who hath his fan in his hand, and will thoroughly purge his floor, and gather the wheat into his garner, and burn up the chaff with unquenchable fire.   [For

Margin references:
1 Peter iii. 21.
Matt. iii. 11. Luke iii. 11.
Mal. iii. 3. 1 Cor. iii. 11—15. Matt. iii. 12.

A SHORT CATECHISM, &c.

[For further thoughts on Baptism, see the Appendix.]

Q. *What is the Lord's Supper?*

A. The Lord's Supper is an institution of Christ, wherein his love is brought to remembrance, in gathering together the whole purchased possession into one, in himself, as the many grains are gathered into one bread, or the many grapes into one cup, his body being given, and his blood shed, not only for his immediate disciples, but for the life of the world; and his disciples breaking bread and drinking wine, in remembrance of him, hereby shew forth to the world their satisfaction in, professed subjection to, and dependence upon, a crucified, risen Saviour, as their only hope of eternal life.

1 Cor. xvi. 17.

Luke xxii. 19, 20. John vi. 33, 51.

1 Cor. xi. 26.

Q. *Who among the sinful children of men may be encouraged to partake in the Lord's Supper?*

A. Every destitute, lost, guilty creature, that sees enough in the perfect character and finished work of Christ, as witnessed in his resurrection, for his complete salvation, and the salvation of the whole world, and professes hearty subjection to him.

Q. *What is required of them that would worthily partake of the Lord's Supper?*

A. The Apostle saith, " Let a man examine himself, and so let him

1 Corinth. xi. 28.

him eat of that bread, and drink of that cup."

Q. What in particular is a man to examine himself about, in order thereto?

A. Our examination respects ourselves and others.

Q. How doth it respect ourselves?

A. Our iniquity is, whether we discern ourselves as members of the Lord's body, so that our hope of eternal salvation is built entirely on what Jesus Christ, as our head, has wrought for us in his life, finished in his death, and witnessed in his resurrection, exclusive of any supposed personal excellency in ourselves; which is examining, whether we are in the faith.

Q. Doth not our examination respect our practice?

1 Cor. x. 14, 21.

A. Yes; we have to examine, do I understand that partaking in the bread and cup, is a voluntary profession of my obligation to flee every departure from the Lord, particularly to be on my guard against every of those things which occasioned the overthrow of the children of Israel in the wilderness.

Q. How doth our self-examination respect others?

John xii. 32.

Heb. ii. 9.

A. As Christ is the head of every man, drew all men unto him, and tasted death for every man, we are to inquire, whether we discern every man as members of Christ (though

(though not yet brought into subjection to him) as well as ourselves, so that we can remember and commemorate the love of God in Christ to the whole human race in faith, that, according to the mystery of his will, which he hath made known, according to his good pleasure, he will, in the dispensation of the fulness of times gather together all things in Christ, without which we shall eat and drink to our own self-condemnation, not discerning the Lord's body, but encouraging ourselves from some other quarter than that God was in Christ, reconciling the world to himself, not imputing their trespasses unto them. *Heb. ii. 8. Eph. i. 9, 10.*

[That you may see how the above answers are drawn from 1st of Corinthians, x. and xi. chapters, see the Conclusion.]

Q. *What is to be understood by the condescending action of Jesus Christ, in washing his disciples' feet?*

A. There appears a literal and spiritual meaning in that transaction; literally, it teaches the disciples of the Saviour to be ready to attend to every office of kindness one to another; to be ready to wash one another's feet, whenever there shall be an occasion for it, so as to be an act of kindness. The apostle mentions it as a good work, together with relieving the afflicted. *John xiii. from verse 4. 1 Tim. v. 10.*

Q. *What*

Q. What instructions are hereby conveyed, as the spiritual meaning of that transaction?

Phill. ii. 6, 7.

A. The first thing that calls our attention is the inconceivable condescension of Him, who, being in the form of God, thought it not robbery to be equal with God, but made himself of no reputation, and took upon him the form of a servant,

1st Sam. xxv. 41.

and manifested it by taking the place of a servant in washing his servants' feet, who he taught, Except they were washed, they had no part in him.

Q. Why was the feet only washed?

A. Jesus Christ gave Peter the answer, He that is washed, needeth not, save to wash his feet, but is clean every whit; the tempter was

Gen. iii. 15.

to bruise the heel, the human nature: And when the Psalmist, speaking in the person of Jesus, as en-

Psalm xlix. 5

compassed with our transgressions, calls them the iniquities of my heels, the head of every man not needing

Heb. vii. 26.

washing, being holy, harmless and undefiled.

Q. What further instructions have we herein?

A. That nothing but his washing can cleanse us. "If I wash thee not, thou hast no part in me." Our defilement is so deep, that neither our tears, repentance, reformation, nor

Zech. xiii. 1.

any works of our own, can ever wash it away; nothing short of the fountain

fountain opened in Christ Jesus to purify from sin and uncleanness.

Q. *Why is the Christian salutation so often enjoined on the first churches, called* HOLY. *"Greet ye one another with a* HOLY *kiss."*

A. It may refer to that perfect holiness that is made manifest in the embrace of mercy and truth, righteousness and peace in Christ Jesus; and to that purity with which the disciples of Christ ought to salute one another, as partakers therein, and to distinguish it from all others.

Rom. xvi. 16.
1 Cor. xvi. 20.
2d Cor. xiii. 12.

Psalm lxxxv. 10.

Q. *How is it to be distinguished from all others?*

A. As the giving a cup of cold water in the name of a disciple is distinguished from the giving one merely from civil courtesy, viz. because ye belong to Christ, it is respect to Christ, and to his disciples for his sake, that distinguishes; which respect being exercised about the boundless grace of the Gospel, may be called love; and when this salutation is performed from love to Christ, and his disciples for his sake, it may be called, in the language of Peter, " The kiss of charity."

Mark ix. 41.

1 Peter, v. 14.

Q. *How is that direction in James v. 14, to be understood, that speaks of anointing the sick with oil, in the name of the Lord?*

A. It appears to have respect to miraculous healing; the prayer of faith *shall* save the sick, even the faith that Paul perceived in the impotent

Acts xiv. 9.

potent man at Lystra, who had faith to be healed; and it is mentioned with casting out devils, as what was done by miraculous power.

Mark vi. 13.

Q. *What is prayer?*

A. Prayer is an offering up of those desires to God, for things agreeable to his will, that are excited in us by his Spirit, in the name of Christ, with confession of our sins, and thankful acknowledgment of his mercies.

Rom. viii. 26.
Eph. vi. 18.

Q. *What rule hath God given for our direction in prayer?*

A. Every part of the scripture is of use to direct us in prayer, but the special rule of direction is that form of prayer which Christ taught his disciples, commonly called the Lord's prayer.

Matt. vi. 9—13.

Q. *As there are different apprehensions in the minds of Christians about the Lord's prayer, some supposing it was designed only for the use of the disciples during the days of his humiliation, and had its accomplishment in the death, resurrection and ascension of Christ, and the gift of the Holy Ghost; who take notice of this prayer by giving thanks, that thy kingdom is come, and thy will is done in Christ Jesus, and that we have this Gospel-day our daily bread, &c. Others look upon it as a form still to be used by Christ's disciples: How then is it a rule of direction in prayer?*

A. It

A. It is a rule of direction to both, to pattern after; for those that believe it was fulfilled in Christ, must know that while we see not yet all things put under him, there are yet glorious things to be accomplished concerning his kingdom, until the seventh angel soundeth, and the kingdoms of this world become the kingdoms of our Lord and of his Christ, and he shall reign forever and ever. And those who constantly use this form, must know that Jesus hath glorified the Father's name, that his kingdom come, or was made fully manifest, after the Holy Ghost was given on the day of Pentecost, his will being done in him; therefore it is necessary that the use of this prayer should be with understanding; and to each sentiment, it is a rule of direction in prayer. Heb. ii. 8.

Rev. xi. 15.

Q. *What doth the preface of the Lord's prayer teach us?*

A. The preface of the Lord's prayer, which is, " Our Father who art in Heaven," teaches us, in union with Jesus Christ, to draw near to God with all holy reverence and confidence, as children to a father, able and ready to help us, and that we should pray with and for others. Gal. iv. 6.

Q. *How are the several petitions to be used as our direction in prayer?*

A. Every thing we are directed to pray for, in the Scriptures, is comprehended

comprehended in the glory of the Divine Name, the advancement of his kingdom, and his will being done in earth as it is in Heaven, in our being supplied with daily bread, by being enabled daily to feed on the bread of life, trusting in, and looking to him for the necessary support of the outward man; the forgiveness of trespasses, from him who hath power to forgive sins, and our being blessed in him, with an ability to forgive those that trespass against us, being kept from temptation, and delivered from the evil one, may comprehend all we are directed to pray for.

Phill. iv. 6.

1 Peter, iv. 7.

Q. *What doth the conclusion of the Lord's prayer teach us?*

A. By the conclusion of the Lord's prayer, which is, " For thine is the kingdom, the power, and glory, for ever, Amen," We are taught to take our encouragement in prayer from God only, and in our prayers to praise him, ascribing, kingdom, power and glory to him; and in testimony of our desires and assurance to be heard, we say, Amen.

Matt. vi. 13.

Psalm xxii. 28.
Obadiah 21.

APPENDIX.

APPENDIX.

WHILE the law dispensation lasted, Jesus Christ, who was made under it, is said, to make and baptize more disciples than John, though Jesus himself baptized not, but *<i>his disciples;</i> John hearing this, saith, He must increase, but I must decrease, intimating, that his baptism was to go out by decrease, and that the baptism, that was to take place after the ascension of Christ, must increase, which was the baptism of the Holy Ghost: which Jesus told his disciples to tarry at Jerusalem for; and while they were there assembled, the Holy Ghost came upon them; and according to his promise to them, that he should take of mine, and shew it unto you, they received a clear understanding of the doctrine of Christ, and power to be his witnesses at Jerusalem; and as many as gladly received the word, were baptized; if by gladly receiving the word, is to be understood, a clear understanding of the truth of the Apostles doctrine, so as to gain full credit in their minds, enabling them to count all things loss for the excellency of this knowledge, their minds being immersed in the doctrine of Christ, they were baptized with the Holy Ghost; which was the baptism the Apostles and believers were tarrying at Jerusalem for, according to the direction given them by Jesus Christ before his ascension; and when we consider three thousand were added in one day, it is difficult to conceive that so many could in one day be baptized with water.

It

---

* A learned aged person has assured me that he had in his youth an ancient Greek Testament (the loss of which he lamented) in which this passage is thus read, "Though Jesus himself baptized not, but discipled."

It is true, we have two passages that expresly speak of baptizing with water after the ascension, viz. Phillip baptizing the Eunuch, and Peter at Cornelius's house: and it also seems probable that Paul baptized Crispus and Gaius, and the houshould of Stephanus, with water; but he thanked God that he baptized no other; (which makes it very likely that the disciples Paul found at Ephesus were not baptized with water by him; if they had been, it would make a greater number than he had spoken of, for the men were about twelve, who, when they HEARD, were baptized in the name of the Lord Jesus:) For, saith he, Christ sent me not to baptize, but to preach the Gospel. It is probable, he might not at first so fully understand his commission, as John's baptism was to go out by decrease, the like may be said of Peter, who, though he said at the house of Cornelius,* Who can forbid water that these should not be baptized, who have received the Holy Ghost, yet after, in one of his epistles, saith, baptism doth now save us, not the putting away the filth of the flesh, (which is all water can do) but the answer of a good conscience towards God, by the resurrection of Christ.

However, those who think themselves bound to practice water baptism, must know, if they do it understandingly, that it can be no more than a visible profession of christianity, and they ought to beware of the error that puts it in the place of Christ Jesus, as necessary to salvation, which has so far prevailed, as to cause parents to mourn as without hope, if any thing prevented the baptizing of a child before its death, who would have had no anxiety if the child had been baptized, as if the salvation by Jesus Christ was incomplete, till finished by the actions of his creatures. But

---

* In the same Greek Testament this passage is thus read, "Can any man dispute about water baptism, seeing these have received the Holy Ghost as well as we, and he commanded them to be enrolled among the disciples."

But it may be said, salvation appears connected with baptism, in *Mark* xvi. 16, "He that believeth, and is baptized, shall be saved; and he that believeth not shall be damned." If this is understood of the baptism of CHRIST, it is easy and plain to conceive, that when the mind is baptized in the doctrine of CHRIST, and finds full rest in his perfect work and sacrifice, as witnessed by his resurrection, as its complete and only salvation, or finds the answer of a good conscience toward GOD by the resurrection of CHRIST, that it is freed or saved, from the fearful expectation of the curse of the law, justly due as a transgressor; while he that believeth not, remains under that sense of condemnation, which cannot be removed but by the belief of the Gospel.

CONCLUSION.

CONCLUSION.

INQUIRING for the meaning of the apostle in the exhortation, Let a man examine himself, and so let him eat of that bread, and drink of that cup—I find the apostle in the tenth chapter of the first of Corinthians, taking notice of the Israelites who were baptized into Moses, in the cloud, and in the sea, and did all eat the same spiritual meat, and did all drink of the same spiritual drink, for they drank of that spiritual rock that followed them, and that rock was Christ. But with many of them God was not well pleased, for they were overthrown in the wilderness, and mentions them as our example, to the intent we should not lust after evil things, as they also lusted; and when he had gone over those things which proved their overthrow in the wilderness, he says, " Wherefore, my beloved, flee from idolatry; the cup of blessing which we bless, is it not the communion of the blood of Christ; the bread which we break, is it not the communion of the body of Christ; for we being many, are one bread, and one body, for we are all partakers of that one bread;" as if an attendance on the Lord's-supper, in its native simplicity, was a most efficacious call from idolatry, and from every species of the above-mentioned errors of the children of Israel. Being all partakers of that one bread, why should it not satisfy, and save us from murmuring under every dispensation of providence? why should we tempt Christ? being discouraged because of the way, by loathing what he provides for us, (who is our manna, our daily bread;) the realizing that we are one bread, and of the one body, that our bodies are the temples of the Holy Ghost, should ever excite

CONCLUSION.

us to flee fornication, and not to take the members of Chrift and join them to a harlot; and that finglenefs towards Chrift, which partaking of the Lord's-fupper we are called to, which calls us off from idolatry, for, faith the Apoftle, ye cannot drink the cup of the Lord, and the cup of the devils; ye cannot be partakers of the Lord's table and the tables of the devils. This compared with the rebuke he gives to the Corinthians, in the next chapter, for their conduct when they came together; for one taking before another his own fupper, and one is hungry and another is drunken, looks as if they had flid into their former practices in their ftate of Gentilifm (that was then in practice among the Gentiles) and called it the Lord's fupper. Even as the feaft made to the golden calf, was by Aaron called a feaft to the Lord, when the people fat down to eat and drink, and rofe up to play. The Apoftle tells them, this is not to eat the Lord's fupper: for which conduct he could not praife them; and then to call them off from such conduct, carries their minds to an attention to it, as he had received of the Lord, which he backs with the confideration, that whoever eats and drinks unworthily, eateth and drinketh judgment to himfelf, or felf-condemnation, being condemned of himfelf for not judging a right of the Lord's body; for which caufe many are weak and fickly among you, and many fleep. It is eafy to conceive of excefs in eating and drinking, together with felf-condemnation arifing therefrom, bringing on weaknefs and ficknefs, &c.

Therefore, let a man examine himfelf, and fo let him eat of that bread, and drink of that cup. Now when we confider the apoftle in the midft of thefe things, of which we have taken notice; fay I, would have you know, that the head of every man is Chrift, we are taught, if the head of every man is Chrift, then the whole human nature are taken into him, were drawn to him, when he was lifted up, and he tasted death for every man, is this my encouragement, as the ground of my acceptance, upon a level with the vilest? Or have I some preference on account of something personal that encourages me to eat before another my own supper? this is not to eat the Lord's supper; for in that we being many, are one bread and one body; all former difference between the several grains of wheat being lost in one bread, so all distinction is lost in Christ Jesus, he being all in all. Our encouragement being exclusively from him, produces the highest sense of our obligation to yield ourselves, with all our hearts, to him; which is what every one that attends on the Lord's supper, with understanding, is sensible of.

Or, on the other hand, do I, for want of a sense of the complete fulness that is in Christ, wish for some other excellency, wish to be like some other whom I esteem, as if I should then have an encouragement which I could not find exclusively in Christ, and come to look for it there, in order to make one of that body, and to partake in the one bread. The Apostle says, we are one body, and one bread, for we are all partakers of that one bread.

Further, we may inquire, do I understand the obligation, that partaking in the bread and cup, I consider myself voluntarily under, to flee every species of departure from the Lord, or the tendency of that singleness towards Christ, with which I should partake in the Lord's supper, to cause me to beware of every of those things, which occasioned the overthrow of the children of Israel in the wilderness.

These thoughts being persued, in order to find an answer to the question, what is a man to examine himself about, in order to partaking of the Lord's supper? Are here inserted, that any one may judge of the propriety of the answer to that question, and those consequent upon it.

SECTION

SECTION XI.

The RIGHT *and* WRONG WAY, *with their* TENDENCY *and* EFFECTS.

THERE often arises much perplexity of mind from different apprehensions of several texts of scripture, and various expositions of them by writers and preachers, who often run counter, not only to each other, but sometimes appear inconsistent with themselves, so that in attending to them, the mind is ready to sigh out a wish, O that I knew the right way. It is a short, but a comprehensive ejaculation.

In order to treat of it distinctly, it may be useful to say,

First. There is the way of our acceptance with God.

Secondly. The way of our peace.

Thirdly. The way of our duty, or the way in which we ought to walk; these are all connected, but for clearer understanding, may be considered distinctly.

First, For the way of our acceptance with God, Jesus Christ hath told us, *I am the way*; and the apostle tells us, *He hath made us accepted in the beloved.* Take special notice of the single syllable *in*, and it will tend to help the understanding of the passage: It is not said he hath made us accepted for the sake of the beloved, but *in* the beloved; if we are accepted in him, we are in him. The human nature, is considered in the first Adam, as their head in the transgression; he being the figure of him that was to come, they are considered *in* the substance of that figure: For as in Adam all die, so *in* Christ shall all be made alive, 1st of *Corinth.* xv. 22. The apostle

again

again makes it even in *Romans* v. 22, *As sin reigned unto death, even so might grace reign through righteousness, unto eternal life by Jesus Christ our Lord.*

The head of every man is Christ, the human nature is considered in union with him, as members in the head, as branches in the vine, or as the marriage-union, *Thy maker is thy husband, the Lord of hosts is his name, the God of the whole earth shall he be called.* In vew of this union, we understand the particle *in*, he hath made us accepted *in the* beloved, which agrees with the gospel preached to Abraham, *In thy seed shall all the families of the earth be blessed.* With the lxxii psalm, *Men shall be blessed in him.* With the prophet Jeremiah, *The nations shall bless themselves in him, and in him, shall they glory.* The prophet Isaiah saith, *The Lord laid on him the iniquities of us all*, and he appeared to put them away by the sacrifice of himself. The apostle Peter saith, *He bear our sins in his own body to the tree.* The apostle Paul saith, *He died for our offences, and rose again for our justification.* Hence we are said *to be justified in him*, 1st of Corinth. vi. 11, and as we stood in need of sanctification in our state of pollution, as well as to be justified from guilt and condemnation, *Jesus Christ is made to us of God sanctification.* So the apostle speaks of being *sanctified IN Christ Jesus.* When we reflect on any spiritual blessings we enjoy or hope for, we are led to bless the God and Father of our Lord Jesus Christ, who hath blessed us with all spiritual blessings in heavenly things *in Christ Jesus;* and if that expression should cast the eye of our mind back to the fountain from whence they flow, the following words will direct the mind to the center—*According as he hath chosen us in him before the foundation of the world.*

We are said to be *chosen in him*, to be gathered together *in him; rooted and built up in him;* made to sit together

gether in heavenly places, *in Christ Jesus*. Sitting is a posture of rest, where we might pause to reflect on the exceeding riches of grace herein made manifest. These considerations may serve to excite us to look for acceptance, justification, sanctification, and all spiritual blessings, where they are, and not in ourselves where they are not; which would be to seek the living among the dead.

What has been offered may help to an understanding of the words of our Lord and Saviour, who says, *I am the way, no man cometh to the Father but by me.* 'Tis what is called by the prophet, *the old path, the good way*, referring to the gospel preached to Adam, in the seed of the woman; to Abraham *in* thy seed shall all the nations of the earth be blessed. The way made known to Moses and the children of Israel in all the tipes and sacrifices, under that dispensation, pointing to, and centering in, Christ Jesus, called by the Psalmist, the way everlasting, because the God of Abraham, the God of Isaac, and the God of Jacob, is *his name for ever, and his memorial to all generations.*

When Jesus, the way, is made manifest, the Apostle calls it *the new and living way, the way to the holiest of all, by the blood of Jesus*: Thus you have an attempt to point out the scripture account of the right way of our acceptance with God.

Objection. Doth not the scripture speak of repentance, faith and obedience, as necessary to salvation.

For answer, I would say, I conceive repentance to be an alteration of mind; upon the manifestation of a truth that was hid before, as when John preached, repent ye for the kingdom of heaven is at hand, and Jesus began to preach, and to say, Repent for the kingdom of Heaven is at hand, they preached to the Jews who were in expectation that the Messiah should
have

have an earthly kingdom, and should deliver them from the Romans, under whom they were in bondage; they are called to alter their minds, it was the kingdom of Heaven that was at hand. After the death and resurrection of Christ, we have no account of the Apostles repeating the same expressions, the kingdom was come, and repentance, and remission of sins, were to be preached in his name. To use a similitude---Suppose a traveller to have lost his way, and yet knew it not, and had progressed far in a wrong way, should he be overtaken by a faithful, skilful guide, that was able to convince him that he was wrong, had lost his way; and to shew him the right way, consequent on this he would turn, undoubtedly grieving he had been so long lost, and had gone so far out of the way.

Now it is natural for the children of men universally to suppose that something must be wrought in in them, or done by them, in order to their acceptance with God. Wherewithal shall I come before the Lord, is the universal inquiry of every thoughtful mind, if they are convinced that burnt offerings, calves, rivers of oil, yea, even the first born, will not atone for transgression, nor the fruit of the body for the sin of the soul: Yet they are ready to think, if I had true repentance, then I should be accepted for Christ's sake. And the inquiry is, how shall I get it, how shall I exercise it, how shall I know it is sincere, how indeed! until Jesus is known as the way.

When the mind is thus lost, looking for acceptance in or from himself in a greater or less degree, it will never come to full rest in the sincerity and uprightness of his own repentance. What lack I yet? will still distress the mind, and sometimes prevail to that degree that is described, Job xxxiii. 19, He is chastened with pain upon his bed, and the multitude

of

of his bones with strong pain; so that his life abhorreth bread, and his soul dainty meat; his flesh is consumed away, that it cannot be seen, and his bones that were not seen, stick out; yea, his soul draweth near to the grave, and his life to the destroyer.

The following words appear to shew the effect of the good news of the Gospel:—

If there be a messenger, an interpreter, one of a thousand, to shew to man his uprightness, (namely the uprightness of Jesus Christ made manifest by the Holy Spirit, who Jesus Christ promised to send to testify of him, for the scripture tells us there is none upright among men) then he is gracious unto him, and faith deliver him, for I have found a ransom. The satisfaction of mind consequent hereupon, is manifested in the following words. His flesh shall be fresher than a child's, he shall return to the days of his youth—he shall pray unto God, and he will be gracious unto him, and he shall see his face with joy. Thus have I written of Jesus Christ as the way; and of our being accepted in the beloved; as knowing we shall always progress in the way of self-righteousness, until we are led into the new and living way.

The like may be said of faith; for how shall they believe on him, of whom they have not heard: It is a fruitless business to labour to work faith in our hearts, and exercise it, and evidence it by obedience while we are ignorant of the truth to be believed, and the evidence of it.

Therefore have I written of the truth to be believed, viz. that he hath made us accepted in the beloved, that Jesus is the way; if this can be evidenced to the mind to be a certain truth from the scriptures, can the person help believing it, and is it possible for all the labour of the mind, with all the assistance of others, to produce faith, unless the gospel is thus evidenced to be true. There

There arifes another objection to what hath been said, concerning our being accepted in the beloved.

The Apoftle Peter, when he went to Cornelius, faid, I perceive that God is no refpector of perfons; but in every nation, he that feareth God and worketh righteoufnefs is accepted of him.

For anfwer it may be inquired, who is he that feareth God, and worketh righteoufnefs; was it Cornelius or Jefus Chrift? it may be faid, that the three men who were fent to Peter, called Cornelius a juft man, and one that feareth God: That was their opinion of him, and teftimony concerning him. But the teftimony of the fcripture concerning all mankind is, they are all under fin, there is none righteous, no, not one; there is no fear of God before their eyes, therefore Peter appears to have refpect to Jefus Chrift, as he that feareth God, and worketh righteoufnefs, the fame of whom the Pfalmift fpeaks in the 112th Pfalm, Bleffed is the man that feareth the Lord. (The man is the fingular.) This will appear,

1ft. From the end for which Cornelius fent for Peter, which was to hear words whereby he and all his houfe fhould be faved. Acts xi. 14.

2dly. It appears from the defign of the vifion that appeared to Peter, to prepare him to go to Cornelius the Gentile. The gofpel that was to be preached among all nations, was to begin at Jerufalem, and the Apoftles were forbidden at firft to go to the Gentiles; what Peter was taught by the vifion, was that he fhould call no man common, or unclean, as the Jews until then, looked upon the Gentiles.

So then when Peter had come to Cornelius, and had heard the occafion of his fending for him, confirming what he had already been taught by the vifion, he opened his mouth and faid, I perceive that God is no refpector of perfons, but in every nation he

that

that feareth God, and worketh righteousness, is accepted of him, as if he had said, I perceive Jesus Christ's perfect work is accepted in behalf of the Gentile, as well as the Jew: This is the *mystery that in other ages was not made known to the sons of men.* As it is now revealed to his holy Apostles and Prophets by the spirit, that the Gentiles should be fellow heirs, and of the same body, and partakers of his promise in Christ, by the gospel.

3dly. It appears from Peter's preaching to Cornelius—See how it proceeds in every nation, he that feareth God, and worketh righteousness is accepted with him, *according to* the word which God sent to the children of Israel, preaching peace by Jesus Christ, he is Lord of all. Read on in Acts x. from the 36th to 43d verse, which closes with, to him give all the prophets. Witness that through his name, whosoever believeth in him, shall receive the remission of sins. As he spake these words, the Holy Ghost fell on all them which heard the word; the Holy Ghost was not given by the works of the law, but by the hearing of faith, or the preaching of Jesus. Now putting these things together, the end for which Peter was sent for, and for which he had the vision preparatory to his going, and Peter's preaching Jesus to him, and bringing in the evidence of all the prophets to this truth; it appears from this passage that he hath made us both Jews and Gentiles accepted in the beloved.

OBJECTION. Jesus Christ saith, *Except a man be born again he connot see the kingdom of God;* of what avail will the work of Christ be to me unless I am born again?

For answer it may be said, the scriptures testify of Christ as the head of every man, and when we read them as testifying of men, we have not the key that will open them, to the rest and satisfaction of our minds;

perhaps this scripture text has been thus perverted as much as any other portion, of scripture. Let us look of the passage:

Nicodemus says, *We know that thou art a teacher sent from God, or proceeding from God. For no man can do these miracles that thou dost, except God be with him.* Jesus answered and said unto him except some one were born from above he cannot see the kingdom of God, as it is read in the Greek Testament the words, *A man and again,* are not there, therefore it appears that Jesus Christ is speaking of himself as if he had said, you are so far right, Nicodemus, in saying I am a teacher, proceeding from God, for no man can do these miracles, except God be with him; for except such a one were born from above, he cannot see the kingdom of God. Here arises a question, What is the kingdom of God? Let the apostle answer. He saith the kingdom of God is righteousness, peace and joy in the Holy Ghost. Now where can this be seen in any man born after the flesh? The current testimony of scripture is, that there is none righteous, no, not one; they are all gone out of the way; there is none upright among men. Hence except some one be born from above, he cannot see the kingdom of God. As righteousness, so peace is exclusively in him, for *the work of righteousness is peace, and the effect of righteousness is quietousness, and assurance for ever.* Hence Jesus Christ says—*My peace I give unto you, in the world ye shall have tribulation, but in me ye shall have peace.*—And the apostles *preached peace by Jesus Christ.* Hence the spirit that Jesus Christ promised was to testify of him, not to speak of himself, or of his own work in the hearts of men, persuading them that they are born again, that they have a new nature, an inwrought principle of grace and holiness in themselves, which makes them not like other men; but *he shall glorify me, he shall take of mine and shew it unto you:* For saith the apostle, *No man can say that Jesus is the Lord but by the Holy Ghost.* Nicodemus

Nicodemus not understanding our Lord, speaking of himself, saith, How can a man be born when he is old, can he enter the second time into his mother's womb and be born. Jesus answered, *Verily verily I say unto thee, except some one be born of water and of the spirit he cannot enter into the kingdom of God.*

When Jesus went to John to be baptized of him, he said to John, *Thus it becometh us to fulfil all righteousness; and when he was baptized, went up straightway out of the water, and lo the heavens were opened unto him, and he saw the spirit of God descending like a dove, and lighting upon him; and lo a voice from heaven, saying, this is my beloved son in whom I am well pleased.* This was the truth he heard of God, confirming to him the prophesy in Isaiah xlii.1, Preparing him for his fasting and temptations in the wilderness, and for his public ministry.

That which is born of the flesh is flesh, and that that is born of the spirit, is spirit: That Jesus was born of the spirit is evident from what was said to Mary, in answer to her inquiry, how shall these things be, seeing I know not a man; the angel answered and said unto her, *the holy Ghost shall come upon thee, and the power of the highest shall overshadow thee, therefore also that holy thing that shall be born of thee, shall be called the Son of God,* this is the holy one born from above. John saith, verse 31, He that cometh from above, is above all, he that cometh from Heaven is above all, and Jesus Christ saith again in John viii. 23. I am from above, 'tis the same word that is translated again in the 3d verse.

OBJECTION. But it is said, verse 7th, marvel not that I said unto you, *ye* (in the plural) must be born again.

For answer it may be remembered that the Apostle saith, the head of every man is Christ, he is called the second Adam, the Lord from Heaven; and the head is not without the members, nor the members without the head; either in birth, life, death, resurrection,

rection, or ascension: The Apostle saith, we are his workmanship, *created in Christ Jesus*, when therefore we look for the new birth in ourselves, the voice behind us points us to Christ Jesus, saying, this is the way.

If we would look for marks, compare John i. 12, 13, with 1st of John, v. 1, and we have the Apostolick account of this matter, *He that believeth that Jesus is the Christ is born of God.*

The Spirit bloweth where it listeth, and thou hearest the sound thereof, but canst not tell whence it cometh, nor whether it goeth ; so is every one that is born of the Spirit, the word, that is, is not in the Greek Testament ; so is every one born of the Spirit.

Nicodemus *answered and said unto him, how can these things be?* Jesus answered, *art thou a master in Israel, and knowest not these things?* As if he had said, do not you, that are a teacher in Israel, know that part of Isaiah's prophesy that is ushered in with a note of attention, Behold! Behold a virgin shall conceive and bear a son, and thou shall call his name Imanuel, or do you not recollect the other prophesy of the same prophet, unto us a child is born, unto us a son is given, whose name is the wonderful counseller, the mighty God, the everlasting Father, the Prince of peace, with the prophesy of Mica, but thou Bethlehem Ephratah, though thou be little among the thousands of Judah, out of thee shall he come forth to me, to be ruler in Israel, whose going forth have been from of old, from everlasting.

Verily, verily I say unto thee, we speak that we do know, and testify that which we have seen, and ye receive not our witness ; if I have told you earthly things, and ye believe not, how shall ye believe, if I tell you of heavenly things. If I have used a similitude from earthly things to speak of my being born from above, and ye believe not, how shall you believe, if I tell you of

heavenly

heavenly things. In what follows, to the end of the 21ſt verſe, where the account of the converſation with Nicodemus cloſes, unleſs you believe me to be born from above, how can ye believe me to be the antitype of the brazen ſerpent or the Saviour of the world.

Viewing this paſſage as teſtifying of Chriſt, there appears a connexion between Nicodemus's addreſs and our Saviour's anſwer to him, the whole pointing to himſelf as the world's Saviour, agreeable to the apoſtles expreſſion, to the praiſe of the glory of his grace, wherein he hath made us accepted in the beloved.

Is there not an objection ariſing from what has been ſaid to Cain, *If thou doſt well, ſhalt thou not be accepted; but if thou doſt not well, ſin lieth at the door.*

For anſwer, it may be ſaid, that Abel offered the firſtling of the flock, and of the fat thereof, pointing to the one ſacrifice, the Lamb of God, that taketh away the ſin of the world. The apoſtle ſays, by faith Abel offered a more acceptable ſacrifice than Cain, which ſhew that he looked to be accepted in the beloved.

Cain being very wroth that his offering was not accepted, which is mentioned before Abel's, was thus anſwered, and in that anſwer the goſpel appears to be preached to him. If thou doſt not well, ſin lieth at the door: If we inquire who is the door, Jeſus himſelf gives the anſwer, I am the door, by me if any man enter, he ſhall be ſaved (any man not excluding Cain.)

The paſſage goes on, and his deſire (viz. the deſire of Jeſus the door) ſhall be unto thee, and thou ſhalt rule over him. Chriſt's deſire was unto Cain, though the ſame ſpirit that influenced Cain, ruled over him, or prevailed to put him to death; his deſire was towards them that were thus influenced, expreſſed in

his

his prayer, *Father forgive them, for they know not what they do.*

Having thus considered the objections to the first head, the way of our acceptance with God, let us proceed to consider

2dly, The way of our peace. The prophet Isaiah saith, *the chastisement of our peace was upon him, neither shall the covenant of my peace be removed, saith the Lord, that hath mercy on thee;* the apostle saith, *he is our peace,* and they preached peace *by Jesus Christ,* he hath made peace by the blood of his cross; that being an unshaken truth, that can never fail; as true if we do not believe it, as if we do; yet it puts no man in possession of peace in his own mind and conscience, until the gospel that reports this truth is believed; the things of our peace are written that we might believe, it is believing we have life through his name. Life and peace are so connected, that we cannot enjoy life without peace; hence it is said, *we which have believed do enter into rest.* The apostle speaking of Christ dying for our sins, and rising again for our justification, adds, *Therefore, being justified, by faith* or beliving this truth, *we have peace with God through our Lord Jesus Christ.*

3dly. For the way in which we should go:

Negatively, it is not to make our peace with God, that is made by the blood of the cross.

When any that visit the sick and dying, ask them whether they have made their peace with God, and exhort them to it immediately, they do not appear to be messengers of peace, a messenger of peace would rather comfort a distressed sinner, by bringing to his view, *all we like sheep have gone astray, and the Lord laid on him the iniquities of us all; he was wounded for our transgressions, he was bruised for our iniquities; the chastisement of our peace was upon him, and by his stripes we are healed; when we were without strength,*

strength, to make our peace, *Christ died for the ungodly.*

Positively it is to attend to the will of God in Christ Jesus, revealed in the scriptures; and as man cannot be profitable to God, we can render him no things but thanksgiving; therefore he hath directed us to manifest our gratitude to him, by our conduct one to another. Hence it is emphatically included in what is called the new commandment, *that ye love one another, as I haved love you,* this is my commandment, *that ye love one another.* The exercise of it, is directed by that precept, *Therefore all things whatsoever ye would that men should do unto you, do ye even so to them, for this is the law and the prophets*: Therefore, wherefore because your heavenly father is more ready to give good things to them that ask him, than earthly parents are to give bread to their children.

Love thus directed, worketh no ill to his neighour. Thanfgiving includes every exercise we are called to. Prayer has its foundation in Thanksgiving, that there is a new and living way, by which we draw nigh to God, that it is said, that if any among you are afflicted, let him pray that we are allowed in every thing by prayer and supplication, to make known our requests to God, is always ground of thanksgiving : Faith and repentance are inseparable from thanksgiving. The gospel being believed true, will fill the mind with joy and thankfgiving. The discovery of the right way to a lost traveller, will fill his mind with joy and thanksgiving, mingled with grief and sorrow for his progressing so far in the contrary path.

If any act of obedience is performed, it is from this quarter : Every act of benevolence, that is rightly performed, is a thank-offering to the Lord.

If a number of disciples eat and drink together in remembrance of the dying, rising Lord, what is it but a season of thanksgiving; thus I think the whole of
the

the exercise of piety towards God, may be included in thanksgiving, which is a grateful commemoration of his love and mercy, that promotes an attention to the observation of his will, which hath been before said to be, that we love one another: Love one to another includes that fellowship we have one with another, in drawing nigh to God in Christ, in expressions of thanksgiving, and in a benevolent care to perform those mutual good offices we may have an oportunity for, or are called to one to another.

It may be of use after having meditated on the way of our acceptance, the way of peace and the way wherein we should go, to remark the consequences of going out of the way, or to meditate on the wrong way. The wise man saith, the way of transgressors is hard, and we read in the 89th psalm, which is spoken prophetically of Jesus Christ, *if his children forsake my law, and walk not in my statutes, I will visit their transgression with a rod, and their iniquities with stripes, nevertheless my loving kindness will I not take from him, nor suffer my faithfulness to fail*: The loving kindness shall not be taken from him, from Christ Jesus, yet if his children forsake my law, *I will*, there is the word of truth, for it I will visit their transgressions with a rod, and their iniquities with stripes, the rod and stripes follow transgression, as the shadow follows the substance. To instance in our first parents, after transgression they hid themselves, were afraid because they were naked; fear, shame and nakedness were the consequence, never could they recover the robe of innocence by all the figleaves they could sew together, but must forever have remained naked, had not the Lord God cloathed them.

Suppose you or I had never told a lie, but were innocent in that respect, upon our being once guilty, it were impossible to recover that robe of innocence, we should be immediately exposed to self-condemnation,

nation which as stripes with a rod, would distress our minds with shame and remorse, when ever we reflected on the nature and aggravations of such an evil.

Suppose our covetousness prompts us to overreach and defraud our neighbors, that we might get unjust gain, what a source of trouble and distress should we open on our own minds? Perhaps in time of temptation, we think of no other difficulty, than what arises from the hiding it from the knowledge of those whom we may deceive; and are not afraid of being harrassed by the reflections of our own minds. We do not mean to worry ourselves about such matters; but purpose to divert them from such gloomy thoughts: But riper age, sickness, or unavoidable wakefulness in the night, which we are exposed to, will bring on thinking, whether we will or no: Or the meeting with something similar from others, may force conviction on our minds, when we are ready loudly to say what they deserve: Or heavy losses and disappointments in business, may force the mind to inquire, if they are not providentially ordered as a rod and stripes for thus going astray. It is said, that the children of Israel, when from time to time they were carried into captivity, not only brought to remembrance later transgressions against the law of God, but were ready to say, there was an ounce of the golden calf in all their afflictions.

When Joseph's brethren were in affliction in Egypt, what they had done many years before, afflicted their minds in such a manner, that they could not keep it in, but said one to another, *We are verily guilty concerning our brother, in that we saw the anguish of his soul, when he besought us, and we would not hea , therefore is all this evil come upon us.* They had doubtless been under the rod and stripes for the succeeding years, while they endeavored to conceal their conduct towards their brother. How much aching of heart they endured? what fear leaft they fhould be found out? What a fenfe of ingratitude and difobedience they labored under, which they concealed? But now from home the rod and ftripes came fo heavy, that they could not help crying out in Egypt under the fmart. Thus we fee the tendency of going afide from the rule of doing to others, as we would they fhould do unto us.

If we were to take notice of the tendency of every vice, every ftep out of the right way, we might fee the above connection between erring from the way, and the confequent forrow and affliction.

The confequences of intemperance, are often made manifeft, both in the bodily health and outward eftate of thofe of us, who unhappily indulge in thofe exceffes;* thefe are vifible, while the reflections of our own minds may be almoft intolerable to ourfelves, though we may labour to conceal them from others.

If we fhould reflect on the tendency of debauchery, it would open a field of diftreffing confequences, which would ferve to illuftrate the truth of the apoftles expreffion, He that committeth fornication, finneth againft his own body: As well as that of the wife man, and thou mourn at the laft, when thy flefh and body is confumed.

Thus taking a view of the different ways, we fee the tendency of each. The path of the juft one, is as a rifing light, which fhines more and more unto the perfect day, while the way of the wicked is as darknefs. The certainty of the truth of thefe obfervations,

---

* Dr. RUSH, in his "Inquiry into the Effects of Spirituous Liquors," after having fpoken of their effects, on the body, producing difeafe, goes on to mention their effects on property, having among the inhabitants of cities they produce Debt, Difgrace and Bankruptcy, among farmers they produce Idlenefs, with its ufual confequences, fuch as houfes without windows, barns without roofs, gardens without inclofures, fields without fences, hogs without yokes, sheep without wool, maugre cattle, feeble horfes, and half-clad, dirty children, without principles, morals or manners.

tions, may be gathered from the scriptures of the Old and New Testament, it is said, *He that diggeth a pit, shall fall therein; he that breaketh a hedge, the serpent shall bite him; there is no serpent in the high way, no lion shall be there, nor any ravenous beast,* but on breaking the hedge to go out of the way, the serpent *shall bite,* not may possibly, but shall. Our blessed Saviour says, *With what measure ye mete, it shall be measured to you again.* And the apostle saith, *Whatsoever a man soweth, that shall he also reap: He that soweth to the flesh, shall of the flesh reap corruption, but he that soweth to the spirit, shall of the spirit reap life everlasting.* And when he is speaking to servants, he says, *He that doth wrong, shall receive for the wrong, that he hath done, and there is no respect of persons,* no not those who may be esteemed high in the divine favour: The passage in the 89th psalm, first mentioned, may here be recollected, *If his children forsake my law, I will visit their transgression with a rod,* &c. It may be inquired, how doth this consist with the doctrine of forgiveness, I will forgive their iniquities, and remember their sins no more.

For answer, the case of the children of Israel, may be mentioned, who fell in the wilderness, for whom Moses prayed. Pardon the iniquity of this people, &c. who was answered, I have pardoned according to thy word; not I will, but I *have,* yet it is said, Surely they shall not see the land, which I promised to their fathers; though they were pardoned, their carcasses fell in the wilderness, and they were not suffered to go into the promised land: The psalmist appears to have this in view, psalm xcix. 8, *Thou wast a God that forgavest their iniquities, though thou tookest vengeance of their inventions.* It is, if *his children* forsake my law, I will visit *their* transgressions with a rod, &c. agreeable to the passage in the Hebrews, whom the Lord loveth, he chasteneth and scourgeth, *Every son*

son whom he receiveth. In Matthew xviii. 27, it is said, *The Lord of that servant was moved with compassion, and forgave the debt.* But this forgiven servant, put his fellow servant into prison for an hundred pence, consequent on this, was delivered to the tormentors, not for the debt that was forgiven, but in consequence of the hardness of heart, he discovered towards his brother after his forgiveness, till he should pay the utmost farthing, till he should indure the misery consequent on his transgression, according to the law of retribution, thus expressed: With what measure you mete, it shall be measured to you again, which doth not militate with the doctrine of reconciliation, according to psalm xcix. 8.

We have been ready to look on the afflictions, distresses and miseries of the children of men, as if they denominated them the hated of God; evidences of their being cast off by him, especially when their afflictions are very great; but there is this consolation, that he whose name is Father and Redeemer from everlasting, is unchangeable.

Among ourselves, the disobedience and consequent misery of a son, doth not destroy the relation; but his happiness in his Father's presence, is in proportion to his dutiful behaviour.

I have known several instances of two sons of one man. The one brought up without a blow or a stroke of the rod, the other so disobedient and stubborn, that the father hath been obliged with aching heart, to multiply the stripes of the rod of correction; yea, I have known the instance when the disobedient son, still refractory, despised the correction, and refused to return. This disobedient son consequently shunned his father's presence, and looked on him as an enemy, while at the same time the bowels of the compassion of his father, strongly exercised, were manifest in his earnest application to the Father of mercies,

mercies for the disobedient son, who was, notwithstanding his disobedience, a beloved son still, though he never could be happy in the apprehension of his father's love, while he continued in his stubbornness and disobedience; while the other brother was all the while happy in his father's presence, enjoying his smile.

I knew a mother who had three children that lived to grow up, who said she was obliged to whip each of them once in their childhood, and never had occasion to repeat it, they being ever after ready to submit to her authority—the rod and reproof appeared to give wisdom.

I mention this to show the happy tendency of being in subjection to the Father of our spirits, who doth not afflict willingly, nor grieve the children of men, while stubbornness, under the correcting hand of God, causes a behaviour like a bullock unaccustomed to the yoke, wishing to get away, would fain flee out of his hand, and looks on him as an enemy. While this stubbornness continues, it is impossible to enjoy happiness.

I wish that we might entertain a just apprehension of the Gospel, and the dispensations of Providence, that while we conceive the hope of eternal life by Jesus Christ, as brought to view in the gospel, we may have a just sense of every promise of chastisement and correction, that we meet with in the Scriptures, which set before us life and good, death and evil, and excite us to choose life that we may live.—Where is our life? In the enjoyment of God—In thy favor is life. Eternal life is the gift of God, through Jesus Christ our Lord—doth not depend on any thing wrought in us, or done by us. But life and good, death and evil, are set before us according to the way in which we walk. If we walk in the high way, nothing hath any right to annoy us, and we have

no

no right to go out of the way, for if we go aside and break the hedge, the biting of the serpent is connected with it; and can any man enjoy himself thus bitten, or can he be relieved but by the antitype of the brazen serpent.—I would further say, there are most beautiful representations of the way in the Scriptures. Suppose we look into some passages of the prophet Isaiah, where it is repeatedly called a highway; the thought is enough to gladden the heart of a traveller, that though ever so poor, he hath an equal right with others to travel on the high way. Glory be to him who calls it my high way. 'Tis the friend of the poorest subject—they shall have protection in the high way: Yes! they shall be protected from injury from their fellow subjects.

It may be inquired, But may not the travellers be exposed to wild beasts.

Answer. *No lion shall be there, nor any ravenous beast.*

Q. What Company may be found in the way.

A. Negatively, *The unclean shall not pass over it.*
Positively, *The redeemed of the Lord shall walk there.*

Q. But are they not a melancholy, sorrowful, cast-down, company.

A. *They shall return and come to Zion, with songs and everlasting joy upon their heads, they shall obtain joy and gladness, and sorrow and sighing shall flee away.*

Q. But is it not a difficult way by reason of low miry places some part of the way, and mountains in the other.

A. The King, the Lord of hosts hath said, *I will make all my mountains a way, and my high ways shall be exalted;* and hath directed a cast up way over the low places, *prepare ye the way of the people, cast up, cast up the high way: gather out the stones, take up the Stumbling-Block, out of the way of my people.*

Q. Is not the way through the wilderness, where we may be exposed to hunger and thirst?

A. He hath said, *I will make a way in the wilderness, and streams in the desert;* it is said of the children of Israel, *They thirsted not when he led them through the desert, he caused the water to flow out of the rock for them.* Respecting hunger, read Isaiah xlix. 8, 9, 10, *Thus saith the Lord, in an accepted time have I heard thee, and in a day of salvation have I helped thee, and I will preserve thee, and give thee for a covenant of the people to establish the earth; to cause to inherit the desolate heritage, that thou mayest say to the prisoners, go forth to them that sit in darkness, shew yourselves.*

Mark the following most gracious word, " They shall feed in the way, and their pastures shall be in all high places, they shall not hunger nor thirst, neither shall the heat or sun smite them; but he that hath mercy on them shall lead them even by the spring of water, shall he guide them."

Alas! among men it often happens that poor prisoners, when liberated from the prison, are in very destitute circumstances, having nothing to satisfy hunger or thirst, and exposed to the inclemency of the season; but our gracious deliverer hath provided plentifully, and hath said, *he that cometh unto me shall never hunger, and he that believeth on me shall never thirst.*

It follows—*and I will make all my mountains a way, and my high ways shall be exalted,* so as to remove all obstructions from all parts: Behold, observe the notes of attention: Behold, and lo, *behold, these shall come from far, and lo, these from the north, and from the west, and these from the land of Sinim,* or the South Country.

When we meditate on this most delightful passage, can we help looking on the 13th verse with
joyful

joyful admiration, *Sing O heavens, and be joyful O earth, break forth into singing O mountains, for the Lord hath comforted his people, and will have mercy on his afflicted.* Thus you have my endeavour to lead your mind to some passages of scripture that speaks of the way; it is from them I wish you to take your ideas, and take nothing from me that is not agreeable to them.

Taking my leave of my readers, I would bring to view 2d of Corinthians, xiii. 11, Finally brethren, farewell, be perfect, be of good comfort, be of one mind, live in peace and the God of peace shall be with you.

Finally: As if the apostle, about to leave them, as it were, paused, to recollect how he might sum up all he had said, in a few comprehensive words, full of affection,

My brethren, how comprehensive the expression, implying relation, affection and equality, as children of one father, leading our minds to the consideration of Jesus Christ, who is not ashamed to call us brethren, who graciously sent to his disciples after his resurrection, saying, *Go to my brethren, and say unto them, I ascend to my Father and your Father, to my God and your God.* The expressions include in them love, honour, reverence, submission, trust and confidence, joy and consolation; in God, in Christ as our father, and every expression of ardent affection we may be called to, and have ability and opportunity for one towards another. Is not Jesus Christ ashamed to call us brethren? How shall I then express my shame, that my poor brother has been treated with such cold indifference by me this day.

But what has the apostle to say to his brethren?

Farewell, as if he had said, the doctrine I have taught among you since I have determined to know nothing among you, save Jesus Christ and him crucified is a

saving,

saving, soul-satisfying testimony, calculated for your welfare: Hold fast the grace therein contained, and you will fare well, however your circumstances may be in the world, for we are complete in him.

Be perfect: As if he had said, keep in view what I have preached and wrote to you concerning Christ Jesus; viewing his perfect character and finished work as witness in his resurrection, as your head in behalf of all his members.

View him as the first born among many brethren; the brother born for adversity, the kinsman who had right to redeem—keep this in view, and you are complete in him—your perfection is there.

Be of good comfort; is there enough in Jesus Christ for your welfare and perfection, enjoy it; be of good comfort; let it be your comforting cordial in all your afflictions and distresses in life and death.

Live in peace, peace being preached by Jesus Christ, he being our peace, having made peace by the blood of his cross, given his peace to, and left it with his disciples, how refreshing the tidings; on his resurrection, *the same day at even, when the doors were shut, when the disciples were assembled for fear of the Jews—came Jesus and stood in the midst, and said, peace unto you, and when he had so said, he shewed them his hands, and his side, gave them evidences to their satisfaction and joy, that it was he! Then were the disciples glad when they saw the Lord.* In which there appeared a fulfilment of Psalm cxix. 74. *They that fear thee will be glad when they see me, because I have hoped in thy word.*

When the disciples were thus convinced and satisfied, he saith unto them again, peace unto you; and after eight days the disciples were within, and Thomas with them; then came Jesus and stood in the midst, and said, peace unto you. His gift of peace flowed from unchangeable love, notwithstanding they had all forsook him and fled, and some of them had so shamefully denied him in the time of his deep humiliation: Though they were changable and forsook him, he being, *the same yesterday, to day, and forever,* forsook not them, but manifested the truth of what he had said, when he gave them his peace, *Not as the world giveth, give I unto you, let not your hearts be troubled, neither let it be afraid.* The world gives peace, and offences break it; but though the mountains shall depart, and the hills be removed, my kindness shall not depart from thee, neither shall the covenant of my peace be removed, saith the Lord, that hath mercy on thee.

To them was confirmed, thus repeatedly he sent his apostles forth to preach peace by Jesus Christ, agreeable to the prophecy, *I create the fruit of the lips, peace, peace to them that are far off, and to them that are nigh.* How becoming those, that are blessed with these glad tidings, to live in peace, according to the apostles wish, in his farewell to them: Agreeable to the exhortation given elsewhere, if it be possible, as much as in you lies, live peaceable with all men, be at peace among yourselves; it becomes every disciple of Jesus Christ, to be a peaceable member of society, and a peaceable member of the family, where they are planted in the providence of God.

And the God of peace shall be with you. Is it possible to be otherwise? Only bring all into one point; *the God of peace, who brought again from the dead, our Lord Jesus Christ; that great shepherd of the sheep, through the blood of the everlasting covenant,* hath hereby provided for our welfare, perfection, consolation, union and peace; and in the view of this, while we are at peace one with another, he is graciously and sensibly present with us.

While, if we indulge the works of the flesh, which is hatred, wrath, strife, &c. it raises a cloud that intercepts

cepts the view of the God of peace, agreeable to Isaiah lix. 2, *Your iniquities have separated between you and your God*: Observe it is your God; notwithstanding, O the grace, its because he is God and not man, and to Jeremiah v. 25, *Your iniquities have turned away these things, and your sins have withholden good from you.*

Thus have I taken a view of the Apostles taking leave of his Corinthian brethren, and taking my leave of my readers, I would say, brethren, as I know no other hope of faring well, perfection, good comfort, or peace, for my self, but what is here hinted at, it has been one motive in my writings to lead my readers to view and consider those scripture truths, that has led my mind to these consolations: Therefore, bringing to view the Apostles expression in Galations iv. 12, *Brethren I beseech you, be as I am, for I am as ye are.* Wherein he appears to persuade them to be satisfied with the perfect work of Christ, as the alone ground of their acceptance, as it was his, he being a fellow sinner with them. I would close with my hearty wish that seeing we are complete in him, we may all join with Psalm cxv. 1, *Not unto us! Not unto us, but to thy name, give glory for thy mercy, for thy truths sake, for of him and through him, and to him, are all things, to whom be glory for ever,*

A M E N.

AGED

AGED ADVICE *to a* YOUNG MAN *setting out in the world.*

YOUNG man, I wish you to remember you belong to your Creator, Preserver, and Redeemer; who is our master and Lord. Though you are now free from your earthly master, it is your happiness and honor, and the only way to enjoy liberty, to consider you have a master in Heaven, and make it the rule of your conduct to inquire what is his will concerning you, and to endeavour to pursue a conduct agreeable thereto.

In dealing with your fellow men, his direction is all things whatsoever ye would that men should do to you do ye even so to them.

In our enjoyments, the greatest of which begin the week, by bringing to view the resurrection of Jesus Christ, the foundation of the Christian hope; let it then be our inquiry how would my master and Lord have me spend the day: Not how would my acquaintance, or my corrupt inclination lead me. And thus from day to day through the week.——When any day of relaxation from business, or diversion arrive, let it be persued with a lively, joyful sense of his presence, for he is not far from every one of us, for in him we live and move, and have our being, for we are all his offspring. Are we all his offspring? A reviving thought! How happy are little children to have their father go with them on a holiday, shew them what is to be seen, tell them the meaning, and what use to make of what they see, what dangers to shun, what enjoyments they may partake in! How safe they feel themselves under his protection, till they return safe home under his care; while such as reject parental care often get hurt, abused, and lose themselves, and brought home, greatly dissatisfied; children of 12 and upwards may get a hint of instruction from them. A sense

A sense of the presence of our Father with us, may be a powerful motive to shun that profaneness of speech which is so common and fashionable among too many of our young people. It is a vice altogether unprofitable. Can an instance be produced of one that ever got any thing by it, to clothe or feed himself or family?

Again: It is a foolish practice. A very profane person, being in a tavern where was much company, who were disturbed with his profaneness, one of them addressed the tavern keeper thus, "Do you allow of such profaneness in your house?" Who answered, I must impute it to lack of good sense; a man of good sense can entertain his company without it, but where good sense is wanting, it is often brought in to fill up a vacancy.

Again, it is a hurtful vice, as it has a hurtful tendency, among thoughtless youth. If a young man, that is hired as foreman of a shop, indulge himself herein, it is a wonder if it do not spread among all the apprentices, and if some of them don't go beyond him in it, so as even to call for a rebuke from him, that was instrumental of leading him therein: Besides a young man has the hopes and prospects of a family, and perhaps has no caution on his mind, while his children are in infancy, and ere he is aware, the weed takes root, and springs up with their learning to speak, and grows with rapidity, with the growth of the children; to prevent which let every young man take care he does not save, nor sow the seed.

Again: It is the most dishonourable to God, whose name is the Great God our Saviour, to call on him to do the work of the destroyer.

Jesus Christ says, the thief cometh not but for to steal, and to kill, and to destroy: I am come that they might have life, and that they might have more abundantly. Now if any person will indulge himself to say, " God damn you, it, me, him or them," what is it but to call on the just God and the Saviour, to do the work of the thief, the murderer and destroyer; to take from himself the fruit of his purchase; to kill those that he came to give life to, and destroy what he came to save. Can our adversary the devil, with all his devices, contrive any thing more dishonourable to the Great God our Saviour.

A sober thought on the unprofitableness, the folly, the hateful tendency, and above all, of its being dishonourable to God, will, I hope, guard your mind from every appearance of this evil.

Upon the whole, on our setting out and travelling through the present world, our safety and happiness is to keep the high way; the high way of the upright you know is to depart from evil. The upright one has marked it out—has given order to cast up the high way, to gather out the stones, to take out the stumbling blocks out of the way of his people; has engaged that no lion shall be there, nor any ravenous beast. Keep then the high way, and you keep the way of safety, peace and joy. It is the only way to true happiness in the present world.* To wander from this way, leads to darkness, distress and misery.

I doubt not but you will receive this as an evidence of the love of your old friend, that wishes you a happy journey through this present evil world.

* I say, in the present world I need not inform you, except it be to stir up your mind by way of remembrance, of what you already know, that eternal life is the gift of God through Jesus Christ our Lord.

FINIS.

CONTENTS.

SECTION I.

Peace and Joy. Containing the Evidences of the Truth of the Gospel, from page 5 *to* 66

SECTION II.

The Gospel of Peace published among all Nations, in an Inquiry concerning Repentance and Remission of Sins, from the Scriptures of the Old and New-Testament; addressed, 1st, *to the Author of a Pamphlet, entitled,* Divine Glory in the Condemnation of the ungodly; 2dly, *to all for whom Christ died, from page* 66 *to* 92

SECTION III.

The Gospel thus Evidenced and Published, to be preached to every Creature, with an Endeavour to shew that the Doctrine of Election, rightly understood, can be no objection thereunto, from page 92 *to* 113

SECTION IV.

An attention to the Scriptures for a satisfactory answer to the most important Inquiry that can exercise the minds of Man, from page 113 *to* 135

SECTION V.

Several Objections against the Extent of the Gospel Salvation, considered in an Address to Mr. Samuel Mather, *from page* 135 *to* 179

SECTION VI.

A Universal Call to Thanksgiving, for the glad tidings of the Gospel, thus Evidenced and Promulgated, from page 179 *to* 197

SECTION VII.

The Consequent Obligations on the Believers of the Gospel, in a Practical Essay, in Three Parts.
Part 1st, Addressed to Husbands and Wives.
Part 2d, To Parents.
Part 3d, The Case of Children considered, with an Exhortation to them, from page 197 to   257

SECTION VIII.

A Dialogue between Teacher and Scholar, for the benefit of Young Men, from page 257 to   282

SECTION IX.

A small collection of Psalms, Hymns, and Spiritual Songs, from page 282 to   315

SECTION X.

Scripture Truths and Precepts—a short Catechism, from page 315 to   346

SECTION XI.

The Right and Wrong Way, with their Tendency and Effects. To which is added, the Writer's farewell to his Readers, from page 346 to   374

[Published according to Act of Congress.]

www.ingramcontent.com/pod-product-compliance
Lightning Source LLC
Chambersburg PA
CBHW022335230426
43664CB00040B/807